ALSO BY JOHN JEREMIAH SULLIVAN

Blood Horses

PULPHEAD

PULPHEAD

JOHN JEREMIAH SULLIVAN

FARRAR, STRAUS AND GIROUX   NEW YORK

FARRAR, STRAUS AND GIROUX
18 West 18th Street, New York 10011

Distributed in Canada by D&M Publishers, Inc.
Printed in the United States of America
First edition, 2011

These essays originally appeared, most in substantially
different form, in *GQ*, *The Paris Review*, *Harper's Magazine*,
Oxford American, and *Ecotone*.

Library of Congress Cataloging-in-Publication Data
Sullivan, John Jeremiah, 1974–
Pulphead : essays / John Jeremiah Sullivan.
  p. cm.
Summary : "A collection of nonfiction essays"—Provided
by publisher.
  ISBN 978-0-374-53290-1 (pbk.)
  I. Title.

AC8 .S78135 2011
080—dc23
                                        2011024875

Designed by Abby Kagan

www.fsgbooks.com

3   5   7   9   10   8   6   4

For M. and J. and M.J.

And for Pee Wee (1988–2007)

Good-by now, rum friends, and best wishes.
You got a good mag (like the pulp-heads say) . . .

—NORMAN MAILER,
letter of resignation (rescinded), 1960

CONTENTS

PULPHEAD

UPON THIS ROCK

It is wrong to boast, but in the beginning, my plan was perfect. I was assigned to cover the Cross-Over Festival in Lake of the Ozarks, Missouri, three days of the top Christian bands and their backers at some isolated Midwestern fairground. I'd stand at the edge of the crowd and take notes on the scene, chat up the occasional audience member ("What's harder—homeschooling or regular schooling?"), then flash my pass to get backstage, where I'd rap with the artists themselves. The singer could feed me his bit about how all music glorifies Him, when it's performed with a loving spirit, and I'd jot down every tenth word, inwardly smiling. Later that night I might sneak some hooch in my rental car and invite myself to lie with a prayer group by their fire, for the fellowship of it. Fly home, stir in statistics. Paycheck.

But as my breakfast-time mantra says, I am a professional. And they don't give out awards for that sort of toe-tap foolishness. I wanted to know what these people are, who claim to love this music, who drive hundreds of miles, traversing states, to hear it live. Then it came, my epiphany: I would go with them. Or rather, they would come with me. I would rent a van, a plush one, and we would travel there together, I and three or four hard-core buffs, all the way from the East Coast to the implausibly named Lake of the Ozarks. We'd talk through the night, they'd proselytize at me, and I'd keep my little tape machine working all the while. Somehow I knew we'd grow to like and pity one another. What a story that would make—for future generations.

The only remaining question was: How to recruit the willing? But it was hardly even a question, because everyone knows that damaged types who are down for whatever's clever gather in "chat rooms" every night. And among the Jesusy, there's plenty who are super f'd up. He preferred it that way, evidently.

So I published my invitation, anonymously, at youthon therock.com, and on two Internet forums devoted to the good-looking Christian pop-punk band Relient K, which had been booked to appear at Cross-Over. I pictured that guy or girl out there who'd been dreaming in an attic room of seeing, with his or her own eyes, the men of Relient K perform their song "Gibberish" from *Two Lefts Don't Make a Right . . . But Three Do*. How could he or she get there, though? Gas prices won't drop, and Relient K never plays north Florida. Please, Lord, make it happen. Suddenly, here my posting came, like a great light. We could help each other. "I'm looking for a few serious fans of Christian rock to ride to the festival with me," I wrote. "Male/female doesn't matter, though you shouldn't be older than, say, 28, since I'm looking at this primarily as a youth phenomenon."

They seem like harmless words. Turns out, though, I had

failed to grasp how "youth" the phenomenon is. Most of the people hanging out in these chat rooms were teens, and I don't mean nineteen, either, I mean fourteen. Some of them, I was about to learn, were mere tweens. I had just traipsed out onto the World Wide Web and asked a bunch of twelve-year-old Christians if they wanted to come for a ride in my van.

It wasn't long before the children rounded on me. "Nice job cutting off your email address," wrote "mathgeek29," in a tone that seemed not at all Christlike. "I doubt if anybody would give a full set of contact information to some complete stranger on the Internet . . . Aren't there any Christian teens in Manhattan who would be willing to do this?"

A few of the youths were indeed credulous. "Riathamus" said, "i am 14 and live in indiana plus my parents might not let me considering it is a stranger over the Internet. but that would really be awsome." A girl by the name of "LilLoser" even tried to be a friend:

> I doubt my parents would allow their baby girl to go with some guy they don't and I don't know except through email, especially for the amount of time you're asking and like driving around everywhere with ya . . . I'm not saying you're a creepy petifile, lol, but i just don't think you'll get too many people interested . . . cuz like i said, it spells out "creepy" . . . but hey—good luck to you in your questy missiony thing. lol.

The luck that she wished me I sought in vain. The Christians stopped chatting with me and started chatting among themselves, warning one another about me. Finally one poster on the official Relient K site hissed at the others to stay away from my scheme, as I was in all likelihood "a 40 year old kidnapper." Soon I logged on and found that the moderators of the site had removed my post and its lengthening thread of accusations altogether, offering no explanation. Doubtless at that moment they were faxing alerts to a network of moms. I recoiled in dread. I called my lawyer, in Boston, who told me to "stop using computers" (his plural).

In the end, the experience inspired in me a distaste for the whole Cross-Over Festival as a subject, and I resolved to refuse the assignment. I withdrew.

The problem with a flash mag like the *Gentlemen's Quarterly* is that there's always some overachieving assistant editor, sometimes called Greg, whom the world hasn't beaten down yet, and who, when you phone him, out of courtesy, just to let him know that "the Cross-Over thing fell through" and that you'll be in touch when you "figure out what to do next," hops on that mystical boon the Internet and finds out that the festival you were planning to attend was in fact not "the biggest one in the country," as you'd alleged. The biggest one in the country—indeed, in Christendom—is the Creation Festival, inaugurated in 1979, a veritable Godstock. And it happens not in Missouri but in ruralmost Pennsylvania, in a green valley, on a farm called Agape. This festival did not end a month ago; it starts the day after tomorrow. Already they are assembling, many tens of thousands strong. Good luck to you in your questy missiony thing.

I had one demand: that I not be made to camp. I'd have some sort of vehicle with a mattress in it, one of these pop-ups, maybe. "Right," said Greg. "Here's the deal. I've called around. There are no vans left within a hundred miles of Philly. We got you an RV, though. It's a twenty-nine-footer." Once I reached the place, we agreed (or he led me to think he agreed), I would certainly be able to downgrade to something more manageable.

The reason twenty-nine feet is such a common length for RVs, I presume, is that once a vehicle gets much longer, you need a special permit to drive it. That would mean forms and fees, possibly even background checks. But show up at any RV joint with your thigh stumps lashed to a skateboard, crazily waving your hooks-for-hands, screaming you want that twenty-nine-footer out back for a trip to you ain't sayin' where, and all they want to know is: Credit or debit, tiny sir?

Two days later, I stood in a parking lot, suitcase at my feet. Debbie came toward me. Her face was as sweet as a birthday cake beneath spray-hardened bangs. She raised a powerful arm and pointed, before either of us spoke. She pointed at a vehicle that looked like something the ancient Egyptians might have left behind in the desert.

"Oh, hi, there," I said. "Listen, all I need is, like, a camper van or whatever. It's just me, and I'm going five hundred miles . . ."

She considered me. "Where ya headed?"

"To this thing called Creation. It's, like, a Christian-rock festival."

"You and everybody!" she said. "The people who got our vans are going to that same thing. There's a bunch o' ya."

Her husband and coworker, Jack, emerged—tattooed, squat, gray-mulleted, spouting open contempt for MapQuest. He'd be giving me real directions. "But first let's check 'er out."

We toured the outskirts of my soon-to-be mausoleum. It took time. Every single thing Jack said, somehow, was the only thing I'd need to remember. White water, gray water, black water (drinking, showering, le devoir). Here's your this, never ever that. Grumbling about "weekend warriors." I couldn't listen, because listening would mean accepting it as real, though his casual mention of the vast blind spot in the passenger-side mirror squeaked through, as did his description of the "extra two feet on each side"—the bulge of my living quarters—which I wouldn't be able to see but would want to "be conscious of" out there. Debbie followed us with a video camera, for insurance purposes. I saw my loved ones gathered in a mahogany-paneled room to watch this footage; them being forced to hear me say, "What if I never use the toilet—do I still have to switch on the water?"

Jack pulled down the step and climbed aboard. It was really happening. The interior smelled of spoiled vacations and amateur porn shoots wrapped in motel shower curtains and left in the sun. I was physically halted at the threshold for a moment. Jesus had never been in this RV.

What do I tell you about my voyage to Creation? Do you want to know what it's like to drive a windmill with tires down the Pennsylvania Turnpike at rush hour by your lonesome, with darting bug-eyes and shaking hands; or about Greg's laughing phone call "to see how it's going"; about hearing yourself say "no No NO NO!" in a shamefully high-pitched voice every time you try to merge; or about thinking you detect, beneath the mysteriously comforting blare of the radio, faint honking sounds, then checking your passenger-side mirror only to find you've been straddling the lanes for an unknown number of miles (those two extra feet!) and that the line of traffic you've kept pinned stretches back farther than you can see; or about stopping at Target to buy sheets and a pillow and peanut butter but then practicing your golf swing in the sporting-goods aisle for a solid twenty-five minutes, unable to stop, knowing that when you do, the twenty-nine-footer will be where you left her, alone in the side lot, waiting for you to take her the rest of the way to your shared destiny?

She got me there, as Debbie and Jack had promised, not possibly believing it themselves. Seven miles from Mount Union, a sign read CREATION AHEAD. The sun was setting; it floated above the valley like a fiery gold balloon. I fell in with a long line of cars and trucks and vans—not many RVs. Here they were, all about me: the born-again. On my right was a pickup truck, its bed full of teenage girls in matching powder-blue T-shirts; they were screaming at a Mohawked kid who was walking beside the road. I took care not to meet their eyes—who knew but they weren't the same fillies I had solicited days before? Their line of traffic lurched ahead, and an old orange Datsun came up beside me. I watched as the driver rolled down her window, leaned halfway out, and blew a long, clear note on a ram's horn. I understand where you might be coming from in doubting that. Nevertheless it is what she did. I have it on tape. She blew a ram's horn, quite capably, twice. A yearly rite, perhaps, to announce her arrival at Creation.

My turn at the gate. The woman looked at me, then past me to the empty passenger seat, then down the whole length of the twenty-nine-footer. "How many people in your group?" she asked.

I pulled away in awe, permitting the twenty-nine-footer to float. My path was thronged with excited Christians, most younger than eighteen. The adults looked like parents or pastors, not here on their own. Twilight was well along, and the still valley air was sharp with campfire smoke. A great roar shot up to my left—something had happened onstage. The sound bespoke a multitude. It filled the valley and lingered.

I thought I might enter unnoticed—that the RV might even offer a kind of cover—but I was already turning heads. Two separate kids said "I feel sorry for him" as I passed. Another leaped up on the driver's-side step and said, "Jesus Christ, man," then fell away running. I kept braking—even idling was too fast. Whatever spectacle had provoked the roar was over now: The roads were choked. The youngsters were streaming around me in both directions, back to their campsites, like a line of ants around some petty obstruction. They had a disconcerting way of stepping aside for the RV only when its front fender was just about to graze their backs. From my elevated vantage, it looked as if they were waiting just a tenth of a second too long, and that I was gently, forcibly parting them in slow motion.

The Evangelical strata were more or less recognizable from my high school days, though everyone, I observed, had gotten better-looking. Lots were dressed like skate punks or in last season's East Village couture (nondenominationals); others were fairly trailer (rural Baptists or Church of God); there were preps (Young Life, Fellowship of Christian Athletes—these were the ones who'd have the pot). You could spot the stricter sectarians right away, their unchanging antifashion and pale glum faces. When I asked one woman, later, how many she reckoned were white, she said, "Roughly one hundred percent." I did see some Asians and three or four blacks. They gave the distinct impression of having been adopted.

I drove so far. You wouldn't have thought this thing could

go on so far. Every other bend in the road opened onto a whole new cove full of tents and cars; the encampment had expanded to its physiographic limits, pushing right up to the feet of the ridges. It's hard to put across the sensory effect of that many people living and moving around in the open: part family reunion, part refugee camp. A tad militia, but cheerful.

The roads turned dirt and none too wide: Hallelujah Highway, Street Called Straight. I'd been told to go to "H," but when I reached H, two teenage kids in orange vests came out of the shadows and told me the spots were all reserved. "Help me out here, guys," I said, jerking my thumb, pitifully indicating my mobile home. They pulled out their walkie-talkies. Some time went by. It got darker. Then an even younger boy rode up on a bike and winked a flashlight at me, motioning I should follow.

It was such a comfort to yield up my will to this kid. All I had to do was not lose him. His vest radiated a warm, re-assuring officialdom in my headlights. Which may be why I failed to comprehend in time that he was leading me up an almost vertical incline—"the Hill Above D."

Thinking back, I can't say which came first: a little bell in my spine warning me that the RV had reached a degree of tilt she was not engineered to handle, or the sickening knowl-edge that we had begun to slip back. I bowed up off the seat and crouched on the gas. I heard yelling. I kicked at the brake. With my left hand and foot I groped, like a person drowning, for the emergency brake (had Jack's comprehen-sive how-to sesh not touched on its whereabouts?). We were losing purchase; she started to shudder. My little guide's eyes showed fear.

I'd known this moment would come, of course, that the

twenty-nine-footer would turn on me. We had both of us understood it from the start. But I must confess, I never imagined her hunger for death could prove so extreme. Laid out below and behind me was a literal field of Christians, toasting buns and playing guitars, fellowshipping. The aerial shot in the papers would show a long scar, a swath through their peaceful tent village. And that this gigantic psychopath had worked her vile design through the agency of a child—an innocent, albeit impossibly confused child . . .

My memory of the next five seconds is smeared, but I know that a large and perfectly square male head appeared in the windshield. It was blond and wearing glasses. It had wide-open eyes and a Chaucerian West Virginia accent and said rapidly that I should "JACK THE WILL TO THE ROT" while applying the brakes. Some branch of my motor cortex obeyed. The RV skidded briefly and was still. Then the same voice said, "All right, hit the gas on three: one, two . . ."

She began to climb—slowly, as if on a pulley. Some freakishly powerful beings were pushing. Soon we had leveled out at the top of the hill.

There were five of them, all in their early twenties. I remained in the twenty-nine-footer; they gathered below. "Thank you," I said.

"Aw, hey," shot back Darius, the one who'd given the orders. He talked very fast. "We've been doing this all day—I don't know why that kid keeps bringing people up here—we're from West Virginia—listen, he's retarded—there's an empty field right there."

I looked back and down at what he was pointing to: pastureland.

Jake stepped forward. He was also blond, but slender. And handsome in a feral way. His face was covered in stubble as pale as his hair. He said he was from West Virginia and wanted to know where I was from.

"I was born in Louisville," I said.

"Really?" said Jake. "Is that on the Ohio River?" Like Darius, he both responded and spoke very quickly. I said that in fact it was.

"Well, I know a dude that died who was from Ohio. I'm a volunteer fireman, see. Well, he flipped a Chevy Blazer nine times. He was spread out from here to that ridge over there. He was dead as four o'clock."

"Who are you guys?" I said.

Ritter answered. He was big, one of those fat men who don't really have any fat, a corrections officer—as I was soon to learn—and a former heavyweight wrestler. He could burst a pineapple in his armpit and chuckle about it (or so I assume). Haircut: military. Mustache: faint. "We're just a bunch of West Virginia guys on fire for Christ," he said. "I'm Ritter, and this is Darius, Jake, Bub, and that's Jake's brother, Josh. Pee Wee's around here somewhere."

"Chasin' tail," said Darius disdainfully.

"So you guys have just been hanging out here, saving lives?"

"We're from West Virginia," said Darius again, like maybe he thought I was thick. It was he who most often spoke for the group. The projection of his jaw from the lump of snuff he kept there made him come off a bit contentious, but I felt sure he was just high-strung.

"See," Jake said, "well, our campsite is right over there." With a cock of his head he identified a car, a truck, a tent, a fire, and a tall cross made of logs. And that other thing was . . . a PA system?

"We had this spot last year," Darius said. "I prayed about

it. I said, 'God, I'd just really like to have that spot again—you know, if it's Your will.'"

I'd assumed that my days at Creation would be fairly lonely and end with my ritual murder. But these West Virginia guys had such warmth. It flowed out of them. They asked me what I did and whether I liked sassafras tea and how many others I'd brought with me in the RV. Plus they knew a dude who died horribly and was from a state with the same name as the river I grew up by, and I'm not the type who questions that sort of thing.

"What are you guys doing later?" I said.

Bub was short and solid; each of his hands looked as strong as a trash compactor. He had darker skin than the rest—an olive cast—with brown hair under a camouflage hat and brown eyes and a full-fledged dark mustache. Later he would share with me that friends often told him he must be "part N-word." That was his phrasing. He was shy and always looked like he must be thinking hard about something. "Me and Ritter's going to hear some music," he said.

"What band is it?"

Ritter said, "Jars of Clay."

I had read about them; they were big. "Why don't you guys stop by my trailer and get me on your way?" I said. "I'll be in that totally empty field."

Ritter said, "We just might do that." Then they all lined up to shake my hand.

While I waited for Ritter and Bub, I lay in bed and read *The Silenced Times* by lantern light. This was a thin newsletter that had come with my festival packet. It wasn't really a newsletter; it was publisher's flackery for *Silenced*, a new novel by Jerry Jenkins, one of the minds behind the multi-hundred-million-dollar *Left Behind* series—more than a dozen books so far, all about what happens after the Rapture, to folks like me. His new book was a futuristic job, set in 2047. The dateline on the newsletter read: "March 2, 38." Get it? Thirty-seven years have passed since they wiped Jesus from history. *The Silenced Times* was supposedly laid out to look like a newspaper from that coming age.

It was pretty grim stuff. In the year 38, an ancient death cult has spread like a virus and taken over the "United Seven States of America." Adherents meet in "cell groups" (nice touch: a bit of old commie lingo); they enlist the young and hunger for global hegemony while striving to hasten the end of the world. By the year 34—the time of the last census—44 percent of the population had professed membership in the group; by now the figure is closer to half. This dwarfs any other surviving religious movement in the land. Even the president (whom they mobilized to elect) has been converted. The most popular news channel in the country openly backs him and his policies; and the year's most talked-about film is naked propaganda for the cult, but in a darkly brilliant twist, much of the population has been convinced that the media are in fact controlled by—

Wait! I thought. This is all happening in real life. This is Evangelicalism. And yet *The Silenced Times* describes Christians being thrown into jail, driven underground, their pamphlets confiscated. A guy wins an award for ratting out his sister, who was leading a campus Bible study. I especially liked the part where it was reported that antireligion forces had finally rounded up Jenkins himself—in a cave. He's ninety-seven years old but has never stopped typing, and as they drag him away, he's bellowing Scripture.

Ritter beat on the door. He and Bub were ready to hear some Jars of Clay. Now that it was night, more fires were going; the whole valley was aromatic. And the sky looked like a tin punch lantern—thousands of stars were out. There were so many souls headed toward the stage, it was hard to walk, though I noticed the crowd tended to give Ritter a wider berth. He kind of leaned back, looking over people's heads, as if he expected to spot a friend. I asked about his church in West Virginia. He said he and the rest of the guys were Pentecostal, speaking in tongues and all that—except for Jake, who was a Baptist. But they all went to the same "sing"—a weekly Bible study at somebody's house with food and guitars. Did Ritter think everyone here was a Christian?

"No, there's some who probably aren't saved. With this many people, there has to be." What were his feelings on that?

"It just opens up opportunities for witnessing," he said.

Bub stopped suddenly—a signal that he wished to speak. The crowd flowed on around us for a minute while he chose his words. "There's Jewish people here," he said.

"Really?" I said. "You mean, Jew Jews?"

"Yeah," Bub said. "These girls Pee Wee brung around. I mean, they're Jewish. That's pretty awesome." He laughed without moving his face; Bub's laugh was a purely vocal phenomenon. Were his eyes moist?

We commenced walking.

I suspect that on some level—the conscious one, say—I didn't want to be noticing what I noticed as we went. But I've been to a lot of huge public events in this country during the past five years, writing about sports or whatever, and one thing they all had in common was this weird implicit enmity that American males, in particular, seem to carry around with them much of the time. Call it a laughable generalization, fine, but if you spend enough late afternoons in stadium concourses, you feel it, something darker than machismo. Something a little wounded, and a little sneering, and just plain ready for bad things to happen. It wasn't here. It was just, not. I looked for it, and I couldn't find it. In the three days I spent at Creation, I saw not one fight, heard not one word spoken in anger, felt at no time even mildly harassed, and in fact met many people who were exceptionally kind. Yes, they were all of the same race, all believed the same stuff, and weren't drinking, but there were also one hundred thousand of them.

We were walking past a row of portable toilets, by the food stands. As we came around the corner, I saw the stage, from off to the side. And the crowd on the hill that faced the stage. Their bodies rose till they merged with the dark. "Holy crap," I said.

Ritter waved his arm like an impresario. He said, "This, my friend, is Creation."

For their encore, Jars of Clay did a cover of U2's "All I Want Is You." It was bluesy.

That's the last thing I'll be saying about the bands.

Or, no, wait, there's this: the fact that I didn't hear a single interesting bar of music from the forty or so acts I caught or overheard at Creation shouldn't be read as a knock against the acts themselves, much less as contempt for the underlying notion of Christians playing rock. These were not Christian bands, you see; these were Christian-rock bands. The key to digging this scene lies in that one-syllable distinction. Christian rock is a genre that exists to edify and make money off evangelical Christians. It's message music for listeners who know the message cold, and, what's more, it operates under a perceived responsibility—one the artists embrace—to "reach people." As such, it rewards both obviousness and maximum palatability (the artists would say clarity), which in turn means parasitism. Remember those perfume dispensers they used to have in pharmacies—"If you like Drakkar Noir, you'll love Sexy Musk"? Well, Christian rock works like that. Every successful crappy secular group has its Christian off brand, and that's proper, because culturally speaking, it's supposed to serve as a stand-in for, not an alternative to or an improvement on, those very groups. In this it succeeds wonderfully. If you think it profoundly sucks, that's because your priorities are not its priorities; you want to hear something cool and new, it needs to play something proven to please . . . while praising Jesus Christ. That's Christian rock. A Christian band, on the other hand, is just a band that has more than one Christian in it. U2 is the exemplar, held aloft by believers and nonbelievers alike, but there have been others through the years, bands about which people would say, "Did you know those guys were Christians? I know—it's freaky. They're still fuckin' good, though." The Call was like that; Lone Justice was like that. These days you hear it about indie acts like Pedro the Lion and Damien Jurado (or people I've never heard of). In most cases, bands like these make a very, very careful effort not to be seen as playing "Christian rock." It's largely a matter of phrasing: don't tell the interviewer you're born-again; say faith is a very important part of your life. And here, if I can drop the open-minded pretense real quick, is where the stickier problem of actually being any good comes in, because a question that must be asked is whether a hard-core Christian who turns nineteen and finds he or she can write first-rate songs (someone like Damien Jurado) would ever have anything whatsoever to do with Christian rock. Talent tends to come hand in hand with a certain base level of subtlety. And believe it or not, the Christian-rock establishment sometimes expresses a kind of resigned approval of the way groups like U2 or Switchfoot (who played Creation while I was there and had a monster secular-radio hit at the time with "Meant to Live" but whose management wouldn't allow them to be photographed onstage) take quiet pains to distance themselves from any unambiguous Jesus-loving, recognizing that to avoid this is the surest way to connect with the world (you know that's how they refer to us, right? We're "of the world"). So it's possible—and indeed seems likely—that Christian rock is a musical genre, the only one I can think of, that has excellence-proofed itself.

It was late, and the Jews had sown discord. What Bub had said was true: there were Jews at Creation. These were Jews for Jesus, it emerged, two startlingly pretty high school girls from Richmond. They'd been sitting by the fire—one of them mingling fingers with Pee Wee—when Bub and Ritter and I returned from seeing Jars of Clay. Pee Wee was younger than the other guys, and skinny and cute, and he gazed at the girls admiringly when they spoke. At a certain point, they mentioned to Ritter that he would writhe in hell for having tattoos (he had a couple); it was what their people believed. Ritter had not taken the news all that well. He was fairly confident about his position among the elect. There was debate; Pee Wee was forced to escort the girls back to their tents, while Darius worked to calm Ritter. "They may have weird ideas," he said, "but we worship the same God."

The fire had burned to glowing coals, and now it was just we men, sitting on coolers, talking late-night hermeneutics blues. Bub didn't see how God could change His mind, how He could say all that crazy shit in the Old Testament—like don't get tattoos and don't look at your uncle naked—then take it back in the New.

"Think about it this way," I said. "If you do something that really makes Darius mad, and he's pissed at you, but then you do something to make it up to him, and he forgives you, that isn't him changing his mind. The situation has changed. It's the same with the old and new covenants, except Jesus did the making up."

Bub seemed pleased with this explanation. "I never heard anyone say it like that," he said. But Darius stared at me gimlet-eyed across the fire. He knew my gloss was theologically sound, and he wondered where I'd gotten it. The guys had been gracefully dancing around the question of what I believed—"where my walk was at," as they would have put it—all night.

We knew one another fairly well by now. Once Pee Wee had returned, they'd eagerly showed me around their camp. Most of their tents were back in the forest, where they weren't supposed to be; the air was cooler there. Darius had located a small stream about thirty yards away and, using his hands, dug out a basin. This was supplying their drinking water.

It came out that these guys spent much if not most of each year in the woods. They lived off game—as folks do, they said, in their section of Braxton County. They knew all the plants of the forest, which were edible, which cured what. Darius pulled out a large piece of cardboard folded in half. He opened it under my face: a mess of sassafras roots. He wafted their scent of black licorice into my face and made me eat one.

Then he remarked that he bet I liked weed. I allowed as how I might not not like it. "I used to love that stuff," he told me. Seeing that I was taken aback, he said, "Man, to tell you the truth, I wasn't even convicted about it. But it's socially unacceptable, and that was getting in the way of my Christian growth."

The guys had put together what I did for a living—though, to their credit, they didn't seem to take this as a reasonable explanation for my being there—and they gradually got the sense that I found them exotic (though it was more than that). Slowly, their talk became an ecstasy of self-definition. They were passionate to make me see what kind of guys they were. This might have grown tedious, had they been any old kind of guys. But they were the kind of guys who believed that God had personally interceded and made it possible for four of them to fit into Ritter's silver Chevrolet Cavalier for the trip to Creation.

"Look," Bub said, "I'm a pretty big boy, right? I mean, I'm stout. And Darius is a big boy"—here Darius broke in and made me look at his calves, which were muscled to a degree that hinted at deformity; "I'm a freak," he said; Bub sighed and went on without breaking eye contact—"and you know Ritter is a big boy. Plus we had two coolers, guitars, an electric piano, our tents and stuff, all"—he turned and pointed, turned back, paused—"in that Chevy." He had the same look in his eyes as earlier, when he'd told me there were Jews. "I think that might be a miracle," he said.

In their lives, they had known terrific violence. Ritter and Darius met, in fact, when each was beating the shit out of the other in middle-school math class. Who won? Ritter looked at Darius, as if to clear his answer, and said, "Nobody." Jake once took a fishing pole that Darius had accidentally stepped on and broken and beat him to the ground with it. "I told him, 'Well, watch where you're stepping,'" Jake said. (This memory made Darius laugh so hard he removed his glasses.) Half of their childhood friends had been murdered—shot or stabbed over drugs or nothing. Others had killed themselves. Darius's grandfather, great-uncle, and onetime best friend had all committed suicide. When Darius was growing up, his father was in and out of jail; at least once, his father had done hard time. In Ohio he stabbed a man in the chest (the man had refused to stop "pounding on" Darius's grandfather). Darius caught a lot of grief—"Your daddy's a jailbird!"—during those years. He'd carried a chip on his shoulder from that. "You came up pretty rough," I said.

"Not really," Darius said. "Some people ain't got hands and feet." He talked about how much he loved his father. "With all my heart—he's the best. He's brought me up the way that I am.

"And anyway," he added, "I gave all that to God—all that anger and stuff. He took it away."

God in His wisdom had left him enough to get by on. Earlier in the evening, the guys had roughed up Pee Wee a little and tied him to a tree with ratchet straps. Some other Christians must have reported his screams to the staff, because a guy in an orange vest came stomping up the hill. Pee Wee hadn't been hurt much, but he put on a show of tears, to be funny. "They always do me like that," he said. "Save me, mister!"

The guy was unamused. "It's not them you got to worry about," he said. "It's me."

Those were such foolish words! Darius came forward like

some hideously fast-moving lizard on a nature show. "I'd watch it, man," he said. "You don't know who you're talking to. This'n here's as like to shoot you as shake your hand."

The guy somehow appeared to move back without actually taking a step. "You're not allowed to have weapons," he said.

"Is that right?" Darius said. "We got a conceal 'n' carry right there in the glove box. Mister, I'm from West Virginia—I know the law."

"I think you're lying," said the guy. His voice had gone a bit warbly.

Darius leaned forward, as if to hear better. His eyes were leaving his skull. "How would you know that?" he said. "Are you a prophet?"

"I'm Creation staff!" the guy said.

Jake stood up—he'd been watching this scene from his seat by the fire. The fixed polite smile on his face was indistinguishable from a leer.

"Well," he said, "why don't you go somewhere and *create* your own problems?"

I admit that these tales of the West Virginia guys' occasional truculence might appear to gainsay what I claimed earlier about "not one word spoken in anger," et cetera. But it was playful. Darius, at least, seemed to be performing a bit for me. And if you take into account what the guys have to be on guard for all the time back home, the notable thing becomes how successfully they checked their instincts at Creation.

Whatever the case, we operated with more or less perfect impunity from then on. This included a lot of very loud, live music between two and three o'clock in the morning. The guys were running their large PA off the battery in Jake's truck. Ritter and Darius had a band of their own back home, First Verse. They were responsible for the music at their church. Ritter had an angelic tenor that seemed to be coming out of a body other than his own. And Josh was a good guitar player; he had a Les Paul and an effects board. We passed around the acoustic. I had to dig to come up with Christian tunes. I did "Jesus," by Lou Reed, which they liked okay. But they really enjoyed Bob Marley's "Redemption Song." When I finished, Bub said, "Man, that's really Christian. It really is." Darius made me teach it to him; he said he would take it home and "do it at worship."

Then he jumped up and jogged to the electric piano, which was on a stand ten feet away. He closed his eyes and began to play. I know enough piano to know what good technique sounds like, and Darius played very, very well. He improvised for an hour. At one point, Bub went and stood beside him with his hands in his pockets, facing the rest of us, as if guarding his friend while the latter was in this vulnerable trance state. Ritter whispered to me that Darius had been offered a music scholarship to a college in West Virginia; he went to visit a friend, and a professor heard him messing around on the school's piano. The dude offered him a full ride then and there. Ritter couldn't really explain why Darius had turned it down. "He's kind of our Rain Man," Ritter said.

At some juncture, I must have taken up my lantern and crept back down the hill, since I sat up straight the next morning, fully dressed in the twenty-nine-footer. The sound that woke me was a barbaric moan, like that of an army about to charge. Early mornings at Creation were about Praise and Worship, a new form of Christian rock in which the band

and the audience sing, all together, as loud as they can, directly to God. It gets rather intense.

The guys had told me they meant to spend most of today at the main stage, checking out bands. But I'd already checked out a band. My task was to stay in this trailer, jotting impressions.

It was hot, though. As it got hotter, the light brown carpet started to give off fumes from under its plastic hide. I somewhat light-headedly tumbled out the side hatch and went looking for Darius, Ritter, and Bub.

In the light of day, one could see there were pretty accomplished freaks at this thing: a guy in a skirt wearing lace on his arms; a strange little androgynous creature dressed in full cardboard armor, carrying a sword. They knew they were in a safe place, I guess.

The guys left me standing in line at a lemonade booth; they didn't want to miss Skillet, one of Ritter's favorite bands. I got my drink and drifted slowly toward where I thought they'd be standing. Lack of food, my filthiness, impending sunstroke: these were ganging up on me. Plus the air down here smelled faintly of poo. There were a lot of blazing-hot portable toilets wafting miasma whenever the doors were opened.

I stood in the center of a gravel patch between the food and the crowd, sort of gumming the straw, quadriplegically probing with it for stubborn pockets of meltwater. I was a ways from the stage, but I could see well enough. Something started to happen to me. The guys in the band were middle-aged. They had blousy shirts and halfhearted arena-rock moves from the mid-eighties.

What was . . . this feeling? The singer was grinning

between lines, like if he stopped, he might collapse. I could just make out the words:

> There's a higher place to go (beyond belief, beyond belief),
> Where we reach the next plateau (beyond belief, beyond belief) . . .

The straw slipped from my mouth. "Oh, shit, it's Petra."

It was 1988. The guy who brought me in we called Verm (I'm using nicknames; these people don't deserve to be dragooned into my memory voyage). He was a short, good-looking guy with a dark ponytail and a devilish laugh, a skater and an ex-pothead, which had got him kicked out of his house a year or so before we met. His folks belonged to this nondenominational church in Ohio, where I went to high school. It was a movement more than a church—thousands of members, even then. I hear it's bigger now. "Central Meeting" took place in an empty warehouse, for reasons of space, but the smaller meetings were where it was at: home church (fifty people or so), cell group (maybe a dozen). Verm's dad said, Look, go with us once a week and you can move back in.

Verm got saved. And since he was brilliant (he became something of a legend at our school because whenever a new foreign student enrolled, he'd sit with her every day at lunch and make her give him language lessons till he was proficient), and since he was about the most artlessly gregarious human being I've ever known, and since he knew loads of lost souls from his druggie days, he became a champion evangelizer, a golden child.

I was new and nurturing a transcendent hatred of Ohio. Verm found out I liked the Smiths, and we started swapping tapes. Before long, we were hanging out after school. Then the moment came that always comes when you make friends with a born-again: "Listen, I go to this thing on Wednesday nights. It's like a Bible study—no, listen, it's cool. The people are actually really cool."

They were, that's the thing. In fifteen minutes, all my ideas about Christians were put to flight. They were smarter than any bunch I'd been exposed to (I didn't grow up in Cambridge or anything, but even so), they were accepting of every kind of weirdness, and they had that light that people who are pursuing something higher give off. It's attractive, to say the least. I started asking questions, lots of questions. And they loved that, because they had answers. That's one of the ways Evangelicalism works. Your average agnostic doesn't go through life just primed to offer a clear, considered defense of, say, intratextual scriptural inconsistency. But born-agains train for that chance encounter with the inquisitive stranger. And when you're a fourteen-year-old carting around some malnourished intellectual ambitions, and a charismatic adult sits you down and explains that if you transpose this span of years onto the Hebrew calendar, and multiply that times seven, and plug in a date from the reign of King Howsom-ever, then you plainly see that this passage predicts the birth of Christ almost to the hour, despite the fact that the Gospel writers didn't have access to this information! I, for one, was dazzled.

But also powerfully stirred on a level that didn't depend on my naïveté. The sheer passionate engagement of it caught my imagination: nobody had told me there were Christians like this. They went at the Bible with grad-seminar intensity, week after week. Mole was their leader (short for Moloch; he had started the whole thing, back in the seventies). He had a wiry, dark beard and a pair of nail-gun cobalt eyes. My Russian-novel fantasies of underground gatherings—shared subversive fervor—were flattered and, it seemed, embodied. Here was counterculture, without sad hippie trappings.

Verm embraced me when I said to him, in the hallway after a meeting, "I think I might believe." When it came time for me to go all the way—to "accept Jesus into my heart" (in that time-honored formulation)—we prayed the prayer together.

Three years passed. I waxed strong in spirit. Verm and I were sort of heading up the high school end of the operation now. Mole had discovered (I had discovered, too) that I was good with words, that I could talk in front of people; Verm and I started leading Bible study once a month. We were saving souls like mad, laying up treasure for ourselves in heaven. I was never the recruiter he was, but I grasped subtlety; Verm would get them there, and together we'd start on their heads. Witnessing, it's called. I had made some progress socially at school, which gave us access to the popular crowd; in this way, many were brought to the Lord. Verm and I went to conferences and on "study retreats"; we started taking classes in theology, which the group offered—free of charge—for promising young leaders. And always, underneath but suffusing it all, there were the cell-group meetings, every week, on Friday or Saturday nights, which meant I could stay out till the wee hours. (My Episcopalian parents were thoroughly mortified by the whole business, but it's not easy telling your kid to stop spending so much time at church.)

Cell group was typically held in somebody's dining room, somebody pretty high up in the group. You have to understand what an honor it was to be in a cell with Mole. People would see me at Central Meeting and be like, "How is that, getting to rap with him every week?" It was awesome. He really got down with the Word (he had a wonderful old hippie way of talking; everything was something action: "time for some fellowship action . . . let's get some chips 'n' salsa action"). He carried a heavy "study Bible"—no King James for the nondenominationals; too many inaccuracies. When he cracked open its hand-tooled leather cover, you knew it was on. And no joke: the brother was gifted. Even handicapped by the relatively pedestrian style of the New American Standard version, he could twist a verse into your conscience like a bone screw, make you think Christ was standing there, nodding approval. The prayer session alone would last an hour. Afterward, there was always a fire in the backyard. Mole would sit and whack a machete into a chopping block. He smoked cheap cigars; he let us smoke cigarettes. The guitar went around. We'd talk about which brother was struggling with sin—did he need counsel? Or about the end of the world: it'd be soon. We had to save as many as we could.

I won't inflict on you all my reasons for drawing away from the fold. They were clichéd, anyway, and not altogether innocent. Enough to say I started reading books Mole hadn't recommended. Some of them seemed pretty smart—and didn't jibe with the Bible. The defensive theodicy he'd drilled into me during those nights of heady exegesis developed cracks. The hell stuff: I never made peace with it. Human beings were capable of forgiving those who'd done them terrible wrongs, and we all agreed that human beings were maggots compared with God, so what was His trouble, again? I looked around and saw people who'd never have a chance to come to Jesus; they were too badly crippled. Didn't they deserve—more than the rest of us, even—to find His succor, after this life?

Everything about Christianity can be justified *within the context of Christian belief.* That is, if you accept its terms. Once you do, your belief starts modifying the data (in ways that are themselves defensible), until eventually the data begin to reinforce belief. The precise moment of illogic is hard to isolate and may not exist. Like holding a magnifying glass at arm's length and bringing it toward your eye: things are upside down, they're upside down, they're right side up. What lay between? If there was something, it passed too quickly to be observed. This is why you can never reason true Christians out of the faith. It's not, as the adage has it, because they were never reasoned into it—many were—it's that faith is a logical door which locks behind you. What looks like a line of thought is steadily warping into a circle, one that closes with you inside. If this seems to imply that no apostate was ever a true Christian and that therefore, I was never one, I think I'd stand by both of those statements. Doesn't the fact that I can't write about my old friends without an apologetic tone suggest that I was never one of them?

The break came during the winter of my junior year. I got a call from Verm late one afternoon. He'd promised Mole he would do this thing, and now he felt sick. Sinus infection (he always had sinus infections). Had I ever heard of Petra? Well, they're a Christian-rock band, and they're playing the arena downtown. After their shows, the singer invites anybody who wants to know more about Jesus to come backstage, and they have people, like, waiting to talk to them.

The promoter had called up Mole, and Mole had volunteered Verm, and now Verm wanted to know if I'd help him out. I couldn't say no.

The concert was upsetting from the start; it was one of my first encounters with the other kinds of Evangelicals, the hand-wavers and the weepers and all (we liked to keep things "sober" in the group). The girl in front of me was signing all the words to the songs, but she wasn't deaf. It was just horrifying.

Verm had read me, over the phone, the pamphlet he got. After the first encore, we were to head for the witnessing zone and wait there. I went. I sat on the ground.

Soon they came filing in, the seekers. I don't know what was up with the ones I got. I think they may have gone looking for the restroom and been swept up by the stampede. They were about my age and wearing hooded brown sweatshirts—mouths agape, eyes empty. I asked them the questions: What did they think about all they'd heard? Were they curious about anything Petra talked about? (There'd been lots of "talks" between songs.)

I couldn't get them to speak. They stared at me like they were waiting for me to slap them.

This was my opening. They were either rapt or mentally damaged in some way, and whichever it was, Christ called on me now to lay down my testimony.

The sentences wouldn't form. I flipped though the list of dogmas, searching for one I didn't essentially think was crap, and came up with nothing.

There could have ensued a nauseating silence, but I acted with an odd decisiveness to end the whole experience. I asked them if they wanted to leave—it was an all but rhetorical question—and said I did, too. We walked out together.

I took Mole and Verm aside a few nights later and told them my doubts had overtaken me. If I kept showing up at meetings, I'd be faking it. That was an insult to them, to God, to the group. Verm was silent; he hugged me. Mole said he respected my reasons, that I'd have to explore my doubts before my walk could be strong again. He said he'd pray for me. Unless he's undergone some radical change in character, he's still praying.

Statistically speaking, my bout with Evangelicalism was probably unremarkable. For white Americans with my socioeconomic background (middle to upper-middle class), it's an experience commonly linked to the teens and moved beyond before one reaches twenty. These kids around me at Creation—a lot of them were like that. How many even knew who Darwin was? They'd learn. At least once a year since college, I'll be getting to know someone, and it comes out that we have in common a high school "Jesus phase." That's always an excellent laugh. Except a phase is supposed to end—or at least give way to other phases—not simply expand into a long preoccupation.

Bless those who've been brainwashed by cults and sent off for deprogramming. That makes it simple: you put it behind you. This group was no cult. They persuaded, they never pressured. Nor did they punish. A guy I brought into the group—we called him Goog—is still a close friend. He leads meetings now and spends part of each year doing pro bono dental work in Cambodia. He's never asked me when I'm coming back.

My problem is not that I dream I'm in hell or that Mole is at the window. It isn't that I feel psychologically harmed. It isn't even that I feel like a sucker for having bought it all. It's that I love Jesus Christ.

"The latchet of whose shoes I am not worthy to unloose."

He was the most beautiful dude. Forget the Epistles, forget all the bullying stuff that came later. Look at what He said. Read the Jefferson Bible. Or better yet, read *The Logia of Yeshua*, by Guy Davenport and Benjamin Urrutia, an unadorned translation of all the sayings ascribed to Jesus that modern scholars deem authentic. There's your man. His breakthrough was the aestheticization of weakness. Not in what conquers, not in glory, but in what's fragile and what suffers—there lies sanity. And salvation. "Let anyone who has power renounce it," he said. "Your father is compassionate to all, as you should be." That's how He talked, to those who knew Him.

Why should He vex a person? Why is His ghost not friendlier? Why can't I just be a good child of the Enlightenment and see in His life a sustaining example of what we can be, as a species?

Once you've known Him as a god, it's hard to find comfort in the man. The sheer sensation of life that comes with a total, all-pervading notion of being—the pulse of consequence one projects onto even the humblest things—the pull of that won't slacken.

And one has doubts about one's doubts.

"D'ye hear that mountain lion last night?"

It was dark, and Jake was standing over me, dressed in camouflage. I'd been hunched over on a cooler by the ashes for a number of hours, reading and waiting for the guys to get back from wherever they'd gone. I told him I hadn't heard anything.

Bub came up from behind, also in camo. "In the middle of the night," he said. "It woke me up."

Jake said, "It sounded like a baby crying."

"Like a little-bitty baby," Bub said.

Jake was messing with something at my feet, in the shadows, something that looked alive. Bub dropped a few logs onto the fire and went to the Chevy for matches.

I sat there trying to see what Jake was doing. "You got that lantern?" he said. It was by my feet; I switched it on.

He started pulling frogs out of a poke. One after another. They strained in his grip and lashed at the air. "Where'd you get those?" I asked.

"About half a mile that way," he said. "It ain't private property if you're in the middle of the creek." Bub laughed his high expressionless laugh.

"These ain't too big," Jake said. "In West Virginia, well, we got ones the size of chickens."

Jake started chopping their bodies in half. He'd lean forward and center his weight on the hand that held the knife, to get a clean cut, tossing the legs into a frying pan. Then he'd stab each frog in the brain and flip the upper parts into a separate pile. They kept twitching, of course—their nerves. Some were a little less dead than that. One in particular stared up at me, gulping for air, though his lungs were beside him, in the grass.

"Could you do that one in the brain again?" I said. Jake spiked it, expertly, and grabbed for the next frog.

"Why don't you stab their brains before you take off the legs?" I asked. He smiled. He said I cracked him up.

Darius, when he got back, made me a cup of hot sassafras tea. "Drink this, it'll make you feel better," he told me. I'd never said I felt bad. Jake lightly sautéed the legs in butter and served them to me warm. "Eat this," he said. The meat was so tender, it all but dissolved on my tongue.

Pee Wee came back with the Jews, who were forced to tell us a second time that we were damned. (Leviticus 11:12, "Whatsoever hath no fins nor scales in the waters, that shall be an abomination unto you.")

Jake, when he heard this, put on a show, making the demi-frogs talk like puppets, chewing with his mouth wide open so all could see the meat.

The girls ran off again. Pee Wee chased after them, calling, "Come on, they're just playin'!"

Darius peered at Jake. He looked not angry but saddened. Jake said, "Well, if he wants to bring them girls around here, they oughtn't to be telling us what we can eat."

"Wherefore, if meat make my brother to offend," Darius said, "I will eat no flesh while the world standeth."

"First Corinthians," I said.

"Eight thirteen," Darius said.

I woke without having slept—that awful feeling—and lay there steeling myself for the strains of Praise and Worship. When it became too much to wait, I boiled water and made instant coffee and drank it scalding from the lid of the peanut butter jar. My body smelled like stale campfire. My hair had leaves and ash and things in it. I thought about taking a shower, but I'd made it two days without so much as acknowledging any of the twenty-nine-footer's systems; it would have been silly to give in now.

I sat in the driver's seat and watched, through tinted glass, little clusters of Christians pass. They looked like people anywhere, only gladder, more self-contained. Or maybe they just looked like people anywhere. I don't know. I had no pseudo-anthropological moxie left. I got out and wandered.

I sat with the crowd in front of the stage. There was a red-headed Christian speaker up there, pacing back and forth. Out of nowhere, he shrieked, "MAY YOU BE COVERED IN THE ASHES OF YOUR RABBI JESUS!" If I were to try to convey to you how loudly he shrieked this, you'd think I was playing wordy games.

I was staggering through the food stands when a man died at my feet. He was standing in front of the funnel-cake window. He was big, in his early sixties, wearing shorts and a short-sleeve button-down shirt. He just . . . died. Massive heart attack. I was standing there, and he fell, and I don't know whether there's some primitive zone in the brain that registers these things, but the second he landed, I knew he was gone. The paramedics jumped on him so fast, it was weird—it was like they'd been waiting. They pumped and pumped on his chest, blew into his mouth, ran IVs. The ambulance showed up, and more equipment appeared. The man's broad face had that slightly disgruntled look you see on the newly dead.

Others had gathered around; some thought it was all a show. A woman standing next to me said bitterly, "It's not a show. A man has died." She started crying. She took my hand. She was small with silver hair and black eyebrows. "He's fine, he's fine," she said. I looked at the side of her face. "Just pray for his family," she said. "He's fine."

I went back to the trailer and had, as the ladies say where I'm from, a colossal go-to-pieces. I started to cry and then stopped myself for some reason. I felt nonsensically raw and lonely. What a dickhead I'd been, thinking the trip would be a lark. There were too many ghosts here. Everyone seemed so strange and so familiar. Plus I suppose I was starving. The frog meat had been superb, but meager—even Jake had said as much.

In the midst of all this, I began to hear, through the shell of the twenty-nine-footer, Stephen Baldwin giving a talk on the Fringe Stage—that's where the "edgier" acts are put on at Creation. If you're shaky on your Baldwin brothers, he's the vaguely troglodytic one who used to comb his bangs straight down and wear dusters. He's come to the Lord. I caught him on cable a few months ago, some religious talk show. Him and Gary Busey. I don't remember what Baldwin said, because Busey was saying things so weird the host got nervous. Busey's into "generational curses." If you're wondering what those are, apologies. I was born-again, not raised on acid.

Baldwin said many things; the things he said got stranger and stranger. He said his Brazilian nanny, Augusta, had converted him and his wife in Tucson, thereby fulfilling a prophecy she'd been given by her preacher back home. He said, "God allowed 9/11 to happen," that it was "the wrath of God," and that Jesus had told him to share this with us. He also said the Devil did 9/11. He said God wanted him "to make gnarly cool Christian movies." He said that in November we should vote for "the man who has the greatest faith." The crowd lost it; the trailer all but shook.

When Jake and Bub beat on the door, I'd been in there for hours, getting weaker, rereading *The Silenced Times* and the festival program. In the program, it said the candle-lighting ceremony was tonight. The guys had told me about it—it was one of the coolest things about Creation. Everyone gathered in front of the stage, and the staff handed out a candle to every single person there. The media handlers said there was a lookout you could hike to, on the mountain above the stage. That was the way to see it, they said.

When I opened the door, Jake was waving a newspaper. Bub stood behind him, smiling big.

"Look at this," Jake said. It was Wednesday's copy of *The Valley Log*, serving Southern Huntingdon County—"It is just a rumor until you've read it in *The Valley Log*."

The headline for the week read MOUNTAIN LION NOT BE-LIEVED TO BE THREAT TO CREATION FESTIVAL CAMPERS.

"Wha'd we tell you?" Bub said.

"At least it's not a threat," I said.

"Well, not to us it ain't," said Jake.

I climbed to their campsite with them in silence. Darius was sitting on a cooler, chin in hands, scanning the horizon. He seemed meditative. Josh and Ritter were playing songs. Pee Wee was listening, by himself; he'd blown it with the Jewish girls.

"Hey, Darius," I said. He got up. "It's fixin' to shower here in about ten minutes," he said. I went and stood beside him, tried to look where he was looking.

"You want to know how I know?" he said.

He explained it to me, the wind, the face of the sky, how the leaves on the tops of the sycamores would curl and go white when they felt the rain coming, how the light would turn a certain "dead" color. He read the landscape to me like a children's book. "See over there," he said, "how that valley's all misty? It hasn't poured there yet. But the one in back is clear—that means it's coming our way."

Minutes later, it started to rain, big, soaking, percussive drops. The guys started to scramble. I suggested we all get into the trailer. They looked at one another, like maybe it was a sketchy idea. Then Ritter hollered, "Get her done!" We all ran down the hillside, holding guitars and—in Josh's case—a skillet wherein the fried meat of a still-unidentified woodland creature lay ready to eat.

There was room for everyone. I set my lantern on the dining table. We slid back the panes in the windows to let the air in. Darius did card tricks. We drank springwater. Somebody farted; the conversation about who it had been (Pee Wee) lasted a good twenty minutes. The rain on the roof made a solid drumming. The guys were impressed with my place. They said I should fence it. With the money I'd get, I could buy a nice house in Braxton County.

We played guitars. The RV rocked back and forth. Jake wasn't into Christian rock, but as a good Baptist he loved old gospel tunes, and he called for a few, God love him. Ritter sang one that killed me. Also, I don't know what changed, but the guys were up for secular stuff. It turned out that Pee Wee really loved Neil Young; I mean, he'd never heard Neil Young before, but when I played "Powderfinger" for him, he sort of curled up like a kid, then made me play it again when I was done. He said I had a pretty voice.

We all told one another how good we all were, how everybody else should really think about a career in music. Josh played "Stairway to Heaven," and we got loud, singing along. Darius said, "Keep it down, man! We don't need everybody thinking this is the sin wagon."

The rain stopped. It was time to go. Two of the guys planned to leave in the morning, and I had to start walking if I wanted to make the overlook in time for the candlelighting. They went with me as far as the place where the main path split off toward the stage. They each embraced me. Jake said to call them if I ever had "a situation that needs clearing up." Darius said God bless me, with meaning eyes.

Then he said, "Hey, man, if you write about us, can I just ask one thing?"

"Of course," I said.

"Put in there that we love God," he said. "You can say we're crazy, but say that we love God."

The climb was long and steep. At the top was a thing that looked like a backyard deck. It jutted out over the valley, commanding an unobstructed view. Kids hung all over it like lemurs or something.

I pardoned my way to the edge, where the cliff dropped away. It was dark and then suddenly darker—pitch. They had shut off the lights at the sides of the stage. Little pinpricks appeared, moving along the aisles. We used to do candles like this at church, when I was a kid, on Christmas Eve. You light the edges, and the edges spread inward. The rate of spread increases exponentially, and the effect was so unexpected, when, at the end, you had half the group lighting the other half's candles, it always seemed like somebody flipped a switch. That's how it seemed now.

The clouds had moved off—the bright stars were out again. There were fireflies in the trees all over, and spread before me, far below, was a carpet of burning candles, tiny flames, many ten thousands. I was suspended in a black sphere full of flickering light.

Sure I thought about Nuremberg. But mostly I thought of Darius, Jake, Josh, Bub, Ritter, and Pee Wee, whom I doubted I'd ever see again, whom I'd come to love, and who loved God—for it's true, I would have said it even if Darius hadn't asked me to, it may be the truest thing I will have written here: they were crazy, and they loved God—and I thought about the unimpeachable dignity of that, which I never was capable of. Knowing it isn't true doesn't mean you would be strong enough to believe if it were. Six of those glowing specks in the valley were theirs.

I was shown, in a moment of time, the ring of their faces around the fire, each one separate, each one radiant with what Paul calls, strangely, "assurance of hope." It seemed wrong of reality not to reward such souls.

There are lines in a Czeslaw Milosz poem:

And if they all, kneeling with poised palms, millions,
billions of them, ended together with their illusion?
I shall never agree. I will give them the crown.
The human mind is splendid; lips powerful, and the
summons so great it must open Paradise.

If one could only say it and mean it.

They all blew out their candles at the same instant, and the valley—the actual geographical feature—filled with smoke, there were so many.

I left at dawn, while creation slept.

FEET IN SMOKE

On the morning of April 21, 1995, my elder brother, Worth (short for Elsworth), put his mouth to a microphone in a garage in Lexington, Kentucky, and in the strict sense of having been "shocked to death," was electrocuted. He and his band, the Moviegoers, had stopped for a day to rehearse on their way from Chicago to a concert in Tennessee, where I was in school. Just a couple of days earlier, he had called to ask if there were any songs I wanted to hear at the show. I asked for something new, a song he'd written and played for me the last time I'd seen him, on Christmas Day. Our holidays always end the same way, with the two of us up late drinking and trying out our "tunes" on each other. There's something biologically satisfying about harmonizing with a sibling. We've gotten to where we communicate through music, using guitars the way fathers and sons use baseball, as a kind of emotional code. Worth is seven years older than I am, an age difference that can make brothers strangers. I'm fairly sure the first time he ever felt we had anything to talk about was the day he caught me in his basement bedroom at our old house in Indiana, trying to teach myself how to play "Radio Free Europe" on a black Telecaster he'd forbidden me to touch.

The song I had asked for, "Is It All Over," was not a typical Moviegoers song. It was simpler and more earnest than the infectious pop-rock they made their specialty. The changes were still unfamiliar to the rest of the band, and Worth had been about to lead them through the first verse, had just leaned forward to sing the opening lines—"Is it all over? I'm scanning the paper / For someone to replace her"—when a surge of electricity arced through his body, magnetizing the mike to his chest like a tiny but obstinate missile, searing the first string and fret into his palm, and stopping his heart. He fell backward and crashed, already dying.

Possibly you know most of this already. I got many of my details from a common source, an episode of *Rescue 911* (the reality show hosted by William Shatner) that aired about six months after the accident. My brother played himself in the dramatization, which was amusing for him, since he has no memory whatsoever of the real event. For the rest of us, his family and friends, the segment is hard to watch.

The story Shatner tells, which ends at the moment we learned that my brother would live, is different from the story I know. But his version offers a useful reminder of the danger, where medical emergencies are involved, of talking too much about "miracles." Not to knock the word—the staff at Humana Hospital in Lexington called my brother's case "miraculous," and they've seen any number of horrifying accidents and inexplicable recoveries—but it tends to obscure the human skill and coolheadedness that go into saving some-body's life. I think of Liam, my brother's best friend and bandmate, who managed not to fall apart while he cradled Worth in his arms until help arrived, and who'd warned him when the band first started practicing to put on his Chuck Taylors, the rubber soles of which were the only thing that kept him from being zapped into a more permanent fate than the one he did endure. I think of Captain Clarence Jones, the fireman and paramedic who brought Worth back to life, strangely with two hundred joules of pure electric shock (and who later responded to my grandmother's effusive thanks by giving all the credit to the Lord). Without people like these and doubtless others whom I never met and Shatner didn't mention, there would have been no miracle.

It was afternoon when I heard about the accident from my father, who called and told me flatly that my brother had been "hurt." I asked if Worth would live, and there was a nau-seating pause before his "I don't know." I got in the car and drove from Tennessee to Lexington, making the five-hour trip in about three and a half hours. In the hospital parking lot I was met by two of my uncles on my mother's side, frater-nal twins, both of them Lexington businessmen. They es-corted me up to the ICU and, in the elevator, filled me in on Worth's condition, explaining that he'd flatlined five times in the ambulance on the way to the hospital, his heart locked in something that Captain Jones, in his interview for *Rescue 911*, diagnosed as "asystole," which Jones described as "just another death-producing rhythm." As I took him to mean, my brother's pulse had been almost one continuous beat, like a drumroll, but feeble, not actually sending the blood anywhere. By the time I showed up, his heart was at least beating on its own power, but a machine was doing all his breathing for him. The worst news had to do with his brain, which we were told displayed 1 percent activity, vegetable status.

In the waiting room, a heavyset nurse who looked to be in her sixties came up and introduced herself as Nancy. She took me by the hand and led me through two silent, automatic glass doors into Intensive Care. My brother was a nightmare of tubes and wires, dark machines silently measuring every internal event, a pump filling and emptying his useless lungs. The stench of dried spit was everywhere in the room. His eyes were closed, his every muscle slack. It seemed that only the machines were still alive, possessed of some perverse will that wouldn't let them give up on this body.

I stood frozen, staring at him. The nurse spoke to me from the corner of the room in an unexpected tone of admonishment, which stung me at the time and even in retrospect seems hard to account for. "It ain't like big brother's gonna wake up tomorrow and be all better," she said. I looked at her stupidly. Had I not seemed shocked enough?

"Yes, I realize that," I said, and asked to be alone. When the door closed behind me, I went up to the side of the bed. Worth and I have different fathers, making us half brothers, technically, though he was already living with my dad when I was born, which means that I've never known life without him. Nonetheless we look nothing alike. He has thick dark hair and olive skin and was probably the only member of our family in the hospital that night with green as opposed to blue eyes. I leaned over into his face. The normal flush of his cheeks had gone white, and his lips were parted to admit the breathing tube. There was no sign of anything, of life or struggle or crisis, only the gruesomely robotic sounds of the oxygen machine pumping air into his chest and drawing it out again. I heard my uncles, their voices composed with strain, telling me about the 1 percent brain activity. I leaned closer, putting my mouth next to my brother's right ear. "Worth," I said, "it's John."

Without warning, all six feet and four inches of his body came to life, writhing against the restraints and what looked like a thousand invasions of his orifices and skin. His head reared back, and his eyes swung open on me. The pupils were almost nonexistent. They stayed open only for the briefest instant, focusing loosely on mine before falling shut. But what an instant! As a volunteer fireman in college, I had once helped to pull a dead man out of an overturned truck, and I remember the look of his open eyes as I handed him to the next person in line—I'd been expecting pathos, some shadow of whatever had been the last thought to cross his mind, but his eyes were just marbles, mere things. My brother's eyes had been nothing like that. They were, if anything, the terrified eyes of a man who was trying to climb out of a well: the second he moves, he slips back to the bottom. Worth's head fell back onto the pillow motionless, his body exhausted from that brief effort at reentering the world. I put down his hand, which I'd taken without knowing it, and stepped back into the hallway.

Worth spent that night, and the second day and night, in a coma. There were no outward signs of change, but the machines began to pick up indications of increased brain function. The neurosurgeon, an Irishman, explained to us (in what must have been, for him, child's language) that the brain is itself an electrical machine, and that the volts that had flowed from my brother's vintage Gibson amplifier and traumatized his body were in some sense still racing around in his skull. There was a decent chance, the doctor said, that he would emerge from the coma, but no one could say what would be left; no one could say who would emerge. The period of waiting comes back to me as a collage of awful food, nurses' cautious encouragement, and the disquieting presence of my brother supine in his bed, an oracle who could answer all our questions but refused to speak. We rotated in and out of his room like tourists circulating through a museum.

"On the third day" (I would never have said it myself, but Shatner does it for me on the show), Worth woke up. The nurses led us into his room, their faces almost proud, and we found him sitting up—gingerly resting on his elbows, with heavy-lidded eyes, as if at any moment he might decide he liked the coma better and slip back into it. His face lit up like a simpleton's whenever one of us entered the room, and he greeted each of us by our names in a barely audible rasp. He seemed to know us, but hadn't the slightest idea what we were all doing there, or where "there" might be—though he did come up with theories on the last point over the next two weeks, chief among them a wedding reception, a high school poker game, and at one point some kind of holding cell.

I've tried many times over the years to describe for people the person who woke up from that electrified near-death, the one who remained with us for about a month before he went back to being the person we'd known and know now. It would save one a lot of trouble to be able to say "it was like he was on acid," but that wouldn't be quite true. Instead, he seemed to be living one of those imaginary acid trips we used to pretend to be on in junior high, before we tried the real thing and found out it was slightly less magical—"Hey, man, your nose is like a star or something, man." He had gone there. My father and I kept notes, neither of us aware that the other was doing it, trying to get down all of Worth's little disclosures before they faded. I have my own list here in front of me. There's no best place to begin. I'll just transcribe a few things:

Squeezed my hand late on the night of the 23rd. Whispered, "That's the human experience."

While eating lunch on the 24th, suddenly became convinced that I was impersonating his brother. Demanded to see my ID. Asked me, "Why would you want to impersonate John?" When I protested, "But, Worth, don't I look like John?" he replied, "You look exactly like him. No wonder you can get away with it."

On the day of the 25th, stood up from his lunch, despite my attempts to restrain him, spilling the contents of his tray everywhere. Glanced at my hands, tight around his shoulders, and said, "I am not . . . repulsed . . . by man-to-man love. But I'm not into it."

Evening of the 25th. Gazing at own toes at end of bed, remarked, "That'd make a nice picture: Feet in Smoke."

Day of the 26th. Referred to heart monitor as "a solid, congealed bag of nutrients."

Night of the 26th. Tried to punch me with all his strength while I worked with Dad and Uncle John to restrain him in his bed, swinging and missing me by less than an inch. The IV tubes were tearing loose from his arms. His eyes were terrified, helpless. I think he took us for fascist goons.

Evening of the 27th. Unexpectedly jumped up from his chair, a perplexed expression on his face, and ran to the wall. Rubbed palms along a small area of the wall, like a blind man. Turned. Asked, "Where's the piñata?" Shuffled into hallway. Noticed a large nurse walking away from us down the hall. Muttered, "If she's got our piñata, I'm gonna be pissed."

The experience went from tragedy to tragicomedy to outright farce on a sliding continuum, so it's hard to pinpoint just when one let onto another. He was the most delightful drunk you'd ever met—I had to follow him around the hospital like a sidekick to make sure he didn't fall, because he couldn't stop moving, couldn't concentrate on anything for longer than a second. He became a holy fool. He looked down into his palm, where the fret and string had burned a deep, red cross into his skin, and said, "Hey, it'd be stigmata if there weren't all those ants crawling in it." He introduced my mother and father to each other as if they'd never met, saying, "Mom, meet Dad; Dad, meet Dixie Jean." Asked by the neurosurgeon if he knew how to spell his own name, he said, "Well, doctor, if you were Spenser, you might spell it w-o-r-t-h-E."

Another of the nurses, when I asked her if he'd ever be normal again, said, "Maybe, but wouldn't it be wonderful just to have him like this?" She was right; she humbled me. I can't imagine anything more hopeful or hilarious than having a seat at the spectacle of my brother's brain while it re-constructed reality. Like a lot of people, I'd always assumed, in a sort of cut-rate Hobbesian way, that the center of the brain, if you could ever find it, would inevitably be a pretty dark place, that whatever is good or beautiful about being human is a result of our struggles against everything innate, against physical nature. My brother changed my mind about all that. Here was a consciousness reduced to its matter, to a ball of crackling synapses—words that he knew how to use but couldn't connect to the right things; strange new objects for which he had to invent names; unfamiliar people who approached and receded like energy fields—and it was a good place to be, you might even say a poetic place. He had touched death, or death had touched him, but he seemed to find life no less interesting for having done so.

There is this one other remark:

Late afternoon of April 25. The window slats casting bars of shadow all over his room in the ICU. I had asked my mom and dad if they'd mind giving me a moment alone with him, since I still wasn't sure he knew quite who I was. I did know he wasn't aware of being inside a hospital; his most recent idea was that we were all back at my grandparents' house having a party, and at one point he slipped loose and went to the nurses' station to find out whether his tux was ready. Now we were sitting there in his room. Neither of us was speaking. Worth was jabbing a fork into his Jell-O, and I was just watching, waiting to see what would come out. Earlier that morning, he'd been scared by the presence of so many "strangers," and I didn't want to upset him any more. Things went on in silence like this for maybe five minutes.

Very quietly, he began to weep, his shoulders heaving with the force of emotion. I didn't touch him. A minute went by. I asked, "Worth, why are you crying?"

"I was thinking of the vision I had when I knew I was dead."

Certain that I'd heard him right, I asked him again anyway. He repeated it in the same flat tone: "I was thinking of the vision I had when I knew I was dead."

How could he know he'd been dead, when he didn't even know we were in a hospital, or that anything unusual had happened to him? Had a sudden clarity overtaken him?

"What was it? What was your vision?"

He looked up. The tears were gone. He seemed calm and serious. "I was on the banks of the River Styx," he said. "The boat came to row me across, but . . . instead of Charon, it was Huck and Jim. Only, when Huck pulled back his hood, he was an old man . . . like, ninety years old or something."

My brother put his face in his hands and cried a little more. Then he seemed to forget all about it. According to my notes, the next words out of his mouth were, "Check this out—I've got the Andrews Sisters in my milkshake."

We've never spoken of it since. It's hard to talk to my brother about anything related to his accident. He has a monthlong tape erasure in his memory that starts the second he put his lips to that microphone. He doesn't remember the shock, the ambulance, having died, coming back to life. Even when it was time for him to leave the hospital, he had managed only to piece together that he was late for a concert somewhere, and my last memory of him from that period is his leisurely wave when I told him I had to go back to school. "See you at the show," he called across the parking lot. When our family gets together, the subject of his accident naturally bobs up, but he just looks at us with a kind of suspicion. It's a story about someone else, a story he thinks we might be fudging just a bit.

When I can't sleep I still sometimes will try to decipher that vision. My brother was never much of a churchgoer (he proclaimed himself a deist at age fifteen) but had been an excellent student of Latin in high school. His teacher, a sweet and brilliant old bun-wearing woman named Rank, drilled her classes in classical mythology. Maybe when it came time for my brother to have his near-death experience, to reach down into his psyche and pull up whatever set of myths would help him make sense of the fear, he reached for the ones he'd found most compelling as a young man. For most people, that involves the whole tunnel-of-light business; for my brother, the underworld.

The question of where he got Huck and Jim defeats me. My father was a great Mark Twain fanatic—he got fired from the only teaching job he ever held for keeping the first graders in at recess, to make them listen to records of an actor reading the master's works—and he came up with the only clue: the accident had occurred on the eighty-fifth anniversary of Twain's death, in 1910.

I'm just glad they decided to leave my brother on this side of the river.

MR. LYTLE: AN ESSAY

When I was twenty years old, I became a kind of apprentice to a man named Andrew Lytle, whom pretty much no one apart from his negligibly less ancient sister, Polly, had addressed except as Mister Lytle in at least a decade. She called him Brother. Or Brutha—I don't suppose either of them had ever voiced a terminal *r*. His two grown daughters did call him Daddy. Certainly I never felt even the most obscure impulse to call him Andrew or "old man" or any other familiarism, though he frequently gave me to know it would be all right if I were to call him *mon vieux*. He, for his part, called me boy, and beloved, and once, in a letter, "Breath of My Nostrils." He was about to turn ninety-two when I moved into his basement, and he had not yet quite reached ninety-three when they buried him the next winter, in a coffin I had helped to make, a cedar coffin, because it would smell good, he said. I wasn't too helpful. I sat up a couple of nights in a freezing, starkly lit workshop rubbing beeswax into the boards.

The other, older men—we were four altogether—absorbedly sawed and planed. They chiseled dovetail joints. My experience in woodworking hadn't gone past feeding planks through a band saw for shop class, and there'd be no time to redo anything I might botch, so I followed instructions and with rags cut from an undershirt worked coats of wax into the cedar until its ashen whorls glowed purple, as if with remembered life.

The man overseeing this vigil was a luthier named Roehm whose house stood back in the woods on the edge of the plateau. He was about six and a half feet tall with floppy bangs and a deep, grizzled mustache. He wore huge glasses. I believe I have never seen a person more tense than Roehm was during those few days. The cedar was "green"; it hadn't been properly cured. He groaned that it wouldn't behave. On some level he must have resented the haste. Lytle had lain dying for weeks; he endured a series of disorienting pin strokes. By the end they were giving him less water than morphine. He kept saying, "Time to go home," which at first meant he wanted us to take him back to his house, his real house, that he'd tired of the terrible simulacrum we smuggled him to, in his delirium. Later, as those fevers drew together into what seemed an unbearable clarity, like a blue flame behind the eyes, the phrase came to mean what one would assume.

He had a deathbed, in other words. He didn't go suddenly. Yet although his family and friends had known for years about his wish to lie in cedar, which required that a coffin be custom-made, no one had so much as played with the question of who in those mountains could do such a thing or how much time the job would take. I don't hold it against them, against us, the avoidance of duty, owing as it did to fundamental incredulity. Lytle's whole existence had for so long been essentially posthumous, he'd never risk seeming so ridiculous as to go actually dying now. My grandfather had told me once that when he'd been at Sewanee, in the thirties, people had looked at Lytle as something of an old man, a full sixty years before I met him. And he nursed this impression, with his talk of coming "to live in the sense of eternity," and of the world he grew up in—middle Tennessee at the crack of the twentieth century—having more in common with Europe in the Middle Ages than with the South he lived to see. All his peers and enemies were dead. A middle daughter they'd buried long before. His only wife had been dead for thirty-four years, and now Mister Lytle was dead, and we had no cedar coffin.

But someone knew Roehm, or knew about him; and it turned out Roehm knew Lytle's books; and when they told Roehm he'd have just a few days to finish the work, he set to, without hesitation and even with a certain impatience, as if he feared to displease some unforgiving master. I see him there in the little space, repeatedly microwaving Tupperware containers full of burnt black coffee and downing them like Coca-Colas. He loomed. He was so large there hardly seemed room for the rest of us, and already the coffin lid lay on sawhorses in the center of the floor, making us sidle along the walls. At least a couple of times a night Roehm, who was used to agonizing for months over tiny, delicate instruments, would suffer a collapse, would hunch on his stool and bury his face in his hands and bellow "It's all wrong!" into the mute of his palms. My friend Sanford and I stared on. But the fourth, smaller man, a person named Hal, who'd been staying upstairs with Lytle toward the end and acting as a nurse, he knew Roehm better—now that I think of it, Hal must have been the one to tell the family about him in the first place—and Hal would put his hands on Roehm's shoulders and whisper to him to be calm, remind him how everyone understood he'd been allowed too little time, that if he wanted we could take a break. Then Roehm would smoke. He gripped each cigarette with two fingertips on top, snapping it in and out of his lips the way toughs in old movies do. Sanford and I sat in his truck with the heater on and drank vodka from a flask he'd brought, gazing on the shed with its small bright window, barely saying a word.

Weeks later he told me a story that Hal had told him, that at seven o'clock in the morning on the day of Lytle's funeral— which strangely Roehm did not attend—Hal woke to find Roehm sitting at the foot of his and his wife's bed, repeating the words "It works," apparently to himself. I never saw him again. The coffin was art. Hardly anyone got to see it. All through the service and down the street to the cemetery it wore a pall, and when people lined up at the graveside to take turns shoveling dirt back into the pit, the hexagonal lid, where inexplicably Roehm had found a spare hour to do scrollwork, grew invisible after just a few seconds.

There had been different boys living at Lytle's since not long after he lost his wife, maybe before—in any case it was a recognized if unofficial institution when I entered the college at seventeen. In former days these were mainly students whose writing showed promise, as judged by a certain well-loved, prematurely white-haired professor, himself a former protégé and all but a son during Lytle's long widowerhood. As years passed and Lytle declined, the arrangement came to be more about making sure someone was there all the time, someone to drive him and chop wood for him and hear him if he were to break a hip.

There were always those who saw it as a privilege, especially among the English majors. We were students at the University of the South, and Lytle was the South, the last Agrarian, the last of the famous "Twelve Southerners" behind *I'll Take My Stand*, a comrade to the hallowed Fugitive Poets, a friend since youth of Allen Tate and Robert Penn Warren, a mentor to Flannery O'Connor and James Dickey and Harry Crews and, as the editor of *The Sewanee Review* in the sixties, one of the first to publish Cormac McCarthy's fiction. Bear in mind that by the mid-nineties, when I knew him, the so-called Southern Renascence in letters had mostly dwindled to a tired professional regionalism. That Lytle hung on somehow, in however reduced a condition, represented a flaw in time, to be exploited.

Not everybody felt that way. I remember sitting on the floor one night with my freshman-year suitemate, a ninety-five-pound blond boy from Atlanta called Smitty who'd just spent a miserable four years at some private academy trying to convince the drama teacher to let them do a Beckett play. His best friend had been a boy they called Tweety Bird. The day I met Smitty, I asked what music he liked, and he shot back, "*Trumpets*." That night he went on about Lytle, what a grotesquerie and a fascist he was. "You know what Andrew Lytle said?" Smitty waggled his cigarette lighter. "Listen to this: 'Life is melodrama. Only art is real.'"

I nodded in anticipation.

"Don't you think that's *horrifying*?"

I didn't, though. Or I did and didn't care. I didn't know what I thought. I was under the tragic spell of the South, which you've either felt or haven't. In my case it was acute because, having grown up in Indiana with a Yankee father, a child exile from Kentucky roots of which I was overly proud, I'd long been aware of a faint nowhereness to my life. Others wouldn't have sensed it, wouldn't have minded. I felt it as a physical ache. Finally I was somewhere, there. The South . . . I loved it as only one who will always be outside it can. Merely to hear the word *Faulkner* at night brought gusty emotions. A few months after I'd arrived at the school, Shelby Foote came and read from his Civil War history. When he'd finished, a local geezer with long greasy white hair wearing a white suit with a cane stood up in the third row and asked if, in Foote's opinion, the South could have won, had such and such a general done such and such. Foote replied that the North had won "that war" with one hand behind its back. In the crowd there were gasps. It was thrilling that they cared. How could I help wondering about Lytle, out there beyond campus in his ancestral cabin, rocking before the blazing logs, drinking bourbon from heirloom silver cups and brooding on something Eudora Welty had said to him once. Whenever famous writers came to visit the school they'd ask to see him. I tried to read his novels, but my mind just ricocheted; they seemed impenetrably mannered. Even so, I hoped to be taken to meet him. One of my uncles had received such an invitation, in the seventies, and told me how the experience changed him, put him in touch with what's real.

The way it happened was so odd as to suggest either the involvement or the nonexistence of fate. I wasn't even a student at the time. I'd dropped out after my sophomore year, essentially in order to preempt failing out, and was living in

Ireland with a friend, working in a restaurant and failing to save money. But before my departure certain things had taken place. I'd become friends with the man called Sanford, a puckish, unregenerate back-to-nature person nearing fifty, who lived alone, off the electric grid, on a nearby communal farm. His house was like something Jefferson could have invented. Springwater flowed down from an old dairy tank in a tower on top; the refrigerator had been retrofitted to work with propane canisters that he salvaged from trailers. He had first-generation solar panels on the roof, a dirt-walled root cellar, a woodstove. He showered in a waterfall. We had many memorable hallucinogenic times that did not improve my grades.

Sanford needed very little money, but that he made doing therapeutic massage in town, and one of his clients was none other than Andrew Lytle, who drove himself in once a week, in his yacht-size chocolate Eldorado, sometimes in the right lane, sometimes the left, as he fancied. The cops all knew to follow him but would do so at a distance, purely to ensure he was safe. Often he arrived at Sanford's studio hours early and anxiously waited in the car. He loved the feeling of human hands on his flesh, he said, and believed it was keeping him alive.

One day, during their session, Lytle mentioned that his current boy was about to be graduated. Sanford, who didn't know yet how badly I'd blown it at the school, or that I was leaving, told Lytle about me and gave him some stories I'd written. Or poems? Doubtless dreadful stuff, but maybe it "showed promise." Toward the end of summer airmail letters started to flash in under the door of our hilltop apartment in Cork, their envelopes, I remember, still faintly curled from having been rolled through the heavy typewriter. The first one was dated, "Now that I have come to live in the sense of eternity, I rarely know the correct date, and the weather informs me of the day's advance, but I believe it is late August," and went on to say, "I'm presuming you will live with me here."

That's how it happened, he just asked. Actually, he didn't even ask. The fact that he was ignoring the proper channels eventually caused some awkwardness with the school. At the time, none of that mattered. I felt an exhilaration, the unsettling thrum of a great man's regard, and somewhere behind that the distant onrushing of fame. His letters came once, then twice a week. They were brilliantly senile, moving in and out of coherence and between tenses, between centuries. Often his typos, his poor eyesight, would produce the finest sentences, as when he wrote the affectingly commaless "This is how I protest absolutely futilely." He told me I was a writer but that I had no idea what I was doing. "This is where the older artist comes in." He wrote about the Muse, how she tests us when we're young. As our tone grew more intimate, his grew more urgent, too. I must come back soon. Who knew how much longer he'd live? "No man can forestall or evade what lies in wait." There were things he wanted to pass on, things that had taken him, he said, "too long to learn." Now he'd been surprised to discover a burst of intensity left. He said not to worry about the school. "College is perhaps not the best preparation for a writer." I'd live in the basement, a guest. We'd see to our work.

It took me several months to make it back, and he grew annoyed. When I finally let myself in through the front door, he didn't get up from his chair. His form sagged so exaggeratedly into the sofa, it was as if thieves had crept through and stolen his bones and left him there. He gestured at the smoky stone fireplace with its enormous black andirons and said, "Boy, I'm sorry the wood's so poor. I had no idea I'd be alive in November." He watched as though paralyzed while I worked at building the fire back up. He spoke only to critique my form. The heavier logs at the back, to project the heat. Not too much flame. "Young men always make that mistake." He asked me to pour him some whiskey and announced flatly his intention to nap. He lay back and draped across his eyes the velvet bag the bottle had come tied in, and I sat across from him for half an hour, forty minutes. At first he talked in his sleep, then to me. The pivots of his turn to consciousness were undetectably slight, with frequent slippages. His speech was full of mutterings, warnings. The artist's life is strewn with traps. Beware "the machinations of the enemy."

"Mr. Lytle," I whispered, "who is the enemy?"

He sat up. His unfocused eyes were an icy blue. "Why, boy," he said, "the bourgeoisie!" Then he peered at me for a second as if he'd forgotten who I was. "Of course," he said. "You're only a baby."

I'd poured myself two bourbons during nap time and felt them somewhat. He lifted his own cup and said, "Confusion to the enemy." We drank.

It was idyllic, where he lived, on the grounds of an old Chautauqua called the Assembly, one of those rustic resorts deliberately placed up north, or at a higher altitude, which began as escapes from the plagues of yellow fever that used to harrow the mid-Southern states. Lytle could remember coming there as a child. An old judge, they said, had transported the cabin entire up from a cove somewhere in the nineteenth century. You could still see the logs in the walls, although otherwise the house had been made rather elegant over the years. The porch went all the way around. It was usually silent, except for the wind in the pines. Besides guests, you never saw anyone. A summer place, except Lytle didn't leave.

He slept in a wide carved bed in a corner room. His life was an incessant whispery passage on plush beige slippers from bed to sideboard to seat by the fire, tracing that perimeter, marking each line with light plantings of his cane. He'd sing to himself. The Appalachian one that goes, "A haunt can't haunt a haunt, my good old man." Or songs that he'd picked up in Paris at my age or younger: "Sous les Ponts de Paris" and "Les Chevaliers de la Table Ronde." His French was superb, but his accent in English was best, that extinct mid-Southern, land grant pioneer speech, with its tinges of the abandoned Celtic urban Northeast ("boyned" for *burned*) and its raw gentility.

From downstairs I could hear him move and knew where he was in the house at all times. My apartment had once been the kitchen; servants went up and down the back steps. The floor was all bare stone, and damp. And never really warm, until overnight it became unbearably humid. Cave crickets popped around as you tried to sleep, touching down with little clicks. Lots of mornings I woke with him standing over me, cane in one hand, coffee in the other, and he'd say, "Well, my lord, shall we rise and entreat Her Ladyship?" Her ladyship was the Muse. He had all manner of greetings.

For half a year we worked steadily, during his window of greatest coherence, late morning to early afternoon. We read Flaubert, Joyce, a little James, the more famous Russians, all the books he'd written about as an essayist. He tried to make me read Jung. He chopped at my stories till nothing was left but the endings, which he claimed to admire. A too-easy eloquence, was his overall diagnosis. I tried to apply his criticisms, but they were sophisticated to a degree my efforts couldn't repay. He was trying to show me how to solve problems I hadn't learned existed.

About once a day he'd say, "I may do a little writing yet, myself, if my mind holds." One morning I even heard from downstairs the slap-slap of the typewriter keys. That day, while he napped, I slid into his room and pulled off the slipcover to see what he'd done, a single sentence of between thirty and forty words. A couple of them were hyphened out, with substitutions written above in ballpoint. The sentence stunned me. I'd come half expecting to find an incoherent mess, and afraid that this would say something ominous about our whole experiment, my education, but the opposite confronted me. The sentence was perfect. In it, he described a memory from his childhood, of a group of people riding in an early automobile, and the driver lost control, and they veered through an open barn door, but by a glory of chance the barn was completely empty, and the doors on the other side stood wide open, too, so that the car passed straight through the barn and back out into the sunlight, by which time the passengers were already laughing and honking and waving their arms at the miracle of their own survival, and Lytle was somehow able, through his prose, to replicate this swift and almost alchemical transformation from horror to joy. I don't know why I didn't copy out the sentence—embarrassment at my own spying, I guess. He never wrote any more. But for me it was the key to the year I lived with him. What he could still do, in his weakness, I couldn't do. I started listening harder, even when he bored me.

His hair was sparse and mercury silver. He wore a tweed

jacket every day and, around his neck, a gold-handled tooth-pick hewn from a raccoon's sharpened penis bone. I put his glasses onto my own face once and my hands, held just at arm's length, became big beige blobs. There was a thing on his forehead, a cyst, I assume, that had gotten out of control. It was about the size and shape of a bisected Ping-Pong ball. His doctor had offered to remove it several times, but Lytle treated it as a conversation piece. "Vanity has no claim on me," he said. He wore a gray fedora with a bluebird's feather in the band. The skin on his face was strangely young-seeming. Tight and translucent. But the rest of his body was extraterrestrial. Once a week I helped him bathe. God alone knew for how long the moles and things on his back had been left to evolve unseen. His skin was doughy. Not saggy or lumpy, not in that sense—he was hale—but fragile-feeling. He had no hair anywhere below. His toenails were of horn. After the bath he lay naked between fresh sheets, needing to feel completely dry before he dressed. All Lytles, he said, had nervous temperaments.

I found him exotic; it may be accurate to say that I found him beautiful. The manner in which I related to him was essentially anthropological. Taking offense, for instance, to his more or less daily outbursts of racism, chauvinism, anti-Semitism, class snobbery, and what I can only describe as medieval nostalgia, seemed as absurd as debating these things with a caveman. Shut up and ask him what the cave art means. The self-service and even cynicism of that reasoning are not hard to dissect at a distance of years, but I can't pretend to regret it, or that I wish I had walked away.

There was something else, something less contemptible, a voice in my head that warned it would be unfair to lecture a man with faculties so diminished. I could never be sure what he was saying, as in stating, and what he was simply no longer able to keep from slipping out of his id and through his mouth. I used to walk by his wedding picture, which hung next to the cupboard—the high forehead, the square jaw, the jug ears—and think as I passed it, "If you wanted to contend with him, you'd have to contend with that man." Otherwise it was cheating.

I came to love him. Not in the way he wanted, maybe, but not in a way that was stinting. *Mon vieux*. I was twenty and believed that nothing as strange was liable to happen to me again. I was a baby. One night we were up drinking late in the kitchen and I asked him if he thought there was any hope. Like that: "Is there any hope?" He answered me quite solemnly. He told me that in the hallways at Versailles, there hung a faint, ever-so-faint smell of human excrement, "because as the chambermaids hurried along a tiny bit would always splash from the pots." Many years later I realized that he was half-remembering a detail from the court of Louis XV, namely that the latrines were so few and so poorly placed at the palace, the marquesses used to steal away and relieve themselves on stairwells and behind the beautiful furniture, but that night I had no idea what he meant, and still don't entirely.

"Have I shown you my incense burner?" he asked.

"Your what?"

He shuffled out into the dining room and opened a locked glass cabinet door. He came back cradling a little three-legged pot and set it down gently on the chopping block between us. It was exquisitely painted and strewn with infinitesimal cracks. A figure of a dog-faced dragon lay coiled on the lid, protecting a green pearl. Lytle spun the object to a particular angle, where the face was darker, slightly orange-tinged. "If you'll look, the glaze is singed," he said. "From the blast, I presume, or the fires." He held it upside down. Its maker's mark was legible on the bottom, or would have been to one who read Japanese. "This pot," he said, "was recovered from the Hiroshima site." A classmate of his from Vanderbilt, one of the Fugitives, had gone on to become an officer in the Marine Corps and gave it to him after the war. "When I'm dead I want you to have it," he said.

I didn't bother refusing, just thanked him, since I knew he wouldn't remember in the morning, or, for that matter, in half an hour. But he did remember. He left it to me.

Ten years later in New York City my adopted stray cat, Holly Kitty, pushed it off a high shelf I didn't think she could reach, and it shattered. I sat up most of the night gluing the slivers back into place.

Lytle's dementia began to progress more quickly. I hope it's not cruel to note that at times the effects could be funny. He insisted on calling the K-Y Jelly we used to lubricate his co-lostomy tube Kye Jelly. Finally he got confused about what it was for and appeared in my doorway one day with his tooth-brush and a squeezed-out tube of the stuff. "Put Kye on the list, boy," he said. "We're out."

Evenings he'd mostly sit alone and rehash forty-year-old fights with dead literary enemies, performing both sides as though in a one-man play, at times yelling wildly, pounding his cane. Allen Tate, his brother turned nemesis, was by far the most frequent opponent, but it seemed in these rages that anyone he'd ever known could change into the serpent, fall prey to an obsession with power. Particularly disorienting was when the original version of the mock battle had been between him and me. Him and the boy. Several times, in reality, we did clash. Stood face-to-face shouting. I called him a mean old bastard, something like that; he told me I'd betrayed my gift. Later, from downstairs, I heard him say to the boy, "You think you're not a slave?"

One day I came in from somewhere. Polly, his sister, was staying upstairs. I loved Miss Polly's visits, everyone did. She made rum cakes you could eat yourself to death on like a goldfish. There were homemade pickles and biscuits from scratch when she came. A tiny woman with glasses so thick they magnified her eyes, her knuckles were cubed with arthritis. Who knew what she thought, or if she thought, about all the nights she'd shared with her brother and his interesting artist friends. (Once, in a rented house somewhere, she'd been forced by sleeping arrangements to lie awake in bed all night between fat old Ford Madox Ford and his mistress.) She shook her head over how the iron skillet, which their family had been seasoning in slow ovens since the Depression, would suffer at my hands. I had trouble remembering not to put it through the dishwasher. Over meals, under the chandelier with the "saltcellar" and the "salad oil," as Lytle raved about the master I might become, if only I didn't fall prey to this, that, or the other hubristic snare, she'd simply grin and say, "Oh, Brutha, how *exciting.*"

On the afternoon in question I was coming through the security gate, entering "the grounds," as cottagers called the Assembly, and Polly passed me going the opposite way in her minuscule blue car. There was instantly something off, because she didn't stop completely. She rolled down the window and spoke to me but continued to idle past, going at most twenty miles per hour (the speed limit in there was twelve, I think). It was as though she were waving from a parade float. "I'm on my way to the store," she said. "We need [mumble] . . ."

"What's that?"

"BUTTAH!"

With a bad feeling I watched her recede. Back at the cabin, Lytle was caning around on the front porch in a panic. He waved at me as I turned into the gravel patch where we parked. "She's drunk!" he barked. "Look at this bottle, beloved. Good God, it was full this morning!"

I tried to make him tell me what had happened, but he was too antsy. He wore pajamas, black slippers without socks, a gray tweed coat, and the fedora.

"Oh, I've angered her, beloved," he said. "I've angered her."

He gave me the story as we sped toward the gate. It was more or less as I suspected. The same argument came up every time Polly visited, though I'd never seen it escalate so. They had family in a distant town with whom she remained on decent terms, but Lytle insisted on shunning these people and thought his little sister should, as well. It had to do with an old scandal about land, duplicity involving a will. A greedy uncle had tried to take away his father's farm. But these modern-day cousins, descendants of the rival party, they weren't pretending, as Lytle believed, not to understand why he wouldn't see them. I think they were genuinely confused. There'd been scenes. He'd stood in the doorway and denounced these people, in the highest rhetoric, "Seed of the usurper." Doubtless they thought he was further gone mentally than he was, that when he uttered these curses he had in mind some carpetbagger from olden days, because the relatives just kept coming back, despite never having been allowed past the porch steps.

Now Miss Polly had let them into the vestibule, nearly

into the Court of the Muse. Lytle viewed this as the v
betrayal. He'd been beastly toward them, when he rose fron.
his nap, and Polly had fled. He seemed shaken to remember
the things he'd said.

"Mister Lytle, what did you say?"

"I told the truth," he said passionately. "I recognized the
moment, that's what I did." But in the defensive thrust of his
jaw there quivered something like embarrassment.

He mentions this land dispute in his "family memoir," *A
Wake for the Living,* his most readable and in many ways his
best book. That's perhaps an idiosyncratic opinion. There
are people who've read a lot more than I have who consider
his novels lost classics. But it may be precisely because of the
Faustian ego that thundered above his sense of himself as a
novelist that he carried a lighter burden into the memoir,
and this freedom thawed in his style some of the vivacity and
spontaneity that otherwise you find only in the letters. There's
a scene in which he describes the morning his grandmother
was shot in the throat by a Union soldier in 1863. "Nobody
ever knew who he was or why he did it," Lytle writes, "he
mounted a horse and galloped out of town." To the end of
her long life this woman wore a velvet ribbon at her neck,
fastened with a golden pin. That's how close Lytle was to the
Civil War. Close enough to reach up as a child, passing into
sleep, and fondle the clasp of that pin. The eighteenth century was just another generation back from there, and so on,
hand to hand. This happens, I suppose, this collapsing of
time, when you make it as far as your nineties. When Lytle
was born, the Wright Brothers had not yet achieved a working design. When he died, *Voyager 2* was exiting the solar
system. What does one do with the coexistence of those details in a lifetime's view? It weighed on him.

The incident with his grandmother is masterfully handled:

> She ran to her nurse. The bullet had barely missed the jugular vein. Blood darkened the apple she still held in her hand, and blood was in her shoe. The enemy in the street now invaded the privacy of the house. The curious entered and stared. They confiscated the air . . . To the child's fevered gaze the long bayonets of the soldiers seemed to reach the ceiling, as they filed past her bed, staring out of boredom and curiosity.

Miss Polly passed us again. Apparently she'd changed her mind about the butter. We made a U-turn and trailed her to the cabin. Back inside they embraced. She buried her face in his coat, laughing and weeping. "Oh, sister," he said, "I'm such an old fool, goddamn it."

I've wished at times that we had endured some meaningful falling out. In truth he began to exasperate me in countless petty ways. He needed too much, feeding and washing and shaving and dressing, more than he could admit to and keep his pride. Anyone could sympathize, but I hadn't signed on to be his butler. One day I ran into the white-haired professor, who shared with me that Lytle had been complaining about my cooking.

Mainly, though, I'd fallen in love with a tall, nineteen-year-old half-Cuban girl from North Carolina, with freckles on her face and straight dark hair down her back. She was a class behind mine, or what would have been mine, at the school, and she liked books. On our second date she gave me her father's roughed-up copy of *Hunger*, the Knut Hamsun novel. I started to spend more time downstairs. Lytle became pitifully upset. When I invited her in to meet him, he treated her coldly, made some vaguely insulting remark about "Latins," and at one point asked her if she understood a woman's role in an artist's life.

There came a wickedly cold night in deep winter when she and I lay asleep downstairs, wrapped up under a pile of old comforters on twin beds we'd pushed together. By now the whole triangle had grown so unpleasant that Lytle would start drinking earlier than usual on days when he spotted her car out back, and she no longer found him amusing or, for that matter, I suppose, harmless. My position was hideous.

She shook me awake and said, "He's trying to talk to you on the thing." We had this antiquated monitor system, the kind where you depress the big silver button to talk and let it off to hear. The man hadn't mastered an electrical device in his life. At breakfast one morning, when I'd made the mistake of leaving my computer upstairs after an all-nighter, he screamed at me for "bringing the enemy into this home, into a place of work." Yet he'd become a bona fide technician on the monitor system.

"He's calling you," she said. I lay still and listened. There was a crackling.

"Beloved," he said, "I hate to disturb you, in your slumbers, my lord. But I believe I might freeze to DEATH up here."

"Oh, my God," I said.

"If you could just . . . lie beside me."

I looked at her. "What do I do?"

She turned away. "I wish you wouldn't go up there."

"What if he dies?"

"You think he might?"

"I don't know. He's ninety-two, and he says he's freezing to death."

73

"*Beloved . . . ?*" She sighed. "You should probably go up there."

He didn't speak as I slipped into bed. He fell back asleep instantly. The sheets were heavy white linen and expensive. It seemed there were shadowy acres of snowy terrain between his limbs and mine. I floated off.

When I woke at dawn he was nibbling my ear and his right hand was on my genitals.

I sprang out of bed and began to hop around the room like I'd burned my finger, sputtering foul language. Lytle was already moaning in shame, fallen back in bed with his hand across his face like he'd just washed up somewhere, a piece of wrack. I should mention that he wore, as on every chill morning, a Wee Willie Winkie nightshirt and cap. "Forgive me, forgive me," he said.

"Jesus Christ, Mister Lytle."

"Oh, beloved . . ."

His having these desires was not an issue—no one could be so naive. His tastes were more or less an open secret. I don't know if he was gay or bisexual or pansexual or what. Those distinctions are clumsy terms with which to address the mysteries of sexuality. But on a few occasions he'd spoken about his wife in a manner that to me was movingly erotic, nothing like any self-identifying gay man I've ever heard talk about women and sex. Certainly Lytle had loved her, because it was clear how he missed her, Edna, his beautiful "squirrel-eyed gal from Memphis," whom he'd married when she was young, who was still young when she died of lung cancer.

Much more often, however, when the subject of sex came up, he would return to the idea of there having been a homoerotic side to the Agrarian movement itself. He told me that Allen Tate propositioned him once, "but I turned him down. I didn't like his smell. You see, smell is so important, beloved. To me he had the stale scent of a man who didn't take any exercise." This may or may not have been true, but it wasn't an isolated example. Later writers, including some with an interest in not playing up the issue, have noticed, for instance, Robert Penn Warren's more-than-platonic interest in Tate, when they were all at Vanderbilt together. One of the other Twelve Southerners, Stark Young—he's rarely mentioned—was openly gay. Lytle professed to have carried on, as a very young man, a happy, sporadic affair with the brother of another Fugitive poet, not a well-known person. At one point the two of them fantasized about living together, on a small farm. The man later disappeared and turned up murdered in Mexico. Warren mentions him in a poem that plays with the image of the closet.

The point is that you can't fully understand that movement, which went on to influence American literature for decades, without understanding that certain of the writers involved in it loved one another. Most "homosocially," of course, but a few homoerotically, and some homosexually. That's where part of the power originated that made those friendships so intense, and caused the men to stay united almost all their lives, even after spats and changes of opinion, even after their Utopian hopes for the South had died. Together they produced from among them a number of good writers, and even a great one, in Warren, whom they can be seen to have lifted, as if on wing beats, to the heights for which he was destined.

Lytle would have beaten me with his cane and thrown

me out for saying all that. To him it was a matter for winking and nodding, frontier sexuality, fraternity brothers falling into bed with each other and not thinking much about it. Or else it was Hellenism, golden lads in the Court of the Muse, William Alexander Percy stuff. Whatever it was, I accepted it. I never showed displeasure when he wanted to sit and watch me chop wood, or when he asked me to quit showering every morning, so that he could smell me better. "I'm pert' near blind, boy," he said. "How will I find you in a fire?" Still, I'd taken for granted an understanding between us. I didn't expect him to grope me like a chambermaid.

I stayed away two nights, but then went back. When I reached the top of the steps and looked through the back porch window, I saw him on the sofa lying asleep (or dead, I wondered every time). His hands were folded across his belly. One of them rose and hung quivering, an actor's wave; he was talking to himself. It turned out, when I cracked the door, he was talking to me.

"Beloved, now, we must forget this," he said. "I merely wanted to touch it a little. You see, I find it the most interesting part of the body."

Then he paused and said, "Yes," seeming to make a mental note that the phrase would do.

"I understand, you have the girl now," he continued. "Woman offers the things a man must have, home and children. And she's a lovely girl. I myself may not have made the proper choices, in that role."

I crept down to bed.

Not long after, I moved out. He agreed it was for the best. I reenrolled at the school. They found someone else to live with him. It had become more of a medical situation by that point, at-home care. I drove out to see him every week, and I like to think he welcomed the visits, but things had changed. He knew how to adjust his formality by tenths of a degree, to let you know where you stood.

It may be gratuitous to remark of a ninety-two-year-old man that he began to die, but Lytle had been much alive for most of that year, fiercely so. There were some needless minor surgeries at one point, which set him back. It's funny how the living will help the dying along. One night he fell, right in front of me. He was standing in the middle room on a slippery carpet, and I was moving toward him to take a glass from his hand. The next instant he was flat on his back with a broken elbow that during the night bruised horribly, blackly. His eyes went from glossy to matte. Different people took turns staying over with him, upstairs, including the white-haired professor, whose loyalty had never wavered. I spent a couple of nights. I wasn't worried he'd try anything again. He was in a place of calm and—you could see it—preparation. His son-in-law told me he'd spoken my name the day before he died.

When the coffin was done, the men from the funeral home picked it up in a hearse. Late the same night someone called to say they'd finished embalming Lytle's body; it was in the chapel, and whenever Roehm was ready, he could come and fasten the lid. All of us who'd worked on it with him went, too. The mortician let us into a glowing side hallway off the cold ambulatory. With us was an old friend of Lytle's named Brush, who worked for the school administration, a low-built, bouncy muscular man with boyish dark hair and a perpetual bow tie. He carried, as nonchalantly as he could, a bowling ball bag, and in the bag an extremely excellent bottle of whiskey.

Brush took a deep breath, reached into the coffin, and jammed the bottle up into the crevice between Lytle's rib cage and his left arm. He turned and said, "That way they won't hear it knocking around when we roll it out of the church."

Roehm had a massive electric drill in his hand. It seemed out of keeping with the artisanal methods that had gone into the rest of the job, but he'd run out of time making the cedar pegs. We stood over Lytle's body. Sanford was the first to kiss him. When everyone had, we lowered the lid onto the box, and Roehm screwed it down. Somebody wished the old man Godspeed. A eulogy that ran in the subsequent number of *The Sewanee Review* said that, with Lytle's death, "the Confederacy at last came to its end."

He appeared to me only once afterward, and that was two and a half years later, in Paris. It's not as if Paris is a city I know or have even visited more than a couple of times. He knew it well. I was coming up the stairs from the metro into the sunshine with the girl, whom I later married, on my left arm, when my senses became intensely alert to his presence about a foot and a half to my right. I couldn't look directly at him: I had to let him hang back in my peripheral vision, else he'd slip away. It was a bargain we made in silence. I could see enough to tell that he wasn't young but was maybe twenty years younger than when I'd known him, wearing the black-framed engineer's glasses he'd worn at just that time in his life, looking up and very serious, climbing the steps to the light, where I lost him.

AT A SHELTER (AFTER KATRINA)

Coming east along the Gulf, you started picking up signs around Slidell that something ungodly had passed through there. Whole stands of mature pine had been chopped down at the knees, as if by shock wave. And the huge black metal poles that hold up highway billboards, many of those were bent in half, the upper parts dangling by spiky hinges. Weirdest of all was the roadkill. There's always plenty in Mississippi, but now, among the raccoons and the deer and the occasional armadillo, you saw dogs, more than a few, healthy-looking apart from being dead, and with collars on—not strays, in other words, or not until a few days before. And the little black vultures they have down there, with gray, beaked faces like Venetian masks, were hopping up out of the brush to pick at them.

That was the outer edge of what the hurricane had done. By the time you reached the coast in Gulfport, there was a smell in the air you couldn't tolerate for longer than forty-five seconds or so. I'd smelled it before but never in the First World. It was the smell of large organic things that had lain dead under a burning sun for days. Dozens of semitrailers and boats—ships, really—had been picked up and hurled half a mile, just spun around and crunched. It looked contrary to the laws of physics, to the point where you saw it in miniature, a toy box overturned by an angry child. Perfectly clean wood frames stood where some very substantial houses had been. The wind and water had simply moved through them, stripping away every brick and board and shingle. Even the toilet bowls were blasted out.

Katrina created what was almost certainly the largest storm surge ever recorded in the United States: official numbers are still forthcoming, but it was around thirty feet. A lot of the people who died in Mississippi did so because this inundation happened horrifically fast. You were listening to the wind at your windows, wondering if you should flee, then you were trying to grab at the uppermost limbs of trees as you went rushing by. One older woman told me a giant sea turtle swam through her kitchen while she perched on the counter.

In the Red Cross shelter at Harrison Central Elementary School in Gulfport, you kept hearing people say they'd "swum out the front door." One was Terry DeShields, a trim, muscular black guy with a neat mustache and a bad, healed burn on his left arm. The hurricane had made landfall on his thirty-fifth birthday. He'd been sitting on his couch and thinking to himself, I'm not gonna run from this thing. He took a nap. He woke up and there was seven feet of water in his house. "I heard the rumbling," he said, "and I thought, Oh, Lord, here we go!" He made it through the door just seconds before the surge "pushed the walls out."

"The wind's blowing me around," he said. "I'm hitting trees. There's snakes swimming around—and I ain't no friend to snakes."

DeShields was tossed through his old neighborhood, searching for something to climb. He was carried to the rear parking lot of a Chinese restaurant. There he saw two convection ovens, one stacked atop the other, and bolted down. The upper one was still above the waterline. He hoisted himself onto it and curled into a ball. The hurricane roared around him for hours. That seemed like a long time to think, so I asked him what he thought about. "Pretty simple," he said. "I am going to die."

When the water fell back, he climbed down and set out, looking for food. "There wasn't no shelters yet," he said. "Least I didn't know where." He had on a pair of underwear and one sock. He wandered for two days in scorching heat. He slept on the ground in the woods. When I talked to him, his hands were still puffed up like mittens from the mosquito bites. Finally, a state trooper passed him and gave him a packet of crackers and a hot can of Coca-Cola and pointed him toward the shelter. "When I saw that cross," he said, "I knew I was saved."

And yet the next night he snuck out, slipping back to a beach not far from where his house had stood. "I couldn't help it," he said. "That was my beach, you know. I had to see it. Gone. All those mansions, casinos. The sidewalk, man. I sat there till four o'clock in the morning and cried."

There was an older man, wiry and dark, who looked to be in his late fifties. He had a single tooth on each side of his smile, perfectly spaced. His name was Ernel Porché, but at the shelter they called him Boots, because he'd escaped his house with a pair of dirty white oversize galoshes on and hadn't wanted to change them since. He told me he was worried about his aunt. "We're a small family," he said. "I don't know if she got out." When the man from the Red Cross had first switched on the TV and put it to CNN, Boots saw a picture of his aunt's neighborhood. It was underwater. "That was very disturbing," he said.

Gone. That was the word everybody used. What about your house? Did it hit your house? "Oh, that's gone, honey. That's all gone." The walls "was blowed out." The future had been ripped away and replaced with a massive blank. You asked people what they were going to do, where they'd end up, how long they'd be allowed to stay at the shelter. They looked at you like they were thinking hard about something else.

It was past lights-out. The generator was powering only a string of emergency lights that lined the middle hallway, where people lay sleeping on bedrolls. I got assigned a spot in a little classroom with construction-paper pictures on the wall. Plenty of folks were still up, though, whispering in clusters. You could hear babies crying. An old, long-bearded white guy with no shirt on and sagging hairy man-breasts was coughing, a terrible hacking cough. "There's a pill sticking sideways in my throat!" he croaked. Another guy kept reminding the shelter manager that he was severely manic and had been off his meds for five days now. "And you know what it's like when you're off your meds!" I'd heard him by then say to at least four people. I heard a woman tell the manager that the Red Cross needed to "put the censorship on the TV," because she'd caught some children in the cafeteria watching a sex movie. "It was the real dirty stuff," she said, "people sucking on each other's nipples and everything."

I got up and went out back and found a little party sitting on a patio, talking by lantern light. They were in wonderfully high spirits. Most of the people who ended up in the shelters had been living pretty close to the bottom already. Some had no reason not to assume that their new FEMA housing would be nicer than what they'd been living in for years.

There on the patio, a big jolly-looking bearded white man named Bill Melton, a shrimper with a neck tattoo, was kicking back in a wooden chair next to a black couple in their forties, R.J. and Jacqueline Sanders. I asked if they'd all known one another before the storm. Mistaking my question (or maybe taking it correctly), Melton said, "There's no color here, man. R.J. and Miss Jackie, they're my brother and sister now." I heard other expressions of this almost Utopian feeling. An old man and woman were talking in the hallway. "All them rich people," he said, "I don't care how much money you got. We all the same now. That's why I'm *always* looking up to God. I don't care how high I get."

Bill and R.J. and Miss Jackie were part of a small group at Harrison Central who appeared to be dealing with their situation by staying constantly, almost frantically active. The Red Cross had more than enough packaged meals for everyone, but this crew had convinced the woman who managed the school lunchroom to unlock the kitchen doors so they could use the food before it went bad. Boots was a cook in a restaurant; he fired up the gas burners and took the helm. They'd been serving meals to everyone, and their energy was shoring up morale. (The next morning, I tasted what Melton called S.O.S.—shit on a shingle, or meat in gravy on a roll—and found it edible.) "We feed eeeeverybody," R.J. said. "Not just our little family here."

"We even feed the officers!" Melton added.

Miss Jackie jumped up and told me I had to see the shower they'd made. Normally, the Red Cross doesn't like to use a site for shelter unless it has shower facilities, but many of the original buildings they'd chosen were destroyed in the storm, so they'd been forced to take over Harrison Central.

Miss Jackie and R.J. led me past a plastic curtain into the shower area. What they'd done was pretty ingenious. With the keys the lunch lady gave them, they'd opened a metal plate in the bricks that shielded an outdoor spigot. Someone rigged a gas burner to heat a water tank inside. They'd scavenged the neighborhood around the school for metal pipe and rigged up a flow. For the showerhead, they'd taken an empty can, one of these curious white cans of tap water that Anheuser-Busch evidently produces during natural disasters, and poked a bunch of holes in the bottom. Then they'd taped it onto the pipe.

"Turn it on, Miss Jackie!" said Bill Melton. Jackie was entrusted with the keys. She opened the metal plate and turned the red knob. Warm water came spraying out of the can, a fountain of water. It made a pattern like a garden spider's web in R.J.'s flashlight.

"We made this happen," Bill Melton said.

"Isn't it beautiful?" Miss Jackie said.

I groped for a response.

"It is beautiful," R.J. said.

———

When after a few days I left the shelter and drove back to Jackson in my rental, I had a *Mad Max*–style experience that I've thought about many times since. I started running low on gas, and the gas situation was bad. People had lined up for miles at the few pumps with any fuel left. My gauge showed well below a quarter tank, so I pulled off. The road to the station ran long and straight. I could see how far we had to go and wondered if I had even enough gas to last the line. It was unsettling to see something like that in America. In all the nuclear war movies that damaged us as kids, wasn't there always a scene where they waited in line for the dwindling gas? Here we were. But so far everybody seemed calm, treating it like any other traffic jam. It was hot and sunny on the asphalt as we slithered over it, bumpers inches from one another, each of us an interlinked segment of some slow, determined insect.

At one point, we intersected with another, smaller road that exited onto ours, the road to the gas. Few people were foolish enough to try entering the line by this road—it was cutting, essentially—but every time someone did, there'd be tension, shouts out the window, the exiting person making upturned "What can I do?" hands. Nothing awful, though. No fighting. The radio played "Sweet Emotion."

There was a traffic light at the intersection of these two roads, and in passing through it, as it reverted from green to red, I did something sort of awkward. An older woman who'd been immediately behind me—for an hour—was attempting to come through the light with me as well. She thought she'd be the last one in our group to make it. But she'd miscalculated, there wasn't room. I'd gone as far forward as I could without hitting the truck in front of me, and the back half of her car was still stranded in the box. Had someone coming the opposite way, on the other side of the highway, tried to turn through our line fast, onto that road, she'd have been smashed. In my rearview mirror, she looked scared, so I did the only thing I could and gradually, with each jolt of the traffic, nosed my car over to the side of the highway, until I could edge the front right bumper up onto the grass there, giving the woman six or so feet to scooch up and out of harm's way. It was no act of heroism on my part, but nor was it an act of sneakiness and cheating, which is what the wiry, drunken, super-pissed-off Mississippian who appeared at my side window accused me of, in the most furious tones. "I saw what you did, asshole," he said. He'd actually climbed out of his own car and walked a good ways up the road, just to unload on me.

"What do you mean?" I said. "I haven't done shit but sit here for hours."

He was pacing around in the road next to my car, pointing his finger at me. The line of traffic was that motionless, that he could do this without worrying about his own car.

"There's people in this line that have been waiting for *miles*," he said. "You can't just jump in the fucking line." He'd seen me execute that little maneuver, you see, to make room for the old lady, and he'd assumed (not irrationally) that he was witnessing the final stages of my inserting myself in front of her, from the side road.

Who knew what the guy had been through in the last few days. His face was bristled with long stubble. His flannel shirt was filthy. The way he wouldn't stop moving, it looked like he was in the desert, raving at God.

The reptilian thing that takes over at moments like that told me not to get mad, but to keep *explaining* what had happened. I said, "You have to listen to me, man! I've been in this lines for miles. *Let* me explain—"

Mainly he shouted over me, but each time I repeated the story—the light, the old lady—it seemed like another sentence would slip through his shield of outrage, and slowly he began to calm down. Finally he walked back to his car. At least I thought he was doing that. In reality he was going back to interrogate the old lady about me. I watched them in my rearview mirror. She was shaking her head and clearly saying the word *no* over and over, looking at my car and saying, *no. Was that old . . . ?*

My tormenter returned. Others in their cars were watching and listening. It was embarrassing. "She says she'd never *seen* your car," he said.

"What?" I turned in my seat and looked back at her with an exaggerated How could you? expression. The woman just looked scared.

The guy kept cursing. "Go back to Tennessee!" he shouted. "You got plenty of gas up there." I didn't live in Tennessee anymore. How did he know I once had? The license plate on the rental—I hadn't even noticed it.

In the end I rolled up my window and blasted the music, and he melted away. There was no option, for either of us. The gas got me to more gas. But I was thinking, the whole rest of the wait, this is how it would start, the real end of the world. The others in their cars, instead of just staring, would have climbed out and joined him. It would be nobody's fault.

GETTING DOWN TO WHAT IS REALLY REAL

It was maybe an hour before midnight at the Avalon Nightclub in Chapel Hill, and the Miz was feeling nervous. I didn't pick up on this at the time—I mean, I couldn't tell. To me he looked like he's always looked, like he's looked since his debut season, back when I first fell in love with his antics: all bright-eyed and symmetrical-faced, fed on genetically modified corn, with the swollen, hairless torso of the aspiring professional wrestler he happened to be and a smile you could spot as Midwestern American in a blimp shot of a soccer stadium. He had on a crisp, cool shirt and was sporting, in place of his old floppy bangs, a new sort-of mousse-Mohawk, just a little ridgelet of product-hardened hair emerging from his buzz cut.

In the parking lot, just past the Dumpster on which some citizen had written in white spray paint MEAT MARKET—BITCHES, a chalkboard sign told passersby that the Miz was inside, if any felt ready to party. He was whipping back gratis shots of some stuff that looked like flavored brandy and chatting with undergraduate girls, more and more of whom were edging closer and closer every minute. As he grinned and chatted with them, he looked so utterly guileless and unselfconscious as to seem incapable of nervousness. Granted, I'd already joined him and the owner, Jeremy (who was a good bro of the Miz's), in doing some generous shots, one of which the Miz had marked with a toast that involved his trademark saying, his motto, as it were—"Be good. Be bad. Be Miz"—prompting a skinny, bearded fellow who was doing the shots with us, as well as several on his own, and whose surname must have been Flangey, to blurt out, "Or be FLANGEY . . ." But I hadn't done that many shots, and to me the Miz looked pumped. Later, however, he would write in his online diary that he'd been nervous, for the simple reason that I was there, with my notepad and my judgments and my dubious but sincere claim of being a "hard-core fan" of MTV's *The Real World* and its various spin-off reality series (of which the Miz is perhaps the best-known and best-liked cast member). And although these club-appearance things are usually cool, are typically bumpin'-bumpin', "sometimes, like, only eight people show," and the scene gets grim. What if tonight were like that and then it were to be written about in a magazine? That would be a fiasco. Or, as the Miz might put it—has put it, in fact, in describing a separate incident on that selfsame diary—a fiascal.

He needn't have worried. The place filled up so fast I thought maybe a bus had arrived. It was like those Asian noodles that explode when they hit hot oil. I went to the bathroom in quiet calm, and when I came back, there was hardly room to lift your drink. It was jumpin'-jumpin'. There were loads of the sort of girls who, when dudes ask them to show their breasts and asses, show their breasts and asses. One girl—a beautiful Indian girl who couldn't have been older than nineteen; I wanted to call a cop and have him drive her home—requested to have her right breast signed. The Miz was given a Magic Marker. He showed, I must say, admirable concentration on his penmanship. Another of these girls—a Hooters employee who was saving up for college in a not-too-nearby town—had driven a long way alone.

"I'm here just to see the Miz," she said, but there was a line to talk to him now, of both chicks and dudes, and she'd seen that the Miz and I were bros, so she kicked it with me for a while.

"Are you a fan of the show?" I asked her.

"Oh yeah," she said, "I've already seen MJ here, and Cameran [two other, more recent *Real World* faves]. There's been a bunch of *Real World* people here."

"I've been watching it since high school," I said.

"Oh, me too!" she said.

Then I reflected that, for me, this meant since the show debuted; for her, it meant since last season; which in turn caused me to reflect mournfully on what a poseur she was. Did she even remember the Miz's cast? Probably she knew him only from *The Real World/Road Rules Challenge*, which—although he is awesome on that—is not the best place to get insight into what makes him such a powerful fun-generator.

On the other hand, this young lady was a veteran of the club-appearance scene, and tonight was my first time. If a little hoochie tunnel leading straight to the Miz's presence hadn't opened right at that moment, causing her to sprint from my side and toward his, I was going to ask her, "What's this all about?" Because she belonged to this thing I'd heard rumors of, what I'd come to get a peep at: this little bubble economy that *The Real World* and its less-entertaining mutant twin, *Road Rules* (essentially *Real World* in an RV), have made around themselves.

I don't know how ready you are to admit your familiarity with the show and everything about it, so let me go through the motions of pretending to explain how it operates. Once a *Real World* season ends, the cast members who have emerged during the filming as the popular ones (a status that can be achieved through hotness, all-American likability, and/or unusually blatant behavioral disorders) are invited into a shadow world that exists just below the glare of the series itself. This world has many rooms of its own: club appearances (like this one in Chapel Hill), spring break (which is essentially an amplified version of the club appearance, at one or another beach resort, with several bars and clubs jammed into several consecutive days of straight wildin'-wildin'), "speaking engagements" (at colleges, or to youth groups or antismoking groups, or what have you—especially advantageous here is if you've revealed some side of yourself on the show, such as gayness, alcoholism, bulimia, unhappiness over your breast implants, severe and unprovoked instantaneous anger, neediness, fainting when you see large ships, or crypto-racism, which speaks to a certain specialty population); "um, product launches"; and finally, most important of all, the highly visible and jealously guarded spots on *The Real World/Road Rules Challenge*, where former cast members team up to compete for—oh, fuck it! You know how it works. It's like a ten-times-as-excellent version of *Battle of the Network Stars*—and of course, this being the twenty-first century and reality having long surpassed our fictions, a few of the *Real World/Road Rules Challenge* standouts, among them the Miz, have been cast in a revived edition of *Battle of the Network Stars.* Point being, one never really leaves *The Real World*, not if one is blessed with ripped abs or a boomin' rack.

The agent who sets up most of these gigs, a guy named Brian J. Monaco—who's been doing it for eleven years and is "the one we trust," according to the Miz and every former *Real World* cast member with whom I spoke—told me that there are even instances of unpopular *Real World*ers and *Road Rules*ers "hustling" on the circuit, desperately offering themselves to club owners who don't really want them, asking only "part of the door." And on *The Real World/Road Rules Challenge*, which has evolved its own *shadow* shadow culture, in which cast members transmit messages to one another via silk-screened T-shirts and nurse trans-seasonal grudges and self-generate weird rivalries (veterans versus new guys) that then become official story lines, I'd even seen two girls rend the veil and fight over something that happened out there, in the "real world," one accusing the other of stealing speaking-engagement business away from her by telling a college administrator that she, the accuser, was "quite demanding" and cursed too much. A whole little picture bloomed in the mind, of all those former cast members out there, a Manson family with perfect teeth, still hanging out, still feuding, still drunkenly hittin' that (a bunch of them even lived on the same block in Los Angeles, I'd been told), all of them just going around being somebody who'd been on *The Real World*, which is, of course, a show where you just be yourself. I mean, my God, the purity of that . . .

A lot of the young people yelling questions into the Miz's face seemed mystified by the particulars of it all. They'd ask him, "What are you doing here?" and the Miz, who's a pro, would always say, "Avalon brought me here."

Apparently stunned, they'd ask him, "Are you getting paid to be here?" And the Miz would say, "Yeah, I do all right." And they'd say, "Just to party?"

Some of the youngsters badgered me, thinking maybe I was the Miz's manager or something. "Does he go all over doing this?" two sophomore dudes in polo shirts wanted to know.

"Oh, yeah," I said, "he's huge."

Then they asked me, "Why are you here?"

And I said, "I'm writing about him."

And they said, "What about him?"

We turned and looked at him then, as though in his face we might find the answer. He was all goldeny. For a moment, it seemed we were unified in the humor and puzzlement of it all. There was music that sounded like a rabbit's heartbeat in the core of your brain. There was a gangster-style guy onstage, sort of conducting the crowd, making them sway from side to side with his hand. "Are you an undercover cop?" one of the two dudes asked me. When I said I wasn't, he said, "Then why is your hair so short?" It gave me pleasure when the Miz refused to buy those two little fuckers beer.

He'd broken away from his fans for a minute and was resting with his back to the bar. One couldn't help but marvel at how fresh he looked. He'd been drinking since he got off the plane. The owner had picked him up and whisked him off to a cookout, where everybody did tequila shots. Then there'd been stops at a couple of bars in town, at the first of which I found him slurping martinis (an activity the Miz referred to as "a little pregame warm-up"). For a minute there, before he decided to put on his "big-boy pants," the Miz had wondered whether he'd even make it to the club. And not only that, but things had been even wilder the night before, in Austin, where the Miz had done a tag-team club appearance with MJ and Landon, two male cast members from the *Real World* season that was currently airing on MTV. There were, like, 280 people at that one. It was thumpin'-thumpin'.

It is a truism by now that every *Real World* cast features some combination of recurring types—the slutty one, the sweet one, the racially ambiguous one, the gay one, the slutty-sweet Southern one, and so on. MJ and Landon were two new versions of the Miz, if you savvy. They were super-ripped white guys from tiny towns who didn't know poop from peanuts, multiculturally speaking, but who were soon to learn, and in learning, they'd grow. Yeah, well, the Miz invented that shit. MJ and Landon took the whole typological thing to another level, by looking disconcertingly alike, with tight curly blond cherub hair and unblinking eyes that had never known fear. They horrified, even before Landon got drooling drunk and half-naked and approached his fellow housemates with a butcher knife behind his back. Naturally, they'd both been superpopular, and you can bet they'd been doing a ton of club appearances. The Miz has been at it for years.

I was like, "Mike"—that's his real name—"doesn't this lifestyle wear you down?"

He goes, "Yeah, but I take care of myself. First thing, dude: I don't mix my drinks. If I'm drinking vodka, I keep with vodka. Shots make that hard, though. Somebody hands you a shot, it's hard to be like, 'Can I have something else?' But for the most part . . ."

"But what about your soul?" I said. "Does it take a toll on your soul?" He looked down at his drink.

Psych! I didn't ask him that.

Some girls came up and started grilling the Miz about the *Real World/Road Rules Challenge* season then showing on MTV. Was so-and-so really a cold bitch? Was so-and-so really as nice as he seemed? Was the Miz's team going to win this season?

The Miz pursed his lips and slowly shook his head. He'd been here before—he's here all the time. You can't give away secrets about upcoming episodes. Corporate no-no with immediate consequences. One of the girls said, "There's one I don't like. Who's that girl, the one—not Veronica, but she kinda reminds you of Veronica. Kinda short. Kinda busty brunet."

The Miz looked perplexed. Who could look like Veronica? Vicious little Veronica, queen of the bathtub threesome, that petite and pneumatic perhaps-lesbian who almost fell to her death after Julie the psychotic Mormon fucked with her safety harness during a heated rope-race challenge?

"You mean Tina?" I asked.

"Yeah, Tina!" the girl said.

The Miz looked at me. He goes, "Damn, dude . . . you're good."

"Yeah, well . . ."

There was a time when people liked to point out that reality TV isn't really real. "They're just acting up for the cameras." "That's staged." "The producers are telling them what to do!" "I hate those motherfuckers!" and so forth. Then there was a sort of *deuxième naïveté* when people thought, Maybe there is something real about it. "Because you know, we can be narcissistic like that." "It's our culture." "It gives us a window onto certain . . ." And such things. But I would argue that *all* these different straw people I've invented are missing the single most interesting thing about reality TV, which is the way it has successfully *appropriated reality*.

In the beginning, back in '92, when *The Real World* debuted, establishing in the process the pattern on which all future reality shows would be based, the game was rather crude and obvious—was a character "aware of the cameras," or did he or she momentarily "forget about the cameras"? Those were your subtle shades. That was before the reality-show form itself went kudzu on the televised landscape, its insta-ratings and all but nonexistent production costs allowing it to proliferate, till pretty soon everybody had a mom or brother-in-law or ex-girlfriend on a show; that was before being cast on a reality show had become a rite of passage, like getting your first apartment or your calf implants. I switched on one new show a few months ago, Richard Branson's *The Rebel Billionaire*, and found one of my oldest childhood friends having tea on top of a hot-air balloon with that weird and whispery mogul-faun, Sir Richard, then saying things I'd never heard him say but had heard so many others say in identical tones, things like, "I am not going to lose a second of this experience worrying about tomorrow." Was he smiling *ironically* when he said it? Impossible to tell.

Came a point at which the people being cast on the shows were for the most part people who thrilled back home to watch the shows, people (especially among the younger generation) whose very consciousness had been formed by the shows. Somewhere, far below, a switch was flipped. Now, when you watch a reality show—when you follow *The Real World*, for instance—you're not watching a bunch of people who've been hurled into some contrived scenario and are getting filmed, you're watching people caught in the act of *being on a reality show*. This is now the *plot* of all reality shows, no matter their cooked-up themes.

Here's the surprising thing about this shift toward greater self-consciousness, this increased awareness of complicity in the falseness of it all—it made things more real. Because, of course, people being on a reality show is precisely what these people are. Think of it this way: if you come to my office and film me doing my job (I don't have one, but that only makes this thought experiment more rigorous), you wouldn't really see what it was like to watch me doing my job, because you'd be there watching me (the Heisenberg uncertainty principle, interior auto-mediation, and so forth). But now add this: What if my job were to be on a reality show, being filmed, having you watching me, interior auto-mediation, and so forth? What if that were my reality, bros? Are your faces melting yet?

This is where we are, as a people. And not just that. No, the other exciting thing that's happened—really just in the last few years—involves the ramping acceleration of a self-reinforcing system that's been in place since the birth of reality TV. Because the population from which producers and casting directors can draw to get bodies onto these shows has come to comprise almost exclusively persons who "get" reality shows and are therefore hip to the fact that one is all but certain to be humiliated and irrevocably compromised on such a show, the producers and casting directors, who've always had to be careful to screen out candidates who are overly self-aware and therefore prone to freeze up and act all "dignified" in front of the cameras, are forever having to work harder and harder to locate "spontaneous" individuals, people who, as the Miz says approvingly, "just can't help being who they are."

Well, the effects of this sequence—by which casting directors must get crazier and crazier with their choices, resulting, once the show has aired and had its effect on the country, in a casting demographic in which one must scrape the barrel that much harder to find people who'd even go near a reality show—remained, for many years, gradual and nearly imperceptible. But now— Have you watched television recently? From what can be gathered, they're essentially emptying group homes into the studio. It has all gotten so very real. Nobody's acting anymore. I mean, sure, they're acting, but it's not like they're ever *not* acting.

People hate these shows, but their hatred smacks of denial. It's all there, all the old American grotesques, the test-tube babies of Whitman and Poe, a great gauntlet of doubtless eyes, big mouths spewing fantastic catchphrase fountains of impenetrable self-justification, muttering dark prayers, calling on God to strike down those who would fuck with their money, their cash, and always knowing, always preaching. Using weird phrases that nobody uses, except everybody uses them now. Constantly talking about "goals." Throwing carbonic acid on our castmates because they used our special cup and then calling our mom to say, in a baby voice, "People don't get me here." Walking around half-naked with a butcher knife behind our backs. Telling it like it is, y'all (what-what). And never passive-aggressive, no. Saying it straight to your face. But crying . . . My God, there have been more tears shed on reality TV than by all the war widows of the world. Are we so raw? It must be so. There are simply too many of them—too many shows and too many people on the shows—for them not to be revealing something endemic. This is us, a people of savage sentimentality, weeping and lifting weights.

The club appearance wasn't enough, reporting-wise. I asked them to dinner—the Miz, Melissa, and Coral. I was curious to see if they were real. If all those years spent being themselves for a living had left them with selves to be, or if they'd maybe begun to phase out of existence, like on a *Star Trek* episode. But then I got distracted. You know how it is, when you're kicking it. I got to telling them about some of my all-time fave moments. I talked about the time Randy and Robin were drinking on the upstairs porch—it was the San Diego season. Big Ran was teaching Robin about his personal philosophical system, involving a positive acceptance of epistemological uncertainty, a little thing he liked to call "Agnostics." When Robin (I thought very sweetly) complimented Ran on his philosophical side, which she hadn't noticed up till then, Big Ran goes: "I have a lot of knowledge to share."

I liked Big Ran. He was who he was—it's like the Miz said, he couldn't help it. He was the kind of guy who was always telling you what kind of guy he was. A few months before, I'd almost had a brush with him. A travel company announced there was a *Real World* cruise planned, in the Caribbean. Big Ran and Trishelle (greatest Southern slut in *Real World* history) were going to be on it. I got tickets. I got all excited. But in the end, I got mind-fucked. They canceled the cruise. I don't know if it was for lack of ticket sales or what, but for a brief period, I wondered if maybe I'd been the only person to purchase a ticket. And then I imagined a scenario in which, for some nitpicky contractual reason, the cruise line had been forced to go through with the package anyway, and it was just me, Big Ran, and Trishelle out there on the seas, drifting around on our ghost ship, eating foam from the chaise cushions. Sure, there'd have been some tears, some wrestling and whatnot, but in the end . . .

The Miz, Coral, and Melissa didn't remember that—they didn't remember Big Ran saying, "I have a lot of knowledge to share." I got the sense they don't really watch the show, not since they were on it. "It's hard," said Coral, "'cause you know better. You know that that ain't really like that."

It took me about twenty minutes to put together what was off about our interview: I was enjoying it. Ordinarily, one is tense interrogating strangers, worried about freezing or forgetting to ask what'll turn out to be the only important question. But since we'd all sat down, I'd been totally, totally at ease. Then I saw that this light, this tremulous, bluish light playing over their faces, was the very light by which I knew them best. I'd instinctively brought them to this place in Beverly Hills, Blue on Blue, that has open cabanas around a pool, and we were lounging in one, and the light was shining on their amazing, poreless skin. How many times had I sat with them like this, by pools and Jacuzzis? How often had we chilled like this, just drinking and making points? Thousands of times. My nervous system had convinced itself we were on the show.

"Yeah," the Miz said, "that's both the good and the bad about being on a reality-TV show." He was drinking a vodka drink (everyone knows clear liquor is easier over time on the colon, prostate, et cetera—plus, as the Miz points out, it's lower in calories). "We'll be eating, and it's 'That muthafucka right THERE! What's up, son?' See, they're not gonna do that to Tom Cruise. They're not even going to do that to a B- or C-list actor. But they feel like they know us, so they can come up to us and say whatever they want . . ."

I was about to point out to the Miz that he might seem

less approachable to folks like me if he'd quit taking money to party with us at places like the Avalon Nightclub, but that seemed like a real dick thing to say to a guy who's given me so much joy over the years. And anyway, Melissa and Coral agreed with him.

Coral was in the Miz's same cast, the "Back to New York" season. They're sort of my generation's Ozzie and Harriet, though as far as I can tell (and to the great chagrin of millions) they've never been "romantic." Their friendship started off shaky. At breakfast one morning, back in 2001, conversation turned to that trusty standby "white people and black people." The Miz let slip that his dad doesn't like to hire black people at his Mr. Hero franchise back in northern Ohio because the inner-city schools there are bad, and black people there are "slow." Coral—who's black and beautiful and possesses a raw and somewhat terrifying intelligence—wasn't really feeling that. The season's main plot line became one of Coral mercilessly making Mike feel like a fool (which he already did). But then the two met up again on *The Real World/Road Rules Challenge*, succeeded in winning the first season's competition together, and although they haven't yet produced multiracial triplets, they do manifest a mutual and patently authentic affection. Coral calls the Miz "Mikey."

Melissa, who is half African American and half Filipino— and blessed, one can't help chastely adding, with an extraordinary upper lip—has been living with Coral, they told me, and they are best friends. Melissa was on the New Orleans season. She's the one we all saw go off on Julie that time, for the speaking-engagement shadiness (our first clue that *The Real World* was a real world). Melissa and Julie had never really been super close, not since Melissa asked Julie to hand her a pudding cup one time, and Julie said, "See, back where

I'm from, if somebody asked us to do that, we'd say, 'What color do I look like?'"

The Miz, Coral, and Melissa had just come back from a speaking engagement at Texas Christian University. It was the three of them and David Burns (another former *Real World*er who, I'm told, is opening a bar in Myrtle Beach called Reality Bites that will be staffed by former cast members—and I might just drop in here the little facty-facty that I live an hour from Myrtle Beach, so y'all can sit on that).

Anyhoo, they did their thing, shared some knowledge, and then, at the end, students were invited to come forward and ask questions. This is the typical format. Also typical is that most students who come forward have the same question to ask, namely, "Can I have a hug?" So the Miz has taken to making an announcement before the question part. He'll say, "Afterwards, we're going to have a meet-'n'-greet. We can do hugs and pictures there. So don't ask about hugs."

Okay, so, the question thing was going good. They were almost out of time. The Miz said, "Last question. Something saucy." This girl got up and goes, "I understand you're not going to do any pictures or any hugs after the show, but I was wondering if I could just sit on your face."

The Miz was staring, obviously still working with it. "I was really quite stunned," he said. "This is Texas *Christian* University."

I wish—for your sakes—that the Miz, Coral, and Melissa had turned out to be more fucked-up, as people. I have a vague sense of owing the reader that. I said some out-there things about people on TV—and it's not like I take any of it back—but all three of these people were fairly well-adjusted-seeming. And smart. (Well, I mean, *smart* might not be a word with which I'd saddle the Miz, but nice and relatively together?

Totally.) For an hour, I worked hard to force onto them my idea about post–*Real World* existence being essentially a form of fun slavery. I told them what the *Real World* über-agent Brian Monaco had told me, that he's starting to hear from former cast members, twenty-eight-year-olds burnt out on the bar/club/speaking-engagement/*Challenge* circuit, who are coming to him and being like, "Bri, what do I do? I've got nothing on my résumé!" But that doesn't really apply to any of the three I took to dinner. The Miz has his sweet wrestling deal (he will later become an actual huge famous wrestling star and send me a box of Cuban cigars); Coral hosts various shows on MTV; Melissa starred on another show, on the Oxygen channel, called *Girls Behaving Badly*, which produced the now-massive Chelsea Handler.

I suppose I could baselessly predict that none of this stuff will work out for any of them (though it probably will); I could maybe point out that "reality fame"—as opposed to "acting fame" or another more legitimate type of entertainment notoriety—is a sort of trap. As Monaco put it, "I've seen these kids go to premieres with movie stars, and they get, like, a huge response on the carpet, but unless somebody's paying for the drinks, they can't afford their own." Even on *The Real World/Road Rules Challenge*, they get "like, a thousand dollars a week." And keep in mind that *The Real World* and its spores have been, off and on, MTV's top-rated shows for about a decade. That's a screw job. A while back, some of the kids even hired lawyers and tried to band together against the network. But as the Miz put it, "Why would they pay us more? There are so many of us. They're just like, 'You won't do it? Oh, okay. I'll call so-and-so.'" Plus, there's that cursed phenomenon again, the way we feel like we know these kids. Who'd want the Miz hosting a top show? That'd be like your brother hosting it. You'd be like, "Oh, there's my bro, Mike"—flip.

Mainly we spoke of Julie, from the New Orleans cast. She's the one who said that weird racial thing to Melissa; she's the one accused of trying to fuck with Melissa's money; she's the one who nearly manslaughtered Veronica on the rope-race challenge by trying to disengage Veronica's safety harness at a height of eighteen stories. (That was another great moment—the whole cast was screaming at Julie; the host even had a megaphone; they were all like, "No, Julie! No!" Veronica was sobbing and screaming. But Julie just gritted her teeth and kept tugging away, bros!) Julie has rediscovered her Mormon faith. Watching her now on the *Challenge* is wild. She's always praying to herself while she's scaling the rock wall or whatever. But then, when one of the challenges is on, she jumps up and down and clenches her fists and shrieks like a woman with devils inside her. She's hands-down one of my all-time fave cast members. Mostly, the talk about Julie went like this.

> ME: Have they ever had a tranny on the show?
> CORAL: Not that we know of. But maybe . . .
> MELISSA: Maybe Julie?
> CORAL: I saw her balls! I saw them!
> MIZ: But the producers want more . . . people that people can relate to.
> CORAL: Dude, there's some trannies that watch *The Real World*!
> ME: Coral, the whole country watches *The Real World*.
> CORAL: [*squinting*] Yeah, but it's funny, you know—they perpetrate like they don't.

Coral was lighting cigarettes and then passing them to me. She also let me see the spider tattoo on her foot (to commemorate the spider that bit her there a few seasons back, causing her to have an allergic reaction, which in turn contributed to her and the Miz's team losing on the *Challenge*). On two separate instances, when the subject came up of whether Coral's mind-clobbering breasts are real, she grabbed them (somewhat violently), squeezed them together while pushing them up from below, and sort of shook them. Were they real? I don't know—are the Blue Ridge Mountains real?

Things were maybe winding down when I said, "Coral, what did you mean earlier, when you said that thing about how you don't watch the show 'cause you know that that ain't like that?"

The Miz jumped in. (I noticed that, if you ask the Miz a question, Coral answers, and vice versa.)

"Say we're talking right here," he said. "There'd be, like, a cameraman right here. There'd be a light guy right here. A director. And there's, like, five people standing right there, [around] the conversation that you're in. So it's like, we know what they're doing . . . We also know that, when you're in interview, they're asking you questions. A type of question would be, like, 'Do you think anyone's talking about you?'"

ME: "They" are asking you questions?
MIZ: Yeah.
CORAL: There's a confessional . . . You're required to do an hour of confessional a week, and there's also interviews that you have every week. And the person who's interviewing you is a psychiatrist.
ME: Are you serious?
MIZ: Yep, swear to God. Dr. Laura.

CORAL: Dr. Laura.

MELISSA: Dr. Laura.

CORAL: Who I love.

ME: From the show?

MIZ: Well, from our show.

ME: Not the Dr. Laura from . . .

MELISSA: Dr. Laura Schlessinger? That would be hilarious . . .

I'd suspected there were puppeteers involved in *The Real World*, invisibly instigating "drama," but to think that the network had gone for it like that and hired a shrink? One who, as the kids went on to assure me, was involved not only in manipulating the cast during shooting but also in the casting process itself? And she's worked on other shows? This explained so much, about *The Real World*, about all of it. When I wrote that business earlier about how the casting people have made the shows crazier and crazier, I didn't know I was right about any of that! This person is an unacknowledged legislator of the real world. Turns out Dr. Laura is a psychologist, not a psychiatrist, which is better, when you think about it, because psychologists don't have to take the Hippocratic oath, and she's definitely, definitely done some harm. No chance I was going to call her.

No, I think I'll picture the Miz instead, and see him as he was when I was walking out of Avalon, when we said goodbye. He was dancing with that girl whose breast he had signed. They were grinding. The night had gone well. He saw that I was leaving and gave me a wave and a look, like, "You're takin' off?" And I shouted, "Yeah, gotta go!" And he shouted, "Cool, bro!" and then he went back to dancing. The colored lights were on his face. People were watching.

In that moment, I found it awfully hard to think anything bad about the Miz. Remember your senior year in college, what that was like? Partying was the only thing you had to worry about, and when you went out, you could feel people thinking you were cool. The whole idea of being a young American seemed fun. Remember that? Me neither. But the Miz remembers. He figured out a way never to leave that place.

Bless him, bros.

MICHAEL

How do you talk about Michael Jackson except that you mention Prince Screws?

Prince Screws was an Alabama cotton-plantation slave who became a tenant farmer after the Civil War, likely on his former master's land. His son, Prince Screws, Jr., bought a small farm. And that man's son, Prince Screws III, left home for Indiana, where he found work as a Pullman porter, part of the exodus of Southern blacks to the Northern industrial cities.

There came a disruption in the line. This last Prince Screws, the one who went north, would have no sons. He had two daughters, Kattie and Hattie. Kattie gave birth to ten children, the eighth a boy, Michael—who would name his sons Prince, to honor his mother, whom he adored, and to signal a restoration. So the ridiculous moniker given by a white man to his black slave, the way you might name a dog, was bestowed by a black king upon his pale-skinned sons and heirs.

We took the name for an affectation and mocked it.

Not to imply that it was above mockery, but of all the things that make Michael unknowable, thinking we knew him is maybe the most deceptive. Let's suspend it.

Begin not with the miniseries childhood of Joseph's endless family practice sessions but with the later and, it seems, just as formative Motown childhood, from, say, eleven to fourteen—years spent, when not on the road, most often alone, behind security walls, with private tutors and secret sketchbooks. A cloud-headed child, he likes rainbows and reading. He starts collecting exotic animals.

His eldest brothers had at one time been children who dreamed of child stardom. Michael never knows this sensation. By the time he achieves something like self-awareness, he is a child star. The child star dreams of being an artist.

Alone, he puts on classical records, because he finds they soothe his mind. He also likes the old Southern stuff his uncle Luther sings. His uncle looks back at him and thinks he seems sad for his age. This is in California, so poor, brown Gary, with its poisonous air you could smell from leagues away—a decade's exposure to which may already have damaged his immune system in fateful ways—is the past.

He thinks about things and sometimes talks them over with his friends Marvin Gaye and Diana Ross when they are hanging out. He listens to albums and compares. The albums he and his brothers make have a few nice tunes, to sell records, then a lot of consciously second-rate numbers, to satisfy the format. Whereas Tchaikovsky and people like that, they didn't handle slack material. But you have to write your own songs. Michael has always made melodies in his head, little riffs and beats, but that isn't the same. The way Motown deals with the Jackson 5, finished songs are delivered to the group from songwriting teams in various cities. The brothers are brought in to sing and add accents.

Michael wants access to the "anatomy" of the music. That's the word he uses repeatedly. *Anatomy.* What's inside its structure that makes it move?

When he's seventeen, he asks Stevie Wonder to let him spy while *Songs in the Key of Life* gets made. There's Michael, self-consciously shy and deferential, flattening himself mothlike against the Motown studio wall. Somehow Stevie's blindness becomes moving in this context. No doubt he is for long stretches unaware of Michael's presence. Never asks him to play a shaker or anything. Never mentions Michael. But Michael hears him. Most of the Jackson siblings are leaving Motown at this moment, for another label, where they've leveraged a bit more creative sway. The first thing Michael does is write "Blues Away," an unfairly forgotten song, fated to become one of the least-dated-sounding tracks the Jacksons do together. A nice rolling piano riff with strings and a breathy chorus—Burt Bacharach doing Stevie doing early disco, and some other factor that was Michael's own, that dwelled in his introverted-sounding vocal rhythms. Sweet, slightly cryptic lyrics that contain an early notion of melancholy as final, inviolable retreat: "I'd like to be yours tomorrow, so I'm giving you some time to get over today / But you can't take my blues away."

By 1978, the year of "Shake Your Body (Down to the Ground)"—cowritten by Michael and little Randy—Michael's methods have gelled. He starts with tape recorders. He sings and beatboxes the little things he hears, the parts. Where do they come from? Above. He claims to drop to his knees and thank Jehovah after he snatches one. His voice coach tells the story of Michael one day raising his hands in the air during practice and starting to mutter. The coach, Seth Riggs, decides to leave him alone. When he comes back half an hour later, it's to Michael whispering, "Thank you for my talent."

Some of the things Michael hears in his head he exports to another instrument, to the piano (which he plays not well but passably) or to the bass. The melody and a few percussive elements remain with his vocal. The rest he assembles around it. He has his brothers and sisters with him. He conducts.

His art will come to depend on his ability to stay in touch with that childlike inner instrument, keeping near enough to himself to heed his own melodic promptings. If you've listened to toddlers making up songs, the things they invent are often bafflingly catchy and ingenious. They compose to biorhythms somehow. The vocal from Michael's earlier, *Off the Wall*–era demo of the eventual *Thriller* hit "Wanna Be Startin' Somethin'" sounds like nothing so much as playful schoolyard taunting. He will always be at his worst when making what he thinks of as "big" music, which he invariably associates with military imagery.

Nineteen seventy-nine, the year of *Off the Wall* and his first nose job, marks an obscure crisis. Around the start of that year, they offer him the gay lead in the film version of *A Chorus Line*, but he declines the role, explaining, "I'm excited about it, but if I do it, people will link me with the part. Because of my voice, some people already think I'm that way—homo—though I'm actually not at all."

People want to know, Why, when you became a man, did your voice not change? Rather, it did change, but what did it change into? Listening to clips of his interviews through the seventies, you can hear how he goes about changing it himself. First it deepens slightly, around 1972–73 or so. (Listen to him on *The Dating Game* in 1972 and you'll hear that his voice was lower at fourteen than it will be at thirty.) This potentially catastrophic event has perhaps been vaguely dreaded by the family and label for years. Michael Jackson without his falsetto is not the commodity on which their collective dream depends. But Michael has never known a reality that wasn't susceptible on some level to his creative powers. He works to develop something, not a falsetto, which is a way of singing above your range, but instead a higher range. He isolates totally different configurations of his vocal cords, finding their crevices, cultivating the flexibility there. Vocal teachers will tell you this can be done, though it's considered an extreme practice. Whether the process is conscious in Michael's case is unknowable. He probably evolves it in order to keep singing Jackson 5 songs every night through puberty. The startling effect is of his having imaginatively not so much castrated himself as womanized himself. He essentially evolves a drag voice. On the early demo for "Don't Stop 'Til You Get Enough," recorded at home with Randy and Janet helping, you can actually hear him work his way into this voice. It is a character, really. "We're gonna be startin' now, baby," he says in a relaxed, moderately high-pitched man's voice. Then he intones the title, "Don't stop 'til you get enough," in a softer, quieter version of basically the same voice. He repeats the line in a still higher register, almost purring. Finally—in a full-on girlish peal—he sings.

A source will later claim that Michael once, in a moment of anger, broke into a deep, gruff voice she'd never heard before. Liza Minnelli also claims to have heard this other voice.

Interesting that these out-flashings of his "natural" voice

occurred at moments when he was, as we would say, not himself.

On the Internet, you can see a picture of him near the end of his life, juxtaposed with a digital projection of what he would have looked like at the same age without the surgeries and makeup and wigs. A smiling middle-aged black guy, handsome in an everyday way. We are meant, of course, to feel a connection with this lost neverbeing, and pity for the strange, self-mutilated creature beside him. I can't be alone, however, in feeling just the opposite, that there's something metaphysically revolting about the mock-up. It's an abomination. Michael chose his true face. What is, is natural.

His physical body is arguably, even inarguably, the single greatest piece of postmodern American sculpture. It must be carefully preserved.

It's fascinating to read the interviews he gave to *Ebony* and *Jet* over the past thirty years. I confess myself disoriented by them, as a white person. During whole stretches of years when the big media were reporting endlessly on his bizarreness and reclusiveness, he was every so often granting these intimate and illuminating sit-downs to those magazines, never forgetting to remind them that he trusted only them, would speak only to them. The articles make me realize that about the only Michael Jackson I've ever known, personality-wise, is a Michael Jackson who's defending himself against white people who are passive-aggressively accusing him of child molestation. He spoke differently to black people, was more at ease. The language and grain of detail are different. Not that the scenario was any more journalistically pure. The John H. Johnson publishing family, which puts out *Jet* and *Ebony*, had Michael's back, faithfully repairing and maintaining his complicated relations with the community, assuring readers that, in the presence of Michael, "you quickly look past the enigmatic icon's light, almost translucent skin and realize that this African American legend is more than just skin deep." At times, especially when the "homo" issue came up, the straining required could turn comical, as in *Ebony* in 1982, talking about his obsessive male fans:

> MICHAEL: They come after us every way they can, and the guys are just as bad as the girls. Guys jump up on the stage and usually go for me and Randy.
>
> EBONY: But that means nothing except that they admire you, doesn't it?

Even so, to hear Michael laid-back and talking unpretentiously about art, the thing he most loved—that is a new Michael, a person utterly absent from, for example, Martin Bashir's infamous documentary, *Living with Michael Jackson*, in which Michael admitted sharing his bedroom with children. It's only after reading *Jet* and *Ebony* that one can understand how otherwise straightforward-seeming people of all races have stayed good friends with Michael Jackson these many years. He is charming; his mind is alive. What a pleasure to find him listening to early "writing version" demos of his own compositions and saying, "Listen to that, that's at home, Janet, Randy, me . . . You're hearing four basses on there . . ." Or to hear him tell less prepackaged anecdotes, such as the one about a beautiful black girl who froze in the aisle and pissed all down her legs after spotting him on a plane, or the blond girl who kissed him in an airport and, when he didn't respond, asked, "What's wrong, you fag?" He grows tired of reminding people, "There's a reason why I was created male. I'm not a girl." He leaves the reason unspoken.

When Michael and Quincy Jones run into each other on the set of *The Wiz*, Michael remembers a moment from years before when Sammy Davis, Jr., had taken Jones aside backstage somewhere and whispered, "This guy is something; he's amazing." Michael had "tucked it away." He knows Jones's name from the sleeves of his father's jazz albums, knows Jones is a serious man. He waits till the movie is done to call him up. It's the fact that Jones intimidates him slightly that draws Jackson to him. He yearns for some competition larger than the old intrafamilial one, which he has long dominated. That was checkers; he wants chess. Fading child stars can easily insulate themselves from further motivation, if they wish, and most do. It's the more human path. Michael seeks pressure instead, at this moment. He recruits people who can drive him to, as he puts it, "higher effort."

Quincy Jones's nickname for him is Smelly. It comes from Michael's habit of constantly touching and covering his nose with the fingers of his left hand, a tic that becomes pronounced in news clips from this time. He feels embarrassed about his broad nose. Several surgeries later—after, one assumes, it had been deemed impolitic inside the Jackson camp to mention the earlier facial self-consciousness—the story is altered. We are told that when Michael liked a track in the studio, he would call it "the smelly jelly." Both stories may be true. "Smelly jelly" has the whiff of Jackson's weird, infantile sayings. Later in life, when feeling weak, he'd say to his people, "I'm hurting . . . blanket me," which could mean, among other things, time for my medicine.

Michael knows he won't really have gone solo until his own songwriting finds the next level. He doesn't want inclusion; he wants awe. Jones has a trusted songwriter in his stable, the Englishman Rod Temperton, of Heatwave fame, who brings in a song, "Rock with You." It's very good. Michael hears it and knows it's a hit. He's not even worried about hits at this point, though, except as a kind of by-product of perfection. He goes home and writes "Don't Stop 'Til You Get Enough." Janet tinks on a glass bottle. Trusted Randy plays guitar. These are the two siblings whom Michael brings with him into the Quincy Jones adventure, to the innermost zone where he writes. We don't think of the family as having anything to do, musically, with his solo career, except by way of guilt favors. But he feels confident with these two, needs to keep them woven into his nest. They are both younger than he. His baby sister.

From the perspective of thirty years, "Don't Stop 'Til You Get Enough" is a much better track than "Rock with You." One admires "Rock with You," but melodically Michael's song comes from a more distinctive place. You hear not slickness but sophisticated instincts.

Michael feels disappointed with *Off the Wall*. It wins a Grammy, spawns multiple number one singles, dramatically raises Jackson's already colossal level of fame, redeems disco in the very hour and flash of disco's dying. Diana Ross, who once helped out the Jacksons by putting her lovely arm around them, wants Michael to be at her shows again, not for his sake now but for hers. She isn't desperate by any means, but something has shifted. Quincy Jones and Bruce Swedien, the recording guru who works with him, both take to be absurd the mere idea of "following up" *Off the Wall* in terms of success. You do your best, but that kind of thing just happens, if it happens. Jones knows that. Not Michael. All he can see of *Off the Wall* is that the year had bigger records. He wants to make something, he says, that "refuse[s] to be ignored."

At home he demos "Billie Jean" with Randy and Janet. When what will be the immortal part comes around, she and Michael go, "Whoo whoo / Whoo whoo."

From Michael's brain, then, through a portable tape recorder, on into the home studio. Bruce Swedien comes over. Being Michael Jackson working on the follow-up to *Off the Wall* means sometimes your demos are recorded at your home by the greatest audio engineer in the world. But for all that, the team works in a stripped-down fashion, with no noise reduction. "That's usually the best stuff," Michael says, "when you strip it down to the bare minimum and go inside yourself and invent."

On this home demo, made between the "writing version" and the album version, you get to hear Michael's early, mystical placeholder vocals, laid down before he'd written the verses. We hear him say, "More kick and stuff in the 'phones . . . I need, uh . . . more bottom and kick in the 'phones."

Then the music. And what sounds like:

[Mumble mumble mum] oh, to say
On the phone to stay . . .
Oh, born out of time.
All the while I see other eyes.
One at a time
We'll go where the winds unwind

She told me her voice belonged to me
And I'm here to see
She called my name, then you said, Hello
Oh, then I died
And said, Gotta go in a ride

Seems that you knew my mind, now live
On that day got it made
Oh, mercy, it does care of what you do
Take care of what you do
Lord, they're coming down

Billie Jean is not my lover
She just a girl that says that I am the one
You know, the kid is not my son

A big round warm Scandinavian type, Swedien comes from Minnesota, made his mark doing classical, but with classical engineering it's all about fidelity, he knew, and he wants to be part of the making, to help shape the songs. So, a frustrated anatomist himself, coming down from high to low formally and meeting Michael on his way up. Quincy, in the middle with his jazz cool, calls Swedien "Svensk." The white man has the endearing habit of lifting both hands to massage the gray walrus wings of his mustache. He has a condition called synesthesia. It means that when he listens to sound, he sees colors. He knows the mix is right only when he sees the right colors. Michael likes singing for him.

In a seminar room in Seattle, at a 1993 Audio Pro recording-geek conference, Swedien talks about his craft. He plays his recording of Michael's flawless one-take vocal from "The Way You Make Me Feel," sans effects of any kind, to let the engineers in the audience hear the straight dope, a great mike on a great voice with as little interference as possible, the right angle, the right deck, everything.

Someone in the audience raises a hand and asks if it's hard recording Michael's voice, given that, as Swedien mentioned before, Michael is very "physical." At first, Swedien doesn't cotton. "Yeah, that is a bit of a problem," he answers, "but I've never had an incident where the microphone has been damaged. One time, though . . ."

The guy interrupts, "Not to do damage, just the proximity thing."

"Oh!" Swedien says, suddenly understanding. His voice drops to a whisper, "He's unbelievable."

He gives the most beautiful description. "Michael records in the dark," he says, "and he'll dance. And picture this: You're looking through the glass. And it's dark. With a little pin spot on him." Swedien lifts his hand to suggest a narrow cone of light shining directly down from overhead. "And you'll see the mike here. And he'll sing his lines. And then he disappears."

In the outer dark he is dancing, fluttering. That's all Quincy and Swedien know.

"And he's"—Swedien punches the air—"right back in front of the mike at the precise instant."

Swedien invents a special zippered covering for miking the bass drum on "Billie Jean." A muffled enclosure. It gives the song that mummified-heartbeat intensity, which you have seen make a dance floor come to life. The layered bass sounds on the one and the three lend a lurching feline throb. Bass drum, bass guitar, double synthesizer bass, the "four basses," all hitting together, doing the part that started as Michael and Janet going whoo whoo whoo whoo, that came from Jehovah. Its tempo is like the pulse of a sleeping person.

Michael finds himself back in the old Motown building for a day, doing some video mixing, when Berry Gordy approaches and asks him to be in the twenty-fifth-anniversary special on NBC. Michael demurs. A claustrophobic moment for him. All that business, his brothers, Motown, the Jackson 5, the past: that's all a cocoon he's been writhing inside of, finally chewing through. He knows that "Billie Jean" has exploded; he's becoming something else. But the animal inside him that is his ambition senses the opportunity. He strikes his legendary deal with Gordy, that he'll perform with his brothers if he's allowed to do one of his own solo, post-Motown hits as well. Gordy agrees.

What Michael does with his moment, given the context, given that his brothers have just left the stage and that the stage belongs to Mr. Berry Gordy, is outrageous. In the by-now totemic YouTube clips of this performance, Michael's preamble is usually cut off. That makes it worth watching the disc (which also happens to include one of Marvin Gaye's last appearances before his murder).

Michael is sweaty and strutting. "Thank you . . . Oh, you're beautiful . . . Thank you," he says, almost slurring with sexiness. You can tell he's worked out all his nerves on the Jackson 5 songs. Now he owns the space as if it were the inside of his cage. Millions upon millions of eyes.

"I have to say, those were the good old days," he rambles on. "I love those songs, those were magic moments, with all my brothers, including Jermaine." (The Jackson family's penchant for high passive-aggression at watershed moments is extraordinary; at Michael's funeral, Jermaine will say: "I was his voice and his backbone, I had his back." And then, as if remembering to thank his agent, "So did the family.")

"Those were good songs," Michael says. "I like those songs a lot, but especially, I like"—his voice fades from the mike for a second, ramifying the liveness till the meters almost spike—"the new songs."

Uncontrollable shrieking. He's grabbing the mike stand

like James Brown used to grab it, like if it had a neck he'd be choking it. People in the seats are yelling, "'Billie Jean'! 'Billie Jean'!"

I won't cloud the uniqueness of what he does next with words except to mention one potentially missable (because it's so obvious) aspect: that he does it so entirely alone. The stage is profoundly empty. Silhouettes of the orchestra members are clapping back in the dark. But unless you count the dazzling glove—conceived, according to one source, to hide the advancing vitiligo that discolors his left hand—Michael holds only one prop: a black hat. He tosses that away almost immediately. Stage, dancer, spotlight. The microphone isn't even on. He snatches it back from the stand as if from the hands of a maddening child.

With a mime's tools he proceeds to do possibly the most captivating thing a person's ever been captured doing on-stage. Richard Pryor, who was not in any account I have ever read a suck-up, approaches Michael afterward and says simply, "That was the greatest performance I've ever seen." Fred Astaire calls him "the greatest living natural dancer."

Michael tells *Ebony*, "I remember doing the performance so clearly, and I remember that I was so upset with myself, 'cause it wasn't what I wanted. I wanted it to be more." It's said he intended to hold the crouching en pointe at the end of the moonwalk longer. But if you watch, he falls off his toes, when he falls, in perfect time, and makes it part of the turn. Much as, closer to the end, he wipes sweat from under his nose in time.

The intensity behind his face looks unbearable.

Quincy always tells him, "Smelly . . . get out of the way and leave room so that God can walk in."

A god moves through him. The god enters, the god leaves.

It's odd to write about a person knowing he may have been, but not if he was, a serial child molester. Whether or not Michael did it, the suggestion of it shadowed him for so long and finally killed his soul. It's said that toward the end, he was having himself put under—with the same anesthesia that may have finished him—not for hours but for days. As though being snuffed. Witnesses to his body on the morgue table report that his prosthetic nose was missing. There were only holes in his face. A mummy. Two separate complete autopsies: they cut him to pieces. As of this writing, no one outside the Jackson camp knows for certain the whereabouts of his body.

I have read a stack of books about him in the past month, more than I ever imagined I would—though not more than I wanted. He warrants and will no doubt one day receive a serious, objective biography: all the great cultural strains of American music came together in him. We have yet to accept that his very racial in-betweenness made him more and not less of an essential figure in our tradition. He grasped this and used it. His marriage to Elvis's daughter was in part an art piece.

Of all those books, the one that troubles and sticks with me is the celebrity journalist Ian Halperin's *Unmasked: The Final Years of Michael Jackson*. Most famous for a book and movie suggesting dubiously that Kurt Cobain's suicide was a disguised murder, Halperin is not an ideal source but neither is he a useless one. Indeed, he accurately predicted Michael's death six months before it happened and seems to have burrowed his way into the Jackson world in several places.

In the beginning, Halperin claims, he'd set out mainly to prove that Michael had sexually molested young boys and used his money to get away with it. I believe him about this original motivation, since any such proof would have generated the most sensational publicity, sold the most copies, and so on. But Halperin finds, in the end, after exhaustively pursuing leads, that every so-called thread of evidence becomes a rope of sand. Somebody, even if it's a family member, wants money, or has accused other people before, or is patently insane. It usually comes down to a tale someone else knows about an alleged secret payoff. Meanwhile, you have these boys, like Macaulay Culkin (whom Michael was once accused of fondling), who have come forth and stated that nothing untoward ever happened with Michael. When he stood trial and got off, that was a just verdict.

That's the first half of the Halperin Thesis. The second half is that Michael was a fully functioning gay man, who took secret male lovers his entire adult life. Halperin says he met two of them and saw pictures of one with Michael. They were young but perfectly legal. One told Halperin that Michael was an insatiable bottom.

As for Michael's interest in children, it's hard to imagine that lacking an erotic dimension of some kind, but it may well have been thoroughly nonsexual. Michael was a frozen adolescent—about the age of those first dreamy striped-sweater years in California—and he wanted to hang out with the people he saw as his peers. Have pillow fights, call each other doo-doo head. It's creepy as hell, if you like, but victimless. It would make him—in rough clinical terms—a partial passive fixated pedophile. Not a crime yet, not until they get the mind-reader machines going.

I don't ask that you agree with Halperin, merely that you

admit, as I feel compelled to do, that the psychological picture he conjures up is not less and perhaps just slightly more plausible than the one in which Michael uses Neverland Ranch as a spiderweb, luring boys to his bed. If you're like me, you've been subconsciously presuming the latter to be basically the case for most of your life. But there's a good chance it was never true and that Michael loved children with a weird but not immoral love.

If you want a disturbing thought experiment, allow these—I won't say facts, but feasibility structures—let them digest, and then go back again to Martin Bashir's 2003 documentary. There's no point adding here to the demonization of Bashir for having more or less manipulated Michael through kindness into declaring himself a complete Fruit of the Loom–collecting fiend, especially when you consider that Bashir was representing us fairly well in the ideas he appears to have carried regarding Michael, that it was probably true about him and kids.

But when you put on the not-so glasses and watch, and see Michael protesting his innocence, asking, "What's wrong with sharing love?" as he holds hands with that twelve-year-old cancer survivor—or many years earlier, in that strange self-released statement, where he describes with barely suppressed rage the humiliation of having his penis examined by the police—dammit if the whole life doesn't look a lot different. There appears to exist a nondismissible chance that Michael was some kind of martyr.

We won't pity him. That he embraced his own destiny, knowing beforehand how fame would warp him, is precisely what frees us to revere him.

We have, in any case, a pathology of pathologization in this country. It's a bourgeois disease, and we do right to call bullshit on it. We moan that Michael changed his face out of self-loathing. He may have loved what he became.

Ebony caught up with him in Africa in the nineties. He had just been crowned king of Sani by villagers in the Ivory Coast. "You know I don't give interviews," he tells Robert E. Johnson there in the village. "You're the only person I trust to give interviews to: Deep inside I feel that this world we live in is really a big, huge, monumental symphonic orchestra. I believe that in its primordial form, all of creation is sound and that it's not just random sound, that it's music."

May they have been his last thoughts.

THE FINAL COMEBACK OF AXL ROSE

1.

He is from nowhere.

That sounds coyly rhetorical—in this day and age, it's even a boast: socioeconomic code for "I went to a second-tier school and had no connections and made all this money myself."

I don't mean it that way. I mean he is from nowhere. Given the relevant maps and a pointer, I know I could convince even the most exacting minds that when the vast and blood-soaked jigsaw puzzle that is this country's regional scheme coalesced into more or less its present configuration after the Civil War, somebody dropped a piece, which left a void, and they called the void "central Indiana." I'm not trying to say there's no there there. I'm trying to say there's no there. Think about it; get systematic on it. What's the most nowhere part of America? The Midwest, right? But once you get into the Midwest, you find that each of the different nowherenesses has laid claim to its own somewhereness. There are the lonely plains in Iowa. In Michigan there's a Gordon

Lightfoot song. Ohio has its very blandness and averageness, faintly comical, to cling to. All of them have something. But now I invite you to close your eyes, and when I say "Indiana" . . . blue screen, no? And we are speaking only of Indiana generally, which includes southern Indiana, where I grew up, and northern Indiana, which touches a Great Lake. We have not even narrowed it down to central Indiana. Central Indiana? That's like, "Where are you?" I'm nowhere. "Go there."

When I asked Jeff Strange, a morning-rock DJ in Lafayette, how he thought about this part of the world—for instance, did he think of it as the South? After all, it's a Klan hot spot (which can be read as a somewhat desperate affectation); or did he think of it as the Midwest, or what—you know what he told me? He said, "Some people here would call it 'the region.'"

William Bruce Rose, Jr.; William Bruce Bailey; Bill Bailey; William Rose; Axl Rose; W. Axl Rose.

That's where he's from. Bear that in mind.

2.

On May 15, he came out in jeans and a black leather jacket and giant black sunglasses, all lens, that made him look like a wasp-man. We had been waiting so long, in both years and hours. It was the third of the four comeback shows in New York, at the Hammerstein Ballroom. It was after eleven o'clock. The doors had opened at seven o'clock. The opening act had been off by eight-thirty. There'd already been fights on the floor, and it didn't feel like the room could get any more wound up without some type of event. I was next to a really nice woman from New Jersey, a hairdresser, who told me her husband "did pyro" for Bon Jovi. She kept texting one of her husband's friends, who was "doing pyro" for this show, and asking him, "When's it gonna start?" And he'd text back, "We haven't even gone inside." I said to her at one point, "Have you ever seen a crowd this pumped up before a show?" She goes, "Yeah, they get this pumped up every night before Bon Jovi."

Then he was there. And apologies to the nice woman, but people do not go that nuts when Bon Jovi appears. People were: Going. Nuts. He is not a tall man—I doubt even the heels of his boots (red leather) put him over five feet ten. He walked toward us with stalking, cartoonish pugnaciousness.

All anybody talks about with Axl anymore is his strange new appearance, but it is hard to get past the unusual impression he makes. To me he looks like he's wearing an Axl Rose mask. He looks like a man I saw eating by himself at a truck stop in Monteagle, Tennessee, at two o'clock in the morning about twelve years ago. He looks increasingly like the albino reggae legend Yellowman. His mane evokes a gathering of strawberry-red intricately braided hempen fibers, the sharply twisted ends of which have been punched, individually, a half inch into his scalp. His chest hair is the color of a new penny. With the wasp-man sunglasses and the braids and the goatee, he reminds one of the monster in *Predator*, or of that monster's wife on its home planet. When he first came onto the scene, he often looked, in photographs, like a beautiful, slender, redheaded twenty-year-old girl. Now he has thickened through the middle—muscly thickness, not the lard-ass thickness of some years back. He grabs his package tightly, and his package is huge. Only reporting. Now he plants his feet apart. "You know where you are?" he asks, and we bellow that we do, we do know, but he tells us anyway. "You're in the jungle, baby," he says, and then he tells us that we are going to die.

He must be pleased, not only at the extreme way that we are freaking out to see him but also at the age range on view: there are hipsters who were probably born around the time *Appetite* got released, all the way up to aging heads who've handed in their giant rock hair for grizzled rattails, with plenty of microgenerations in between. But why should I even find this worth remarking? The readers of *Teen* magazine, less than one year ago, put him at number two (behind "Grandparents") on the list of the "100 Coolest Old People" . . . Axl Rose, who hasn't released a legitimate recording in thirteen years and who, during that time, turned into an almost Howard Hughes–like character—only ordering in, transmitting sporadic promises that a new album, titled *Chinese Democracy*, was about to drop, making occasional startling appearances at sporting events and fashion shows, stuff like that—looking a little feral, a little lost, looking not unlike a man who's been given his first day's unsupervised leave from a state facility. Now he has returned. The guitarists dig in, the drummer starts his I-Am-BUil-DINg-UP-TO-THE!-VERSE! pounding section, and at the risk of revealing certain weaknesses of taste on my own part, I have to say, the sinister perfection of that opening riff has aged not a day.

There's only one thing to do, and you can feel everybody doing it: comparing this with the MTV thing in 2002. If you've seen that, you may find a recounting here of its grotesqueries tedious, but to that I say, never forget. About the guitar player Buckethead. About the other guitar player. About Axl's billowing tentlike football jersey or the heartbreaking way he aborted his snaky slide-foot dance after only a few seconds on the stage projection, like, "You wanna see my snaky dance? Here, I'll do my snaky dance. Oh, no, I think I just had a small stroke. Run away." The audible gasp for oxygen on the second "knees" in Sh-na-na-na-na-na-na-na-na-na-na-na knees, kn[gasp!]ees. The running and singing that came more and more to resemble stumbling and squawking as the interminable minutes groaned by. The constant, geriatric-seeming messing with the earpiece monitor.

My point is, it's different tonight. For one thing, these guys can handle or choose to handle Slash's parts. They aren't fake-booking, like happened on MTV. Buckethead has been replaced by a guy called Bumblefoot, and Bumblefoot can shred. So can Robin Finck, formerly of Nine Inch Nails. Everything's note for note. And although we could get into the whole problem of virtuosity as it applies to popular music— namely, that for some reason people who can play anything will, nine times out of ten, when asked to make something up, play something terrible—still, if you mean to replace your entire band one instrument at a time and tell them, "Do it like this," you'll be wanting to find some monster players.

The whole arc of the show has this very straightforward plot. Crudity is in the service of truth-telling here: it's a battle between the dissonance of seeing all these guys who were not in Guns N' Roses jumping around with Axl and playing Guns N' Roses songs—between the off-putting and even disturbing uncanny dissonance of that—and the enduring qualities of the songs themselves. The outcome will determine whether tonight was badass or "Sort of sad, but hey, it's Axl." For what it's worth, I thought he won. His voice is back, for starters. He was inhabiting the notes. And his dancing—I don't quite know how else to say this. It has matured. From the beginning, he's been the only indispensable white male rock dancer of his generation, the only one worth imitating in mockery. I consider the moment in the "Patience" video when he does the slow-motion snaky slide-foot dance while letting his hands float down as if they were feathers in a draft-less room—one fleeting near-pause in their descent for each note that Slash emphasizes in his transition to the coda—the greatest white male rock dance moment of the video age. What Axl does is lovely, I'm sorry. If I could, I would be do-ing that as I walk to the store. I would wake up and dance every morning like William Byrd of Westover, and that would be my dance. And while I cannot say Axl is dancing as well tonight as he used to, that so fluidly are his heels gliding out and away from his center they look each to have been tapped with a wand that absolved them of resistance and weight, and although he does at particular moments remind one of one's wasted redneck uncle trying to "do his Axl Rose" after a Super Bowl party, he is nevertheless acquitting himself honorably. He is doing "dammit just dropped a bowling ball on my foot spin-with-mike-stand" dance; he is doing "prance sideways with mike stand like an attacking staff-wielding ritual warrior" between-verses dance. And af-ter each line he is gazing at the crowd with those strangely startled yet fearless eyes, as though we had just surprised him in his den, tearing into some carrion.

3.

Conversation with wife, Mariana, June 27, 2006:

ME: Oh, my God.
HER: What?

ME: Axl just bit a security guard's leg in Sweden. He's in jail.

HER: Is that gonna affect your interview with him?

ME: No, I don't think they ever really considered letting me talk to him . . . Biting somebody on the leg, though—it forces you to picture him in such a, like a, disgraced position.

HER: Does anybody help Axl when that happens?

4.

I'd been shuffling around a surprisingly pretty, sunny, newly renovated downtown Lafayette for a couple of days, scraping at whatever I could find. I saw the house where he grew up. I looked at his old yearbook pictures in the public library. Everyone had his or her Axl story. He stole a TV from that house there. Here's where he tried to ride his skateboard on the back of a car and fell and got road rash all up his arm. He came out of this motel with a half-naked woman and some older guys were looking at her and one of 'em threw down a cigarette, not meaning anything by it, but Axl freaked out and flipped 'em off and they beat the crap out of him. Hard to document any of this stuff. Still, enough Wanted On Warrant reports exist for Axl's Indiana years to lend credence to the claim that the city cops and county troopers pretty much felt justified, and technically speaking were justified, in picking him up and hassling him whenever they spotted him out. One doubts he left the house much that they didn't spot him, what with the long, fine, flowing red hair. Not always fun to be Axl.

I went to the city cops. They've mellowed with the town.

In fact, they were friendly. They found and processed the negatives of some never-before-seen mug shots for me, from '80 and '82, the former of which (where he's only eighteen) is an unknown American masterpiece of the saddest, crappiest kind. The ladies in the records department rummaged some and came back with the report connected to that picture, as well, which I'd never seen mentioned in any of the bios or online or anything. It's written by an officer signing himself "1–4." I took it back to the Holiday Inn and spent the rest of the afternoon reading. Call it the Sheidler Incident. It begins:

FULL NAME: BAILEY, WILLIAM BRUCE . . .
ALIASES: BILL BAILEY . . .
CURRENT PLACE OF EMPLOYMENT: SELF EMPLOYED—BAND
CHARGE: W[ANTED]O[N]W[ARRANT] BATTERY . . .
AGE: 18; HEIGHT: 5'9"; WEIGHT: 149; HAIR: RED; EYES: GRN; BUILD: SLENDER; COMPLEXION: FAIR . . .

Here's how it went down that day—"allegedly" (I'll cherry-pick the good bits for you). A little kid named Scott Sheidler was riding his bike in front of the house of an older kid named Dana Gregory. Scott made skid marks on the sidewalk. Dana Gregory ran out, picked Scott up under the armpits, kicked over his bike, and ordered the boy TO GET ON HIS HANDS AND KNEES AND SCRUB THE SKID MARKS OFF THE SIDEWALK. The kid went squealing to his old man, Tom Sheidler. Tom Sheidler went to young Dana Gregory and asked if it was true, what Scotty had said. Dana Gregory said, "YES AND I'M GOING TO BEAT THE FUCK OUT OF YOU." The mom, Marleen, then ran up to the scene and began to shout. Around the same time, BILL BAILEY appeared, red, green, slender, and fair. And here I need to let the report take over, if only temporarily, as I can't begin to simulate its succinctness or authority:

M. Sheidler stated that BAILEY was also arguing with SHEIDLER and that he was using the "F" WORD in front of her kids. M. SHEIDLER stated that she went up to BAILEY and pointed her finger at BAILEY and told him not to use the "F" WORD in front of her kids. M. SHEIDLER stated that BAILEY, who has a SPLINT ON HIS ARM, then struck her on the arm and neck with the splint. I looked at M. SHEIDLER and could see some RED MARKS on her ARM and NECK which could have been made by being struck.

This matter of which hand it was takes over the narrative for a stretch. Marleen Sheidler says "with the SPLINT," and little Scott says "with a SPLINT," but Dana Gregory's younger brother CHRIS 15 says "with the opposite hand that his SPLINT is on" (adding that Bailey struck Sheidler in response to "SHEIDLER STRIKEING [sic]" him). Bill Bailey himself then goes on to say that he "struck M. SHEIDLER in the FACE with his LEFT HAND the hand with out the SPLINT." Once again, this only after "MARLEEN SHEIDLER struck him in the face" (though seconds earlier, by his own admission, he'd told her "to keep her fucking brats at home"). The story ends with a strangely affecting suddenness: "BAILEY stated SHEIDLER then jumped at him and fell on his face, he then left and went home . . ."

The thing I couldn't stop wondering as I read it over was: Why were they so freaked out about the skid marks? Is making skid marks on the sidewalk a bad thing to do? It makes me think I spent half my childhood inadvertently infuriating my entire neighborhood.

The local Lafayette morning-rock DJ Jeff Strange, on Axl's extremely brief but much-reported fisticuffs with the diminutive and seemingly gentle designer of mall clothes Tommy Hilfiger; actually, "fisticuffs" is strong—accounts suggest that the fight consisted mostly of Hilfiger slapping Axl on the arm many times, and photos show Axl staring at Hilfiger with an improbable fifty-fifty mixture of rage and amused disbelief, like, "Should I . . . hurt it?":

"Man, I saw that, and I thought, That is straight Lafayette."

5.

I found Dana Gregory. I called his stepmom. He's Axl's oldest friend and worked for him at one time in L.A., after Guns had gotten big. When I sat down at the table in the back-patio area of a pub-type place called Sgt. Preston's, he had sunglasses on. When he pushed them up into his bushy gray hair, he had unnervingly pale mineral-blue eyes that had seen plenty of sunrises. He'd been there. You knew it before he even spoke. He'd done a spectacular amount of crazy shit in his life, and the rest of his life would be spent remembering and reflecting on that shit and focusing on taking it day by day. The metamorphosis of Bill, the friend of his youth, in whose mother's kitchen he ate breakfast every morning, his Cub Scouts buddy (a coin was tossed: Bill would be Raggedy Ann in the parade; Dana, Raggedy Andy), into—for a while—the biggest rock star on the planet, a man who started riots in more than one country and dumped a supermodel and duetted with Mick Jagger and then did even stranger shit like telling *Rolling Stone* he'd recovered memories of being sodomized by his stepfather at the age of two, a man who took as his legal name and made into a household word the name of a band (Axl) that Gregory was once in, on bass, and that Bill was never even in, man . . . This event had appeared in Gregory's life like a supernova to a prescientific culture. What was he supposed to do with it?

I said, "Do you call him Bill or Axl?"

He smiled: "I call him Ax."

"Still talk to him much?"

"Haven't talked to him since 1992. We had sort of a falling-out."

"Over what?"

He looked away. "Bullshit." Then, after a few pulls and drags, "It might have been over a woman."

He was nervous, but nervous in the way that any decent person is when you sit down in front of him with a notebook and are basically like, "I have to make a two-thirty flight. Can you tell me about the heaviest things in your life? Order more spinach-'n'-artichoke dip, I can expense it."

He finished beers quickly. He used, repeatedly, without the slightest self-consciousness, an idiom I've always loved— "*Right* on," spoken quickly and with the intonation a half octave higher on "Right," to mean not "That's correct" or "Exactly" but simply "Yes," as in "Hey, you like to party?" *Right* on.

"Tell me about L.A.," I said. "You said you were working for him out there. What kind of stuff?"

"Fixing shit that he broke," Gregory said.

"Did he break a lot of shit?" I said.

"His condo had these giant mirrors going all around it. And every now and then, he'd take that spaceman statue they give you when you win an award on MTV and smash up the mirrors with it. Well, he slept till four o'clock in the afternoon every day. Somebody had to let the guy in when he came to fix the mirrors. Shit like that."

He told me another L.A. story, about the time Axl picked up Slash's beloved albino boa constrictor and it shat all over Axl. And Axl had on some expensive clothes. He got so mad he wanted to hurt the snake. He was cussing at it. But Slash picked up his guitar—here Dana imitated a tree-chopping backswing pose—and said, "Don't. Hurt. My. Snake." Axl backed off.

I guess we sat there a pretty long time. Dana has four children and four grandchildren. When I said he seemed young for that (can you imagine Axl with four grandchildren?), he said, "Started young. Like I was saying, there was a lot of experimentation." His ex-wife, Monica Gregory, also knew Axl. She gave him his first PA. Gregory said he talks to her only once a year, "when I have to." He said what he wants is to lower the level of dysfunction for the next generation. He told me about how he and Axl and Monica and their group of friends used to go to a park in Lafayette after dark, Columbian Park—"We ruled that place at night"—and pick the lock on the piano case that was built into the outdoor stage and play for themselves till the small hours. I'd wandered around Columbian Park. It's more or less across the street from where those boys grew up. Not twenty feet from the stage, there's a memorial to the sons of Lafayette who "made the supreme sacrifice in defense of our country," and it includes the name of William Rose, probably Axl's great-great-great-grandpa, killed in the Civil War, which I suppose was fought in defense of our country in some not quite precise way. And now, as Gregory talked, I thought about how weird it was, all those years of Axl probably reading that name a hundred times, not making anything of it, not knowing that it was his own name—he who one day, having discovered his original name while going through some of his mother's papers and taking it as his own, would sing, "I don't need your Civil War," and ask the still-unanswered question, "What's so civil about war, anyway?"

Back then, Gregory said, Axl played all kinds of stuff. He mentioned Thin Lizzy. "But the only time I ever really heard him sing was in the bathroom. He'd be in there for an hour doing God knows what. Prancing around like a woman, for all I know."

"So, what is there of Lafayette in his music, do you think?"

"The anger, man. I'd say he got that here."

"He used to get beat up a lot, right?" (More than one person had told me this since I'd come to town.)

"I beat him up a lot," Gregory said. "Well, I'd win one year, he'd win the next. One time we was fighting in his backyard, and I was winning. My dad saw what was going on and tried to stop it, but his mom said, 'No, let 'em fight it out.' We always hashed it out, though. When you get older, it takes longer to heal."

It was awkward, trying incessantly to steer the conversation back toward the Sheidler business without being too obvious about it. Did Dana honestly have no memory of the fracas? He kept answering elliptically. "I remember the cops wanted to know who'd spray-painted all over the street," he said, smiling.

"The night Axl left for L.A., he wrote, 'Kiss my ass, Lafayette. I'm out of here.' I wish I'd taken a picture of that."

Finally, I grew impatient and said, "Mr. Gregory, you can't possibly not remember this. Listen: You. A kid with a bike. Axl and a woman got into a fight. He had a splint on his arm."

"I can tell you how he got the splint," he said. "It was from holding on to an M-80 too long. We thought they were pretty harmless, but I guess they weren't, 'cause it 'bout blew his fucking hand off."

"But why were you so mad about the skid marks in the first place?" I asked.

"My dad was in construction. Still is. That's what I do. It's Gregory and Sons—me and my brother are the sons. Mostly residential concrete. My brother, he's dead now. He was thirty-nine. A heart thing. My dad still can't bring himself to get rid of the 'Sons.' Anyway, see, we poured that sidewalk. He'd get so pissed if he saw it was scuffed up— 'Goddamm it, you know how hard it is to get that off?' He'd think we done it and beat our ass. So, I saw [little Scott Sheidler's handiwork], and I said, 'No, I don't think that's gonna do.'"

That was all. I couldn't get too many beats into any particular topic with Gregory before his gaze would drift off, before he'd get pensive. I started to get the feeling that this— his being here, his decision to meet with me—was about something, that we had not yet gotten around to the subject he was here to discuss.

"You know," he said, "I've never talked to a reporter before. I've always turned down requests."

"Why'd you agree to this one?" I asked.

"I wasn't going to call you back, but my dad said I should. You oughta thank my dad. My son said, 'Tell him what an asshole that guy was, Dad.' I said, 'Ah, he knows all that shit, son.'"

"Is it that you feel it's been long enough, and now you can talk about all that stuff?"

"Shit, I don't know. I figure maybe he'll see the article and give me a call. It's been a long time. I'd really love just to talk to him and find out what he's really been into."

"Do you still consider him a friend?" I said.

"I don't know. I miss the guy. I love him."

We were quiet for a minute, and then Gregory leaned to the side and pulled out his wallet. He opened it and withdrew a folded piece of white notepaper. He placed it into my hand, still folded. "Put that in your story," he said. "He'll know what it means." I went straight to the car after the interview and remembered about the note only when I was already on the plane. Written on it in pencil were a couple of lines from "Estranged," off *Use Your Illusion II*:

But everything we've ever known's here.
I never wanted it to die.

6.

Axl has said, "I sing in five or six different voices that are all part of me. It's not contrived." I agree. One of them is an unexpectedly competent baritone. The most important of the voices, though, is Devil Woman. Devil Woman comes from a deeper part of Axl than do any of the other voices.

Often she will not enter until nearer the end of a song. In fact, the dramatic conflict between Devil Woman and her sweet, melodic yang—the Axl who sings such lines as "Her hair reminds me of a warm, safe place" and "If you want to love me, then darling, don't refrain"—is precisely what resulted in Guns N' Roses' greatest songs. Take "Sweet Child o' Mine." It's not that you don't love it from the beginning, what with the killer riffs and the oddly antiquated-sounding chorus, yet a sword hangs over it. You think: This can't be everything. Come on, I mean, "Now and then when I see her face / It takes me away to that special place"? What is that?

Then, around 5:04, she arrives. The song has veered minor-key by then, the clouds have begun to gather, and I never hear that awesome, intelligent solo that I don't imagine Axl's gone off somewhere at the start of it, to be by himself while his body undergoes certain changes. What I love is how when he comes back in, he comes in on top of himself ("five or six different voices that are all part of me"); he's not yet all the way finished with I, I, I, I, I, I, I, I when that fearsome timbre tears itself open. And what does she say, this Devil Woman? What does she always say, for that matter? Have you ever thought about it? I hadn't. "Sweet Child," "Paradise City," "November Rain," "Patience," they all come down to codas—Axl was a poet of the dark, unresolved coda—and to what do these codas themselves come down? "Everybody needs somebody." "Don't you think that you need someone?" "I need you. Oh, I need you." "Where do we go? Where do we go now?" "I wanna go." "Oh, won't you please take me home?"

7

When I was about seventeen, I drove back to Indiana with my oldest friend, Trent. We'd grown up in the same small river town there and both went off to school elsewhere at about the same time, so we romanticized our childhood haunts and playmates a little, the way you do. The summer before our senior year of high school, we made a sentimental journey home to drop in on everybody and see how each had fared. This is 1991, when *Use Your Illusion* came out. "Don't Cry" was on the radio all the time and fun to imitate. Still, that turned out to be one of the more colossally bleak afternoons of my life.

To a man, our old chums divided along class lines. Those of us who'd grown up in Silver Hills, where kids were raised to finish high school and go to college, were finishing high school and applying to colleges. Those who hadn't, weren't. They weren't doing anything. There were these two guys from our old gang, Brad Hope and Rick Sissy. Their fathers were working-class—one drove a bus and the other a concrete truck; the latter couldn't read or write. But the public elementary where we met them was mixed in every sense. And there's something about that age, from nine to eleven— your personality has appeared, but if you're lucky you haven't internalized yet the idea that you're any different from anyone else, that there's a ladder in life.

We stopped by Ricky's house first. Ricky had been a kind of white-trash genius, into everything. You know those ads in the back of comics that say you can make a hovercraft out of vacuum-cleaner parts? Ricky was the kid who made the hovercraft. And souped it up. He was taller and chubbier than the rest of us and had a high-pitched voice and used some kind of oil in his hair. Trent would eventually get into the University of Chicago and wind up writing a two-hundred-page thesis on the Munich Conference, and even he would tell you: Ricky was the smartest. One time Ricky and I were shooting pellet guns at cars in the small junkyard his father maintained as a sort of sideline. We were spider-webbing the glass. Suddenly Ricky's dad, who had just been woken up from one of his epic diurnal naps between shifts, hollered from the window of his bedroom, "Ricky, you'd better not be shooting at that orange truck! I done sold the windshield on that."

I'll never forget; Ricky didn't even look at me first. He just ran. Dropping the pistol at his feet, he ran into the forest. I followed. We spent the whole rest of the day up there. We found an old grave in the middle of a field. We climbed to the top of Slate Hill, the highest knob in our town, and Ricky gave me a whole talk on how slate formed, how it was and was not shale. I'll never forget the scared, ecstatic freedom of those hours in the woods.

When Trent and I rediscovered Ricky, he was sitting alone in a darkened room watching a porn movie of a woman doing herself with a peeled banana. He said, "What the fuck is that thing on your head?" I was in a bandanna-wearing phase. This one was yellow. He said, "When I saw you get out of the car, I thought, Who the fuck is that? I 'bout shot you for a faggot." We asked him what was going on. He said he'd just been expelled from school, for trying to destroy one of the boys' restrooms by flushing lit waterproof M-80s down the toilets. Also, he'd just been in a bad jeep accident; his shoulder was messed up somehow. All scabbed over, maybe? This entire conversation unfolded as the woman with the banana worked away. Ricky's dad was asleep in the next room. Retired now. We told him we were headed over to Brad's next. He said, "I haven't seen Brad in a while. Did you hear he dorked a spook?" That's what he said: "dorked a spook."

We were quiet on the way to Brad's. He had a real mustache already. He'd always been an early bloomer. When we knew him well, he was constantly exposing himself. Once I watched him run around the perimeter of a campsite with his underpants at his ankles going, "Does this look like the penis of an eleven-year-old?" It did not. Brad used to plead with his mom to sing "Birmingham Sunday" for us, which she'd do, a cappella, in the kitchen. Now he was all nigger this, nigger that. Trent was dating a black girl in Louisville at the time. Neither of us knew how to behave. Brad must have noticed us squirming, because he looked at me at one point and said, "Ah, y'all probably got some good niggers in Ohio." That's where I was living. "We're fixin' to have a race war with the ones we got here." He had dropped out of high school. It had been only four years since we'd been sleeping over at his house, doing séances and whatnot, and now we had no way to reach each other. A gulf had appeared. It opened the first day of seventh grade when some of us went into the "accelerated" program and others went into the "standard" program. By sheerest coincidence, I'm sure, this division ran perfectly parallel to the one between our respective parents' income brackets. I remember Ricky and me running into each other in the hallway the first day of seventh grade and with a confusion that we were far too young to handle, both being like, "Why aren't you in any of my classes?" When I think about it, I never saw those boys again, not after that day.

Axl got away.

8

There were hundreds of blue flags draped along the south bank of the Nervión in Bilbao, and across the top of each it said GUNS N' ROSES. The flags were of Moorish blue, and they shook against a spotless sky that was only barely more pale than that. Late that night, in the hills over the city, the band would begin headlining a three-day festival, and the river valley echoed the sound so clearly, so helplessly, people in the old part of town would be able, if they understood English, to make out the individual words, but for now Bilbao retained its slightly buttoned-up tranquillity and charm. There's a fountain next to the Guggenheim that fires bursts of water every four or five seconds, and the olive-skinned kids jump up and down in it. They just strip to their underpants and go wild, male and female, and to watch them at it was lovely. Can you imagine, in the center of some major American city, a bunch of twelve-year-old girls in their panties capering in the water, their lank hair flinging arcs of droplets? Hard to say which would be greater: the level of parental paranoia or the actual volume of loitering pervs. Here things seemed so sane. Axl and the boys hadn't landed yet. They were still in the air.

The district where they played is called Kobetamendi. It's high up, and from there you could see the city, the river, the spires, the flashing titanium scales of the museum. When it got dark, you could see the lights. When there aren't stages set up at Kobetamendi, it's just a large empty field with a road and, across the road, some modest farmhouses.

As I reached the crest of the hill, a rap-rock band was playing. The justification for rap rock seems to be that if you take really bad rock and put really bad rap over it, the result is somehow good, provided the raps are being barked by an overweight white guy with cropped hair and forearm tattoos. The women from those few little farmhouses had gathered at their fence; they leaned and mumbled and dangled their canes. One of them was one of the oldest-looking old people I have ever seen, with stiff white hair and that face, like the inside of a walnut shell, that only truly ancient women get. She and her friends were actually listening to the rap rock, and part of me wanted to run over to them and assure them that after they died, there would still be people left in the world who knew how horrifying this music was, and that these people would transmit their knowledge to carefully chosen members of future generations, but the ladies did not appear worried. They were even laughing. I'm sure they remembered traveling circuses in that field in eighteen ninety something, and what was the difference, really?

That night I wheedled my way backstage by doing a small favor for the bassist's Portuguese model girlfriend (I gave her buddy from home a spare media pass they'd accidentally given me). When the security guard on the back ramp leading up to the stage, who did not even make eye contact with the Portuguese model as she floated past him, put his palm against my chest, as if to say, "Whoa, that's a little much," she turned around briefly and said, *"Está conmigo."* She said this with about the level of nervousness and uncertainty with which you might say, to a maître d', "Smoking." Before I could thank her, I was watching Axl dance from such an inconceivable propinquity that if I'd bent my knees, thrust my hands forward, and leapt, I'd have been on the front page of the entertainment section of *El País* the next day for assaulting him in front of twenty-five thousand people.

I've been a part of virtual seas of screaming sweaty kids

before, but to see one from the stage, from just above, to see that many thousand people shaping with their mouths some words you made up in your head one time while you were brushing your teeth (needless to say, I was trying to imagine I'd written them), that was heady. "Guns and RO-SES, Guns and RO-SES" . . . Axl was pounding with the base of his mike stand on the stage in time to the chant. A kid with a beard looked at us, me and the model and her friend, every ten minutes or so, put his hands on his ears, and mouthed the word *pyro*. Then we were supposed to put our hands on our ears, because the explosion was about to take place ten feet away. Sometimes the kid would forget—he was busy—and then everyone would go, "Aaaarrrgh!" and clutch their head.

There was a sort of shambling older dude next to me in a newsboy cap, with a guitar in his hands—a tech, I figured. Then he ran out onto the stage, and I was like, "That's Izzy Stradlin" (founding Guns N' Roses guitarist).

Izzy, I know, is the reason the band sounds so much better tonight than they did two months ago in New York. He started joining them on three or four songs the very next night, after the debut, and has been showing up periodically ever since. His presence—or to put it more accurately, the presence of another original member of the band—seems to have made the other guys feel more like they are Guns N' Roses and less like, as *El Diario Vasco* will put it tomorrow, "*una bullanguera formación de mercenarios al servicio del ego del vocalista*," which means "a noisy bunch of mercenaries in the service of the vocalist's ego."

The Spanish press—they weren't kind. They said Axl was a "grotesque spectacle"; they called him "*el divo*"; they talked about the endless, Nigel Tufnel–esque "*solos absurdos*" that he makes each of the band members play, in an effort to get the audience to invest emotionally in the new lineup (it's true that these are fairly ill-advised, as has been the rock solo generally since Jimi died). One article says, *"Las fotos de Axl dan miedo,"* which translates literally and, I think, evocatively as "Pictures of Axl give fear," with his "goatee that gives him the look of a Texas millionaire." In a crowning moment, they say that he has "the voice of a priapic rooster." They say he demands his room be covered in Oriental carpets and that he not be required to interact with the other band members. That he arrived on a separate plane. They say security guards have been ordered never to look him in the eye. They say the other band members also hate one another and demand to be placed on different floors of the hotel. They say he's traveling with a tiny Asian guru named Sharon Maynard, "alias Yoda," and that he does nothing without her guidance, that she chooses the people he should hire by examining their faces. But mostly the Spaniards are fixated, as have been all the European media gangs on this tour, with the secret oxygen chamber into which he supposedly disappears during the shows and from which he emerges *"más fresco que una lechuga"*—fresher than a head of lettuce.

I can't confirm or deny the oxygen thing, and it's hard to say whether the constant mentions of it in the press are evidence of its being real or just a sign that people are recycling the same rumor. The manager of a Hungarian band called Sex Action, which opened for G N' R, claims to have seen the device itself, but Hungarians make up tales like that for entertainment.

What I can tell you, based on my model-side vantage, is that there is a square cell entirely covered in black curtains just to the rear of stage left. You cannot see as much as a crack of light through the curtains, and I tried. Axl runs into this thing about fifteen times during the course of a show. Sometimes he emerges with a new costume on—makes sense—but sometimes he doesn't. Sometimes he goes in there when one of the guys is soloing or something—makes sense—but sometimes he goes in there at a moment when it's really distracting not to have him onstage. I do not know whether Sharon Maynard is in this cell. I do not know what he does in there. If he's huffing reconstituted gas, I don't know whether it's in a Michael Jackson "This is good for me" sort of way or if he has a legitimate lung problem. I don't know anything about what goes on in the cell, only that it exists and that being in there is important to Axl.

Overall, I can't agree with my fellow ink-stained wretches in the Old World about this show. Axl is sounding fuller and fuller. Every now and then the sound guy, just to make sure the board is calibrated, pushes the vocal mike way up in the mix, and we hear nothing but Axl, and the notes are on. Nor is he fat at all. In fact, he looks pretty lithe. At one point, he puts on a rather skimpy T-shirt and sprints from one end of the stage to the other, and it's the sprint of the cross-country runner he used to be. Dana Gregory told me Axl used to run everywhere. Just run and run. Dana Gregory said there was one time out west when G N' R played in a stadium that had a track around it, and Axl just started sprinting around the track during a song. When a security guard, believing him to be a crazed fan, tried to tackle him, Axl kicked the guy in the face. "That happened ten feet in front of me," Gregory said. And now here the bastard was, ten feet in front of me. The moon looked like she was yelling for help because some dark power was erasing her side. They brought out a piano so that he could do "November Rain," and the way they positioned the piano, he was facing me directly.

Like we were sitting across a table from each other. This is as close as I ever got to him. And what I noticed at this almost nonexistent remove was the peace in his features as he tinkled out the intro. Absolute peace. A warm slackness to the facial muscles way beyond what Botox can do, though I'm not saying it didn't contribute. His face was for now beyond the reach of whatever it is that makes him crazy.

After the final encore, he and the rest of the band ran down a ramp, into the open door of a waiting van. Heavy men in black ran alongside them like drill instructors. The van squealed away, taking the model with it. Big, heavy black cars pulled out alongside the van. And then it was quiet. The Basque country. Next morning the flags were still flying by the river, the press was preparing the scathing reviews, but Axl was gone.

They were the last great rock band that didn't think there was something a bit embarrassing about being in a rock band. There are thousands of bands around at any given time that don't think rock is the least bit funny, but rarely is one of them good. With G N' R, no matter how sophisticated you felt yourself to be about pop music (leaving aside for now the paradoxical nature of that very social category), you couldn't entirely deny them. They were the first band I got to be right about with my older brother. It was that way for a lot of people in my generation. All my youth, my brother had been force-feeding me my musical taste—"Def Leppard is shit; listen to the Jam"—and now there was finally one band I wouldn't have to live down; and I recall the tiny glow of triumph, blended with fraternity, that I felt when one day he said, "Dude, you were right about Guns N' Roses. That's a good record." That was *Appetite*, of course. Things got strange after that.

You read things that say Nirvana made Guns N' Roses obsolete. But Guns N' Roses were never made obsolete. They just sort of disintegrated.

Closer to the case is that G N' R made Nirvana possible. When you think about the niche that Nirvana supposedly created and perfected—a megaband that indie snobs couldn't entirely disavow, no matter how badly they wanted to—G N' R got there first. Or almost there. They dressed silly. They didn't seem to know the difference between their good songs and their crap songs. But we have to remember, too, how they came along at a time when bands with singers who looked like Axl and thrust their hips unironically, and lead players who spread their legs and reeled off guitar-god noodling weren't supposed to be interesting, melodically or culturally or in any other way. G N' R were. They were also grotesque and crass and stupid sometimes, even most of the time. Even almost all of the time. But you always knew you were seeing something when you saw them.

Shouldn't the band just get back together? Don't they know how huge that'd be? Dana Gregory told me Slash and Izzy will never play full-time with Axl again: "They know him too well."

I don't know him at all. Maybe if his people had let me talk to him, he'd have bitten and struck me and told me to leave my fucking brats at home, and I could transcend these feelings. As it is, I'm left listening to "Patience" again. I don't know how it is where you are, but in the South, where I live, they still play it all the time. And I whistle along and wait for that voice, toward the end, when he goes, *Ooooooo, I need you. OOOOOOO, I need you.* And on the first *Ooooooo*, he finds this tissue-shredding note. It conjures the image of someone peeling his own scalp back, like the skin of a grape. I have to be careful not to attempt to sing along with this part, because it can make you sort of choke and almost throw up a little bit. And on the second OOOOOOO, you picture just a naked glowing green skull that hangs there vibrating gape-mouthed in a prison cell.

Or whatever it is you picture.

AMERICAN GROTESQUE

The first American revolution was fought over socialism, in 1609. This is rarely mentioned. Even before slavery and the Indian genocides, it's our founding schism.

In that year, a ship called the *Sea Venture* was wrecked off the coast of Bermuda. Shakespeare based *The Tempest* in part on her story. She'd been on her way to relieve the struggling infant Jamestown colony in Virginia. So the ship hadn't even reached here yet—that's how early this was.

Among the passengers were several of separatist tendencies, the Brownists and Familists, whose ideas about society and Christianity had been shaped by the radical sectarian movements that rose up before the English Civil War. These were the parents, then, of the Levellers, Diggers, and Quakers (the people you read about in Christopher Hill's 1972 classic, *The World Turned Upside Down*). Most of those movements contained at least some communitarian element.

The passengers made it ashore and right away set to work building another ship.

Some of them did. The others said, What are we doing? Why are we killing ourselves to get to Jamestown, where they'll put us to work as colonial drones until we starve or get eaten by heathens, when we have everything we need on this island? Fresh fruit, seafood, plenty of space. Let us live here in common, worshipping God and sharing the bounty of the earth, and no man shall be master to any other.

Nor was there any indigenous population in Bermuda. It was *terra pura*, pure soil.

What happened? The ones who intended to go to Jamestown tried to imprison, banish, and execute the ones who wanted to stay. The latter ran off into the forest.

The governor killed one of their leaders, a man named Henry Paine, to set an example. He wanted to hang him, but Paine begged to be shot, as more befitting a gentleman. His last recorded words were "The governor can kiss my arse." Those were his exact words.

In the end, almost everyone went to Jamestown and perished.

Today is September 12, 2009. We are marching.

Actually, at this moment we are massing around a parade float that will guide us from Freedom Plaza to the steps of the Capitol building.

You rarely see a lone parade float, one that's not in a line with others. It gives this thing the look of a ship on a sea of people. The sea is us. (In a different mood it might look like a hayride wagon gone wrong and run into a mob.)

A woman calls to us from the wagon-ship. She's about sixty;

we don't see her well. She has a microphone, but the sound system it's connected to can't compete with this level of crowd noise, so we don't hear much. Another day, this would be annoying. Today it's thrilling. We're too many even for ourselves, and more are coming. As many of the signs say, silent majority no more.

The woman introduces someone; she says we may have seen him on the Internet. In the past week or so, he's become a YouTube sensation. He recorded himself at home with his webcam, just talking, speaking from his heart about what he feels is happening to his nation, the trouble it's headed toward if good people don't make a stand. He's a brown-haired man in his thirties. In the video, he said something, used a phrase that resonated. If you've seen it, you know the phrase; some of us haven't seen it and can't hear well enough to catch the phrase today, but we feel the tone. Something like: "I want my America back." Or, "What happened to my America?"

A guy behind me is holding an ingenious sign he's made. He's cut out the mouth from a giant cardboard poster of House Speaker Nancy Pelosi's face, creating a hole, a gaping maw, and attached a bag to the back of it, like a corn hole at the fair. He's handing out Lipton tea bags to people and urging them to "tea-bag Nancy Pelosi." People are doing it and laughing, even ladies. Pelosi, with her giant crazy eyes, gulps the tea bags eagerly.

It's only fair. Liberals made fun of us because, at first, some of us didn't know what "tea-bagging" meant—that it meant dipping your testicles into a woman's or, if you tend that way, another fella's open mouth—and a few of us, the older ones, may have referred to ourselves for a brief span as "tea-baggers," in ignorance and in innocence. Now we're turning the joke back on them. No one with a sense of humor gets hurt.

Standing on a garbage can and commanding a lot of attention is a strange figure. A small man or woman—you can't see enough of its body to tell—holds a handmade sign that reads YES I AM. The creature wears an Obama mask. When people holler "Obama!" it looks in their direction and does a little shuffle. Atop the Obama mask sits a fake gold crown. Obama thinks he's a king! (Is that what YES I AM means? Yes, I am a king?) The king has on a bright purple pimp's coat with faux-leopard-skin trim. An African king? It looks like something you'd see and turn away from in a Southern antiques shop. We do turn away, after taking a pic.

You can't move sideways as easily as you could a minute ago. The march is slowly moving. To the Capitol!

The date of this march has been carefully chosen. Indeed, the date is the name of the march. This is the 9/12 March. "9/12" refers to a movement begun by Glenn Beck, of Fox News, who's monitoring the events from the studio. Glenn calls on us to return as a nation to the way we were on the day after September 11, when there was no red and blue, no left and right, just Americans, unified, ready. People in New York City had clapped in the streets for Bush, people who hadn't voted for him and wouldn't in 2004 either. He was the president.

Is it strange to feel nostalgia for that day? That was the first day of some kind of war. People's remains still lay smoldering in the wreckage of those buildings. A time of deep psychic trauma for untold numbers of people, it seems a day that only someone with the most distant and abstract connection to it would want to revisit, much less re-create, and that nothing short of a near-galactic narcissism could bring a person to suggest enshrining it as a state of being. But we didn't name the march. Beck named it, although he disavows ownership and is absent today. On TV, in describing his role, he puts it like this: "If you build it, they will come."

Beck is an entertainer. We love him, but he goes over the top.

How many of us are here? As is typical with political-crowd estimates, the question will become charged in the coming weeks, with wildly high guesses (between 1.5 and 2 million, the figure getting passed around today at the march) down to some probably slightly grouchy ones offered later by city employees, who put the number at roughly sixty thousand. Perhaps the fairest count would place it at about seventy-five thousand. What matters at a march is that it feel large, and it doesn't take much to feel like an army.

Every so often someone shouts, "Can you hear us now?" (It's a phrase of the day, like "I want my America back.") The response to these calls is most often a smile and chuckle from people in hearing range. You know how, when you're at a concert and someone shouts something funny from the crowd, there's a tight smile people do while scanning for the one who did it—that's what we do when someone yells, "Can you hear us now?"

This tickled reaction reminds you of something, which is that our march is in part—we could even say mostly—an act of mass irony. Conservatives do not march. We shake our heads and hold signs while lefties march. But today we are marching. We are "marching." (We can march, too.)

That explains why so many of us believe there could be 2 million people here, many more even than came to the

Obama inauguration, which paralyzed the city (whereas we have not even impeded traffic). It's that none of us have ever been in a march before.

For the first time in our history, a black man lives in the White House, and today's is the first massive protest against his administration, and 99.9999 percent of us are white and fan-followers of race-baiting pundits—and mind you, this is in America, where you can't walk into a convenience store without having or witnessing at least three intense, awkward, occasionally inspiring moments of racial tension—but despite all that, today has "nothing to do with race." This phenomenon will be known to future Americans as the "Race Miracle of 9/12."

As evidence, when you approach the Capitol—surely America's most stirring man-made view, where you stare into the gray shadows behind those columns and realize you're witnessing the stone projection of a psychic landscape, a landscape that is not this country but the idea of this country, the very heavenly city of the eighteenth-century philosophers (you're "caught literally and physically," as a quotation inscribed into the asphalt of Freedom Plaza had put it, "in L'Enfant's dream")—an unexpected sight awaits you there: a dark black man, wearing dark glasses, on a video screen. He's here with us in person, but you can't see him because of the crowd. On the screen he turns and speaks directly to the other black man, the one in the White House.

He's the Reverend C. L. Bryant, a conservative preacher from Louisiana. This is his moment.

"Politicians have built walls," he says. "Walls of misunderstanding" (we roar approval), "walls of racism" (louder), "walls of classism" (louder still).

"And to quote Ronald Reagan, when he spoke to Mikhail

Gorbachev at the Berlin Wall," Bryant says, his preacher voice intensifying, our own volume trebling, "Mr. Obama, tear down these walls!"

God knows what this means, but he's on our side.

There is open racism here. Later you'll hear there wasn't, but it's just strangely coded. Perhaps owing to the advanced age of many of us—the same factor, in other words, that caused the tea-bagging embarrassment—we still revert to seventies soul-brother jive talk when we want to be racist. The YES I AM pimp king is one example, but there are plenty of others. A sign shows Obama digging a grave for the Constitution, with the caption I DON'T DIG BARACK. That's too subtle to serve as a convincing example, maybe, but another man holds a sign that reads HEY, BRO, HANDS OFF MY WALLET, next to a picture of a monkey's face. You start to see.

A father and a little boy standing by a tree. Father's sign reads WE KNOW HE SNEAKS CIGARETTES BUT SERIOUSLY IS THE PRESIDENT STILL SMOKING CRACK?

There's music again. A conservative folksinger has taken Reverend Bryant's place, with a song called "We Gotta Get Back" (meaning to our 9/12 ways).

Ronnie Reagan is everywhere. One sign says DIG HIM UP FOR 2012. I ask the young man holding it—Franklin McGuire, a polite, sharp-looking kid from South Carolina who's living in D.C. for the fall semester and interning at a conservative leadership institute—which issue he's here representing, and he says, "Personal responsibility." He's young, but already he feels he's been able to witness his country's decline.

At smaller Tea Party rallies throughout the states, while we wait for speakers like Joe the Plumber to arrive, we play old Reagan speeches from iTunes over PAs and listen to them, standing in fields and parks. We want to remove ourselves from history.

You spot only one counterprotester, if that's what he is. He wears a suit, and his sign reads TAX THE RICH. He stands in the middle of the outgoing flow, so you can't avoid him. His sign puzzles people. One Tea Party patriot in jeans, sneakers, and cap approaches him, demanding to know "What's wrong with rich people? Aren't rich people good?"

"Some of 'em," the man in the suit answers and sort of shrugs, as if he's paid to be here. The back of his sign has Christian stuff on it.

The patriot squints at him, preparing to launch into a stream of abuse, but waves his hand with ah-phooey disgust and stalks off.

Later that evening, in a paid-for suite at the Mandarin Oriental, a tall blond "government-affairs executive at a well-connected industry-trade group" (that is, a lobbyist at one of the top policy "shops" here in the demimonde where private insurance and D.C. politics mingle) was helping me to explore the minibar.

He is my first cousin, with whom I grew up and have stayed close. In the 1940s, our grandfather and two of his childhood friends inherited an insurance company in Kentucky that had been operating since the 1850s. They spent their lives making it into what today is the oldest and, in many years, most successful small firm in the state. My twin uncles run it now. Their sons are being groomed for takeover as we speak. It's the American story. It's an American story. My grandfather drove Buicks; my uncles fly on private jets. My grandfather promised people his vote; my uncles help people get elected. I grew up at the margins of it, dead-middle-class, enjoying the company's benefits at someone's generosity, charging unlimited Cokes at the country club under one of my cousins' names, aware that the whole mechanism of wealth perpetuation would take care of me in a pinch but then settle me back at arm's length.

My family never made me or my siblings feel any of this; they're kind and humor-possessing people, conscientious to a fault, the kind who stress you out trying to feed you, give you spending money, make you stay at their houses instead of hotels, a few of the reasons they've done well—but they never had to make us feel anything. It was Southern class, and we had functioning IQs. In the twilight, from the balcony, it became possible to see my lovable wide-smiled cousin, whose tooth I had once helped pull, as the next logical evolutionary phase, a kind of probe put forward by our provincial-family genome into the D.C. atmosphere to examine possibilities there. Politics, my boy. He was liking it.

We talked about the 9/12 March, some of which we had watched together. I was accusing him and his colleagues of essentially having created it. Didn't the crap those people were spewing originate in the e-mail accounts of lobbyists and "former CEOs" and other cynically interested types? Why else would these citizens purport to fear "socialized medicine" so intensely? An elevated number of them had "marched" in wheelchairs or while manifesting obvious signs of chronic health trouble and obesity, not to mention age—surely Medicare and VA benefits were covering a whopping percentage of all that. These tea-partiers owed their very lives to socialized medicine. You and your dad, I said, are the only people who have any reason to fear it.

My cousin denied any connection. He said he and his colleagues viewed the marchers as at most "a welcome distraction," which I took to mean, they lend a helpful populist sheen to what remains a disagreement among the powerful over how things will be settled.

"That was Palin Nation," my cousin said.

"Yeah," I said, "that was Old People Discover the Internet."

He told me a bunch of them had been in his office earlier that day. "So," I said, "the attitude is, if they want to go on TV shouting against a public option . . ."

"Great!"

I still had the feeling of being down on the street with them in my nerves. The way my cousin talked, this wasn't how they'd seen themselves, not hardly. They were taking back power, seizing a destiny. But even the African pimpking was some kind of pawn, as Bob Dylan might have put it in an eleven-minute impressionistic story song.

We were watching footage of the march on TV, flipping back and forth between that and a sports thing my cousin wanted to see. The distance between up here and down there began to deepen. Had we been marching to keep my relatives rich? Standing up for the rich people, like that guy who'd accosted the counterprotester? What a bizarre turn in American politics. The 9/12 March for Aetna! Vans I'd passed on the highway, driving in, were decorated with handmade pro–Fox News propaganda.

My cousin told me a casual story about a breakfast three months earlier with a leading Republican senator, by the

end of which this senator had vowed to "make the public option radioactive."

I was souring, noticing the conventional unattractiveness
of the crowd. It hinted at undiluted Germanic stock. It had
been wrong to think people like this don't march; they just
do it with torches.

Some text message made my cousin have to run. "Good
luck with the story," he said. We man-hugged.

A sign read THIS TIME WE COME PEACEFULLY AND UN-
ARMED. THIS TIME. But the man holding it was smiling the
same way they do outside the *Today Show* studios.

I arrived at the town-hall meeting in Virginia on time,
but the doors were locked. Too many people inside already;
the fire department had made the call. A bunch of us stood
outside, going through the ritual bonding gesture of greeting
each new person who came up to try the door. "It's locked,"
we muttered in friendly warning. Really? (Trying anyway.)
What the hell? "We know! What the hell!"

I asked a willowy redheaded woman who looked about
forty why she was there. "Because I'm afraid," she said. "I'm
really afraid of this president. I mean, they're starting to talk
about limits on family size, how many children you can have.
In our America."

A guy came up and pulled on the door. "Figures," he said.
"He's a liberal" (meaning the Democratic congressman hosting this town hall).

People around me snort and harrumph, but there are some
guys here from a union. "Oh, some of us are pretty smart," a
white-bearded one of them says.

"Oh yeah?" the guy says.

"Yeah," the labor guy says. "Some of us even have *master's degrees* and *Ph.D.'s*."

Pretty tame, as political combat goes, but you could tell it made the people in our little group edgy. (A couple of days later, somebody would bite off someone else's finger at a health-care-related event. We were ready.)

Three people exited, the fireman let in three, that's how it worked. It took me over an hour to sausage-press my way through this process into the hall itself, where Representative Tom Perriello was facing questions from a constantly self-refreshing queue of disgruntled Republican constituents. It turned out I needn't have worried about missing anything; this meeting would go for hours. It seemed every person who'd come intended to speak.

As we shuffled up the hallway toward the room with the microphones, distinct words began to emerge from the doors. The one we heard clearest and loudest, and that generated the biggest response by a huge measure, was *socialism*.

A man you couldn't see from where I stood got up and said to Perriello—he didn't so much say as intone—"From each according to his abilities; to each according to his needs." He paused. "Karl Marx said that was the credo of communism. Now, I want you to tell me the difference between that . . . and what we're headed for."

It was the one time all day the place really thundered.

"But that's from the Bible," I muttered. "From the New Testament." (Acts 2 and 4: The believers "had all things common . . . as many as were possessors of lands or houses sold them, and brought the prices of the things that were sold, and laid them down at the apostles' feet: and distribution was made unto every man according as he had need.")

The lady next to me looked at me like she'd just caught me sniffing my finger.

"It is!" I said.

The next man up to the mike was very somber, soft-spoken, bearded; a study in browns and khakis; he walked slowly. He had been waiting for this moment. "I have one question," he said to Perriello. "Where in the Constitution does it state that we are required to provide health care for everybody?"

Perriello had given a defense already of the conventional liberal view on this question (that, I imagine, the Constitution is a system for perfecting the never-ending American project, not a chain to keep us fixed in history). The congressman referred to his statement. "We've covered that," he said.

"Thank you," said the man, "you have answered my question." Much cheering.

I liked the man's question. His attitude was belligerent to a level of several hundred percent past what the moment called for, but he embodied something beautiful about the health-care-reform debate as it has evolved this year. Unlike with most questions of national import, even the wars, you can't get into this one without talking about the whole point of America. For the first time in the century or so that it's been an articulated goal of American progressives (beginning with Catholics, moving through labor, into the civil rights and consumer-advocacy struggles), we possess the means, and in some quarters the will, to enact a truly universal "care of the public health," what Benjamin Disraeli said "ought to be, if not the first, at any rate one of the first considerations of a statesman." A majority of the people—not huge but consistent—claims to want it, and we're either going to do it or not. At moments like this one, we remember that we still exist inside the matrix of an eighteenth-century experiment in Enlightenment political thought—we are in a sense the subjects of that experiment—and we interrogate the nature of it. What Would the Founding Fathers Do? becomes not an academic question but in some ways the most relevant one. Is America a place that does this, that cares for everybody? Or is that not our way?

As it happens, Benjamin Franklin, the über–Founding Father, actually got mixed up in health-care reform and the whole public/private funding debate at one point—in 1751, around the time his first papers on electricity appeared. A friend, a surgeon named Thomas Bond, approached him with a suggestion, that they lobby the Pennsylvania Assembly to create in Philadelphia a hospital for "the sick-poor," one modeled on more advanced practices Bond had observed in England and at the Hôtel-Dieu in Paris.

Bond understood that Franklin, perpetually hounded by schemers, would still get behind something new if he thought it made sense. The doctor focused his pitch on the good such an institution could do for the whole province. Treat the sick-poor and you have, for one thing, fewer poor, since prolonged sickness can make and keep us impoverished. Also, epidemics like to begin among the poor or distressed: you suppress those faster. The hard-tested surgeons produced by urban hospitals train others, who export their art to the countryside or the finest clinics. All reasons to spur Franklin.

In a periodical he'd founded, The Pennsylvania Gazette, and in addresses before the assembly, Franklin built a case over weeks. To begin with, he told them, there's no such thing as "the poor." Poor is a way station people pass through, even gentlemen and gentlewomen. "We are in this world mutual hosts to each other," he said, and pointed to the explosive social dynamism of that eighteenth-century Atlantic world outside the window, so familiar to us now, where "the circumstances and fortunes of men and families are continually changing; in the course of a few years we have seen . . . the children of the wealthy languishing in want and misery, and those of their servants lifted into estates."

Franklin proposed an institution that would provide, "free of charge," the finest health care ("diet, attendance, advice, and medicines") to everybody, "whether inhabitants of the province or strangers," even to the "poor diseased foreigners" whose growing numbers in the colony and "dissonant manners" worried many (including Franklin, who wrote that soon everyone would have to learn German).

Franklin had a list of reasons—he cherished lists—but it boiled down to something primal, a sense that it was beyond the pale ever to let human beings suffer because they couldn't pay when means existed to help. This "seems essential to the true spirit of Christianity," Franklin wrote, "and should be extended to all in general, whether deserving or undeserving, as far as our power reaches."

Franklin said to the assembly, You have to build it.

The assembly said, No, you must do it with private donations. You can't tax people in the country to pay for a city hospital.

Franklin said, That won't work, it will never be enough, good health care costs a lot of money, remembering "the distant parts of this province" in which "assistance cannot be procured, but at an expense that neither [the sick-poor] nor their townships can afford."

And besides, Franklin wrote, "the good [that] particular men may do separately, in relieving the sick, is small, compared with what they may do collectively."

The assembly said, The people will never support it. Franklin knew the majority of them already did. He knew the people.

He said to the assembly, Here's the idea. If I and my associates can raise such-and-such an amount of money (an enormous sum for the time), you will match it, and the project moves forward.

The assembly said, Sure! They knew Franklin could never get the funds. This way they looked generous, at no expense.

Franklin went out and quickly raised a good deal more even than the sum he'd named. He used the slightly competitive nature of the matching-funds plan to ratchet up giving. They say we can't do it! The people were ready. The assembly, to which Franklin would soon be elected, and its powerful landed interests had been screwed. Franklin later said he never felt less guilty about an act of deception in his life.

That's how we got: the Pennsylvania Hospital. Whence came: American surgery. Whence came: American psychiatry.

The next year, 1752, Franklin had a visit from yet another friend with yet another sane-sounding idea: modern private insurance.

There was a woman at the town-hall meeting carrying a sign that read NO SOCIALIZED MEDICARE.

I ran into my cousin again at our other cousin's wedding. She was "both our cousin." Four hundred people, black tie, reception at the old club, a soul band that had somehow been teleported in from 1967. It was magnificent. I have a black-and-white cat with a trick bladder, and she had urinated on my bow tie, so I was wearing an actual black necktie with my tuxedo. One of my uncles grabbed it and caught another's eye. "Hey, look," he shouted, acting like he was impressed, "almost there!"

I'd walked away from the town hall and the march and the Tea Party rallies feeling that despite all the crypto-racism and jokes about guns and whatnot, there wasn't anything to fear, or any more to fear than ever, at any rate not an impending Civil War II. These people reminded you of the ancient Russians who came out with pro-Soviet signs every winter. They were capitalism's bizarro reflection of that Cold War nostalgia, victorious version. Mainly they were exercising boredom and frustration. It's not like you couldn't sympathize with half of what they were saying. Most people who are against government probably have a point. It even seemed sane to hope that some good could come from the sheer event of so many Americans educating themselves about policy decisions, getting interested in creating coherence between those decisions and our ultimate hopes for the country.

You did see ominous things like news in *The Boston Globe* that the Secret Service found itself straining to handle the exponential rise in assassination threats since Obama had taken office. And people like Sean Hannity, people with big careers to protect and who are, one assumes, invested in not getting too far out, they were starting to say fairly reckless stuff on the radio, talking openly about the Obama administration as a proto-totalitarian goon squad that would soon be in your living room (the same administration, mind you, that hasn't been able to attempt passage of an ultralite, Euro-style health care public option without occasioning a national crisis). At times it did seem possible to wonder if the old American Caliban was coming out, that thing in us that knows what's right but would sort of rather watch a fight.

On September 23, a small AP article appeared, saying that on the day of the 9/12 March, even as we'd been approaching the Capitol steps, the body of a census worker from London, Kentucky, had been found by horrified tourists in the southeastern part of the state. A lot of those radio hosts, the prophets of the 9/12 marchers, had been encouraging listeners to resist the census: the census was a tentacle of the government, trying to penetrate your life and property. Was this murder a first shot over the bow from the radical right? The magazine was sending me there.

"You're going to London?" my cousin said, and instinctively we both went, "Why leave Kentucky, when you can go to Paris, Athens, London . . ." (the end of an old joke.)

I'd never been to London, at least not the one in Kentucky. I knew we had distant roots in that part of the state. I kept seeing my mother's maiden name on billboards driving in. No doubt the spirit of the place would sense the completion of an ancient circle and welcome a native. Sadly, the captain at the police station seemed intensely displeased, I would even say disgusted, to see me.

"Why are you here?" she asked, leaning against the wall with arms crossed.

I thought she was joking, since there'd been more reporters through London in the past month than in the preceding ten years, and all for the same reason. "Right!" I said gamely. "I guess you know why I'm here!"

"No, I don't," she said more coldly. "*Why are you here?*"

She looked a little like Nancy Grace in a state trooper's uniform. She was younger, and her hair may have lacked the

Magneto-helmet power of that famous crime-show hostess's—whose producers, in my imagination, lower her hair onto her head just before each taping in a darkened chamber where she sits motionless, preparing—but the captain's silhouette was the same, and so was her sneer, full of dismissal.

"That's interesting," I said (implying, I hoped, And a fine day to you, too, sister-protector of our beloved commonwealth!). "You don't think there's a story here?"

The census worker, Bill Sparkman, had been found in a mostly forested county adjacent to this one, naked and tied to a tree. Someone had written the word FED on his chest with a felt-tip marker and stuck his ID badge to his neck, possibly in mocking imitation of a deer tagging. This happened not long after a right-wing U.S. congresswoman from Minnesota had gone on TV telling Americans to remember that the census was used to round up Japanese Americans for the World War II internment camps. I hadn't known but had just learned that they'd found Sparkman on the very day of that rally in D.C. It looked like an antigovernment lynching.

The FBI got involved, but the state police out of London controlled the investigation, and after six weeks they hadn't so much as declared the case a homicide. Now the captain was telling me—one of the few things she would tell me—that the police actively "wanted to squash" that lynching narrative. The census worker's body had been cremated. She claimed to be still awaiting the results of forensic tests.

I don't know about yours, but my onboard story sensor flashed green!

She gave me her card. Actually, by the end of the interview, she was fairly nice. I saw how it would wear on a person, if you were from around here—as she was—and if you loved the place, to have entitled outsiders bursting in the doors, people who remember that your state exists only on Derby Day and when something fantastically horrible happens, and they're demanding (as occurred in nearby Manchester) to be "taken to the crazy hayseeds who killed the government man." The captain knew how people around the country perceived her and her colleagues. She also knew she was good at her job. The combination would irk a person.

Her subordinate, a male officer who stood silent through most of the interview, did say one memorable thing—that he believed, however this case ended up, or if it did, people were going to talk about it for a long time.

They wished me luck.

The hillside cemetery where Bill Sparkman died was visually exquisite in the way that southeastern Kentucky—which has a topographically secretive cove-and-cave-riven landscape—can be abruptly and gasp-inducingly pretty when a small road opens onto some clearing. If Sparkman hanged or garroted himself there, as some believe, it was a dramatic choice of setting. The Ohio tourists who found his body while visiting family graves and came away feeling strongly that Sparkman had not committed suicide but been cruelly murdered, later told reporters that he seemed to have been left on display.

The graveyard rests like an eroded rock stairway against the rim of a natural amphitheater, in the deepest fastnesses of the Daniel Boone National Forest. Without the GPS in the rental, I doubt I'd have gotten within ten miles (although the spot turned out to be not far from a cabin that belonged to my ancestors and which I saw as a kid—we drove through a streambed in someone's truck, and my brother found an old snake-oil bottle stashed in the kitchen wall).

You could hardly imagine how they had physically buried people on this hill, it was that steep. The plots were by necessity almost terraced, with little wooden chairs and benches, since you couldn't stand. The graves went up and up. It took me fifteen minutes to climb to the ridge above. As you ascended, you rose backward through unknown generations of the Hoskins family, from modern tombstones with laminated photographs of guys playing electric guitar, through older concrete slabs with crude lettering and misspellings, back to flat-lying creek rocks with no-longer-legible initials hacked into them, the ur-Hoskinses. Going higher, beyond the graves, you walked on a vast carpet of mosses and lichens, species growing out of other species—the reason the hill had looked oddly green from below, for November.

The death tree itself was glorious, massive. Its leaves clashed incessantly in the wind of a blustery day, like the branches were covered in thin coppery coins. The tree had been here before the first Hoskins.

They found Bill Sparkman strung up to one of its limbs, but not hanging. This last fact had been important (I thought unduly so) to the captain, that the body lay partly in contact with the ground when found. Not suspended there, in other words, the way you see in pictures of lynchings. His hands were bound with duct tape, his mouth stuffed with a red gag. He wore only socks. Apart from the ominous word on his chest, there was the calling attention to his badge. Otherwise, no defensive wounds. He'd died right there, of asphyxiation.

Homicide, suicide, accident—the captain confirmed, incredibly, that none of the three had been ruled out. It was hard to get your mind around. Auto-lynching?

A few days before I'd arrived, a law-enforcement source in another town had speculated to a newspaper reporter that if people wished to understand what had happened to Bill Sparkman, they needed to look into the David Carradine death. Carradine, you'll recall, was found strung up in the closet of his Bangkok hotel room in what appeared to be an auto-erotic episode gone wrong.

Or had this source, in mentioning Carradine, been referring to the actor's family, some of whom continue to insist that his death was a murder made to look like auto-erotic asphyxiation?

I lay down on the moss. It was perfectly soft; it had the softness of a mattress that a billionaire with a bad back would pay to have made for himself. Not the tiniest bit wet or muddy.

If homicide—intentional or accidental—had it been a gay thing? Not the most enlightened question, but it came. You could certainly make Sparkman's biography match up in a wink-wink way, if you wanted. Middle-aged bachelor, former altar boy, raised an adopted son alone, lifelong affiliation with the Boy Scouts, a grade-school substitute teacher, an effeminate voice. I knew the last detail from having heard a speech Sparkman gave, on the Internet, from last year. He was receiving his diploma from an online university. They asked him to serve as class speaker because his story inspired them. While working toward his degree, he'd been battling cancer and seemingly winning. A man with a round, pasty, friendly, bespectacled face and a crop of light reddish hair. In probably the most commonly reproduced photograph of him, he's wearing a toboggan to cover his chemo baldness and reaching down past a young male student's chest to point at something on a piece of paper.

As I lay there, the spheres—pundo, talk radio, and blogo—crackled with talk of what had happened or not happened on this mossy hill. Had Sparkman run into some psychopathic meth cookers on his rounds, asked them how many people lived in their trailer and what they did for a living, and got himself choked to death?

Those leaning left sensed a sweeping under the rug: the Glenn Becks and Michele Bachmanns had Sparkman's blood on their hands. Meanwhile the right seized on every shadowy hint that his death may not even have been homicide, much less a political assassination. See how quick you liberals are to demonize us! The two sides hissed at each other, in a ritual as routine by now as a *West Side Story* number.

Late orange butterflies moved over the moss bed. On the way here I'd passed road signs straight from the family Bible. Brightshade, Barbourville. In Barbourville my great-somethingth-grandmother Kate Adams presented a Union flag to the Home Guard during a ceremony. The college there still displays it. My people were those strange Southerners you don't often read about in histories of the Civil War: white landowners who owned slaves but fought for the North on Republican principles. Kentucky cracked down the middle this way. That's why you hear them say "brother against brother" about us. My ancestors freed their slaves with a kind of "Fine, run off, then" attitude—seeing no other course, maybe in the noblest cases relieved to be doing the right thing at last, to be on the side of furthering the great experiment, not holding it back.

I heard a vehicle come down the road and waited for it to

pass. It didn't pass. That was nerve-racking. They'd seen my car. It's hard to overstate how far back into the park this place is—less than a mile on, the road ends. If you dead-end in the Daniel Boone park, you're pretty far into one of the largest contiguous green blobs of wooded mountainous land left in the United States. It can be seen from space. Coming in along the winding, dipping roads, I'd sighted canebrakes in the river bottoms. Very few of those left. It was time travel, Kentucky-wise. Not wanting to be paranoid, wanting less to be stupid, I waited. Whoever it was drove out of earshot.

When I pulled away, I saw they hadn't moved far. It was a sheriff's deputy, parked in the middle of the road. His finding me here in all Clay County, unless he'd been watching the graveyard day and night, seemed Stephen Hawking–size, oddswise. Was I supposed to stop and get out? I sat behind him with the engine on awkwardly. I decided to pass him. As I went by, we waved. A smiling gray-mustached man with glasses. "Come on back," he said, and just let me go by.

For the next few miles, I was edgy. "Come on back." Had that been creepy? A leeringly cynical mockery of the cherished "Come back, now, y'hear!"? Casually threatening?

No, ironic. Paying attention to strangers who'd gone miles out of their way to visit fresh local crime scenes was solidly under the deputy's aegis. Someone had called him about me. Hadn't I become lost briefly and driven by a junkyard and made the dogs bark? That guy called. The deputy was probably amused by all of us lost-looking rubberneckers showing up with our GPSs, wanting to see the tree where Bill Sparkman died. When the deputy had said, "Come on back," he'd meant, I know you never will. When he implied, I know you never will, he simultaneously meant, And I'm glad, because you're almost certainly an opportunistic reverse-provincial clown who'll go back to the office and try to make me look as stupid and scary as possible in what you write, despite the fact that we've been here since Boone in this forest, surviving, whereas you spend your life hopping around like a flea, chasing money.

He may not have articulated these things when he said "Come on back," but they were present as an undertone. Among Kentuckians, much is exchanged with the volume and tempo of grumbled stock phrases. The deputy and I had achieved perfect social transparency in the fleeting eye contact of that drive-by.

None of which means I didn't take a different, carefully eccentric route back to London, full of circle-backs and stops at country markets, to establish my presence for any future timeline of disappearance. In a gas station I heard a conversation about religion. I almost hesitate to reproduce it, because it sounds made up. The woman behind the counter and a bearded, even cartoonishly hillbilly-looking man who'd just bought a pack of generic cigarettes were talking. The man remarked that there were all sorts of religions right there in that part of Kentucky.

"Did you ever see snakes?" the woman said. She meant snake handlers.

"No," said the man. "Did you?"

"Not right out in the open," the woman said. "But I knew people that had 'em in the back room."

While I paid, they exchanged some pieties on how everyone has his or her own beliefs, et cetera. Then the woman said, "It's just like, ten people see a car accident, every single one is gonna tell the police something different" (a vivid way, I thought, of localizing the story about the blind men feeling an elephant).

"Tell me which one of 'em gets out to help," the man said, "that's the one whose religion I'll listen to."

The woman and I both stood there. I think we each understood in our own way that Snuffy Smith here had just dropped some upper-level wisdom on us through a parting in his tobacco-browned beard-nest.

At my hotel, I called Sparkman's son, Josh, on the phone. I had met him earlier in the driveway of their house, where a sofa laden with heavy junk had been pushed up against the front door like a barricade and a large dog barked in a way that said he would bark until you left. I'd been leaving a note when Josh pulled in. A bearded kid with dark hair and worried eyes, formally polite but then unexpectedly talkative, he'd stopped by just to drop off some stuff. We could connect later.

Josh was adamant that his father hadn't killed himself. He repeated to me what he'd said to others: A man who fights cancer like that does not commit suicide. Bill Sparkman showed every day how badly he wanted to live. It angered Josh that the cops wouldn't come out and at least give his father the dignity of victimhood. As a result of their dithering, a cloud of tawdriness had begun to settle over the whole business. Indeed, two of my formerly cooperative interviewees stood me up on my last day in London. People weren't sure they wanted anything to do with this story anymore.

But Josh's concerns about the delayed determination of death were practical, too. He wanted to hold on to his father's modest ranch house, intended to be his inheritance. Bill Sparkman had worked for sixteen years to keep that house, so that he could leave it to Josh. Without the payout from his father's life-insurance policy, Josh would lose it.

He told me that even before people had begun trying to make his father's death seem like suicide, the insurance company had been giving him problems, claiming his father had missed a payment. Possibly the policy was void before he died. Josh wanted to know if I knew any lawyers.

He and his father had gone through a troubled phase the previous year—while Bill fought cancer, Josh was busted for receiving stolen property and ended up working at a Church's Chicken in Tennessee—but they'd patched things up since then and saw each other not long before Bill died.

The whole thing was sad as hell, if not worse. That was the real question, I suppose: Was it worse? Did it concern anyone but a few people here? The captain had cut straight to it: "Why are you here?" When Josh, too, stood me up the next day and night, I packed and flew home.

The official police pronouncement, when it came weeks later—I watched the captain announce it over a live video feed—was like a dark punch line. Sparkman's death had been all about health care. He was financially ruined from fighting lymphoma without good insurance. Deep in debt, working multiple low-paying jobs to make his mortgage while trying to earn a slightly more lucrative degree, he took the census work as most people take it, out of necessity.

The police investigation concluded that Sparkman had killed himself as part of a tragic insurance scam. He'd taken out two policies on himself not long before dying. The policies became void in the event of suicide, but not if it were murder. He'd just learned that his cancer was back. This was his only way of leaving Josh something. Josh knew nothing about it. One of the ways they solved the case was by studying how FED got written on Sparkman's chest. There were clues in the formation of the letters that the wrist holding the pen had been bent, the way your wrist would be if you were trying to write on your own chest.

I saw my cousin again, at a party in the little lakeside village in northern Michigan where my mother's family has spent every summer since the nineteenth century. It's a kind of Victorian-cottage Utopia, frozen like Brigadoon, a little WASP heaven. The uncles were having a party for another of my cousins, the lobbyist's brother, just back from serving as an intelligence officer in Afghanistan, "taking it to 'em," as he said. And no joke, he'd been over there during the deadliest months since the invasion. I sensed an air of physical relief and lightness in my blond aunt, his mother.

The lobbyist cousin said it was getting rough back in D.C. The public option had gained momentum coming out of the House. The last thing his boss had said to him, that very morning, was "We may be fucked."

From the front porch, we could see a deep green field where we had raced as kids; from the back, the postcard loveliness of the tiny harbor, where the white sails of the sportsmen's boats hung motionless in the afternoon, moths on a pale blue wall. We had grown up here, in what for children was a kind of paradise, all courtesy of private insurance. Now my own daughter was running by, chasing a dog. How could anyone wish it away? It's rather that everyone should have it.

I asked my cousin if he could stay for a few more days or if he had to get back to D.C.

"I have to get back," he said. "This is headed for a showdown on the floor next month. Now's when we go to work."

Lots of breakfasts, lots of office sweep-throughs. A senator was predicting "holy war."

"The circumstances and fortunes of men and families," said Franklin, "are continually changing."

I hoped for my cousin to fail, and wished him luck.

LA•HWI•NE•SKI: CAREER OF AN
ECCENTRIC NATURALIST

For Guy Davenport

All the histories of America are mere fragments or dreams.
—CONSTANTINE SAMUEL RAFINESQUE

The Commonwealth of Kentucky is shaped like an alligator's head. It is also shaped like the Commonwealth of Virginia, as if the latter were advancing westward by generation of mature clones. In a way this is so. The southern borders of these states are keyed to the same horizontal projection, one surveyed by the frontier planter William Byrd in 1728, while the rivers forming their northern extents fall back just opposite each other from the flanks of the Appalachian massif. There's a mirroring there.

In 1818 one of the few people able to give even a semi-coherent accounting of the ancient processes responsible for it neared Louisville, Kentucky, aboard a long covered flatboat, which, following local custom, he called an ark. It was summer. He traveled down the Ohio, along the alligator's eye. For a full ten years he'd gone by his mother's name, Schmaltz—he'd spent them in British-ruled Sicily; one didn't need to sound overly French—but by the time he reached Kentucky, on a botanical trip financed with a hundred dollars he'd wrung from some Pittsburgh bookmongers as advance on a "New and More Accurate Map of the Ohio's Tributaries" (a map he actually drew, but which they never published), he had resumed the name of Constantine Rafinesque.

"Who is Rafinesque, and what is his character?" once asked John Jacob Astor. Rafinesque himself grew dizzy before the complexity of the answer. "Versatility of talents," he wrote, "is not uncommon in America, but those which I have exhibited . . . may appear to exceed belief: and yet it is a positive fact that in knowledge I have been a Botanist, Naturalist, Geologist, Geographer, Historian, Poet, Philosopher, Philologist, Economist, Philanthropist . . ."

The river arks only went downstream. The owners broke them and sold the lumber once they'd made their destinations. They were more like floating islands, often lashed together (as during Rafinesque's trip) into caravans. An 1810 document says they were shaped like "parallelograms." Some were as long as seventy feet. You lived in a cabin or out on deck, other times in a tent, with an open cooking fire. There were animals. To go ashore and come back, which you did whenever you wanted, you took your own, smaller boat, kept tied to the gunwale. Arks went slow when the water was slow, fast when it was fast, and crashed when it was very fast. Typically there were only three rowers. This distinctly American mode of travel sufficed throughout the interior for longer than a century and is now so gone we struggle to reconstitute its crudest features. It had no Twain. Rafinesque liked the arks because he could botanize as they drifted. He felt the vegetable pulse of the continent shuddering down its veins.

The green world whispered to him. He tells us—in his short, hectic, wounded memoir, written near the end—precisely what it said: "You are a conqueror."

The New World had a way of never being new. Ever notice this? I don't mean the Native Americans—that part's obvious. Even in European terms, somebody was always already there. The first person De Soto met in Florida spoke Spanish. Was in fact a Spaniard! And was it the Plymouth voyage that had aboard a group of Indians coming back from a visit to London?

Just so, Rafinesque, that first, famous time he crossed the mountains, had a whole prior American career, a kind of prologue. From 1802 to 1805 he was all through New England, in the fields, at the high tables, driven in jolting carriages by Revolutionary veterans desperate to talk plants. Most places they received him as a boy genius—nineteen when he arrived and recognized internationally for the bold precocity of his juvenile publications. Perhaps one or two better-known naturalists squinted at his "mania" for discovery. It was said he attempted to rename and reclassify the first common weed he spotted on American soil. (True.)

Benjamin Rush, a Declaration signer and the first great American physician, offered Rafinesque an apprenticeship in his practice, medicine and botany being closer together then. Rafinesque refused. His destiny had been revealed to him and did not lie in the city. One must remember when he was here: 1803 to 1805 was the day of Lewis and Clark; Jefferson's Corps of Discovery had reached the Far West. Later expeditions might look to the South, at Louisiana and Arkansas, or toward "the Apalachian mountains, the least known of all our mountains, and which," wrote Rafinesque,

"I pant to explore." He was taken to meet Jefferson, and they started to correspond. The earth, which Rafinesque believed was an "organized animal rolling in space," had arranged for him to be present and correctly positioned at that moment, as a continent of taxonomically pristine vastnesses offered itself to science. He would gladly, *"messer. le president,"* serve as official corps naturalist, being supremely and, though it gave him no pleasure to say so, uniquely qualified for the role. The New World, which Rafinesque called the Fourth World, had long ago been found; now it would be known.

Jefferson either never received or else neglected the letter. He thought of Lewis and Clark as half a military thing and knew the "nine young men from Kentucky" wouldn't stand the deadweight of an eccentric French polymath. Instead he sent Lewis to Philadelphia and paid for him to be tutored by the local savants. Rafinesque, who was teaching in the city and had allowed himself to credit a claim that soon he'd be asked to join the mission, must have seethed. He watched another man's body step into his future, inhabit his moment. The things we'd know if they'd sent Rafinesque to the Pacific! There was his fevered interest in Indian languages alone—almost without parallel for his time. Even as it was, even on his own, he somehow talked the War Department into sending out vocabulary questionnaires to all of its Indian agents. One sees these mentioned with great esteem by linguists who have no idea Rafinesque was behind them.

No less important, the work would have molded and disciplined him as a scientist. For once he'd have known a duty as large as his own self-regard. Every person of learning in the European and East Coast capitals would have awaited his findings on the flora and fauna and tribes. The mountains. He'd have been forced to anticipate scrutiny, to adapt and refine the radically advanced system of natural classification he was then beginning to apply, for he had already begun to peel away slightly from the "indelicate" and arbitrary sexual system of Linnaeus, once his great master and guide. No choice but to go methodically, keeping to what he could see—the number of specimens alone would dictate this.

He chafed at Jefferson's lack of reply and in 1805 sailed for Sicily, muttering that they hadn't been ready for him. This is how it was with Rafinesque, always too quick to take offense, too antsy—untouchable in the field, certainly, but never able to sit. Here his career had barely begun. In the weeks leading up to the departure, the papers openly lamented his decision. He left anyway, trailing a certain petulance that never wholly lifts from the biography.

Three days after his ship weighed anchor, one of his friends in Philadelphia intercepted a letter from Jefferson. A new expedition had formed. This one would seek the Red River. If Rafinesque were still interested, a place could be made. It was a unique provision on Jefferson's part, made expressly with Rafinesque in mind. The former had seen very well what he was in the room with when they met. Now Rafinesque's embarrassed friends had to reply with news of his rashness. The expedition left a year later with a student for naturalist.

I don't know if America ever forgave Rafinesque this betrayal, this weakness of faith. By "America," I mean the land. It had called him. He had not come. Where had he gone?

In Sicily he married the blond Josephine Vacarro. They had a son and daughter. It's said he produced a much-admired brandy vintage without ever tasting a single drop, so strong was his loathing for spirituous liquors, so instinctive his understanding of chemical behavior. The sharpest detail from the Sicilian years is hidden in the journals of William Swainson, an English naturalist of the early nineteenth century who worked for a few years on Italian fishes and visited Rafinesque. Swainson says Rafinesque used to walk down to the fish markets near his house, where the fishermen knew to put aside anything weird for him. He found many new species this way, one while Swainson was there. Yet although Swainson begged him to dry and keep the fish after he'd drawn and named it, Rafinesque insisted on eating it. He lived well. He got involved in some kind of medicinal business and made loads of money. He paid litter bearers to carry him through the hills, laughing that in Sicily only beggars walked. The men slept in the meadows as he herborized. Ten years passed that way.

When at last Rafinesque returned to North America—of course he did; destiny can't be eluded, only perverted—his ship could not make port. She headed for Cape Montauk and was baffled by westerly winds. She tried to cut to Newport, but the wind changed and blew her back northeast, so she turned toward New York again.

Between Long Island and Fisher's Island, across the bottom of the channel, lay a row of tremendous granitic boulders, absorbed by a glacier in Hudson's Bay twenty thousand years ago and extruded as glacial moraine ten thousand years after that, at a place sailors still call the Race. The moon had just changed. There may have been as little as five feet of water above the tip of the biggest rock, which sheared off the keel. It was ten o'clock at night near the beginning of November. The longboat got tangled in rigging and for a moment seemed about to be sucked under, but the ship itself, "being made buoyant by the air in the hold," stopped sinking partway. The passengers cut themselves loose and rowed two hours in the cold toward a lighthouse.

Rafinesque wandered for a period of days in a sort of catatonia. His later memory of the event seems confused—he says he walked "to New London in Connecticut," though we know that's where he landed. At one point some men rowed out to try to save the cargo. The passengers gathered hopefully on the shore to watch. But when the men sawed off the masts, to make the ship more manageable, they upset its equilibrium. It righted and sank "after throwing up the confined air of the hold by an explosion." Rafinesque stood there and watched this occur, he watched the ship explode, saw his prospects all but literally hanging in a balance, then fate like some great sea god turning down its thumb, taking his work, his money, his clothes. The enumeration of losses is nauseating:

> a large parcel of drugs and merchandize, besides 50 boxes
> containing my herbal, cabinet, collections . . . My library.
> I took all my manuscripts with me, including 2000 maps
> and drawings, 300 copperplates, &c. My collection of shells
> was so large as to include 600,000 specimens large and
> small. My herbal was so large . . .

When Josephine heard of the wreck she assumed the worst. It's remarkable in fact the total faith with which she instantly assumed the very worst. It took a mere two weeks for the news that Rafinesque had personally survived to reach Sicily, but she'd already married an actor. Actually what it says in the records is "a comedian." Who turned Rafinesque's only daughter, Emilia, into a singer. Using the insurance money, Rafinesque sent two brigs, the *Indian Chief* and the *Intelligence,* to collect this girl, but she refused to come. Her brother, Charles Linnaeus, had died an infant the year before. Rafinesque was alone.

A letter exists, written and posted during the horrible days after the wreck and addressed to an associate in the Apennines, wherein he reports having identified new species of fish and plants while swimming away from the doomed ship. It is the first of his strange unnecessary lies. The part about swimming away, that is. He had in fact identified a new fish, but it took place on the pier where the lifeboat docked.

The easiest way to fathom what all this did to his mind is to observe the change in his appearance. In the portrait that serves as frontispiece to his *Analyse de la Nature* (1815, the year of the wreck), he is physically shrewlike to a degree that fascinates, with a small nose and a thin, set mouth, his bangs combed forward in oily fronds. He's a French leprechaun with what are remembered as "delicate and refined hands," also "small feet." Women noticed his eyelashes.

Look at him three years on, when he steps away from the ark. He's in Hendersonville, Kentucky, now, hunting for the artist of birds John James Audubon. In Louisville he'd asked for the great man, but they told him Audubon had gone deeper, into the forest, where he'd opened a general store. Rafinesque longed to see Audubon's new paintings of western species, not yet published but already circulating by reputation among the learned. He knew Audubon liked to incorporate local flora into his pictures and was sure he'd find new species of plants in the pictures, hidden, as it were, even from Audubon himself.

Audubon was walking when he noticed the boatmen

staring at something by the landing. It's through Audubon's eyes, which so little escaped, that we can see Rafinesque again, almost, wearing

> a long loose coat of yellow nankeen, much the worse of the many rubs it had got in its time and stained all over with the juice of plants . . . [it] hung loosely about him like a sack. A waistcoat of the same, with enormous pockets, and buttoned up to the chin, reached below over a pair of tight pantaloons . . . His beard was as long as I have known my own to be during . . . peregrinations, and his lank black hair hung loosely over his shoulder. His forehead . . . broad and prominent.

Their meeting was a potentially ghastly slow-motion pileup of awkwardnesses from which they emerged smiling together in perfect good humor. Rafinesque stooped like a peddler under the bundle of dried plants strapped to his back. He walked up to Audubon "with a rapid step" and asked where one could find Audubon, to which Audubon replied, "I am the man." Rafinesque did a little dance and rubbed his hands. He gave Audubon a letter of introduction from some heavyweight back east, probably John Torrey. Audubon read it and said, "Well, may I see the fish?"

"What fish?"

"This says I'm being sent an odd fish."

"It seems I am the fish!"

Audubon stammered. Rafinesque only laughed. After that they never quarreled. Indeed, Audubon is the only person on record as ever having actually liked Rafinesque. Both men worked for money in an age of gentlemen herborizers; as children both had been forced by Revolutionary violence to flee happy Francophone homes (Rafinesque's in Marseilles and Audubon's in Haiti).

Audubon offered to send his servants for the luggage, but the traveler carried only his "pack of weeds," or, as Audubon called them elsewhere, "his grasses." Rafinesque's other things rode in the unexplained huge pockets and included mainly a notebook bound in oiled leather, linen for pressing plants, and a broad umbrella. He refused to ride the many horses he was offered, saying all botanists ought to walk, to stay close to the earth.

The wreck took his materials and his family and his chance at respectability, but it freed him, too. Things that were not essential—tact, cleanliness, appearance of respectability—peeled away. He became the real Rafinesque only after the wreck. Not that it focused him, so much. The "fatal tendency to scatter" only ever worsened, sadly. Indeed there are those who'd make the whole eight-year Kentucky period coincident with the onset of mental degeneration. And it was: *and his genius grew.* His genius grew as his errors and embarrassments multiplied. That's what baffles about Rafinesque and always will—he won't reconcile.

Consider: The Kentucky backwoods are where he gathered most of the material for his masterpiece, *Ichthyologia ohiensis*, rediscovery of which sparked the rehabilitation of Rafinesque's stature. Yet it was on the same trip that the seeds of his academic shame were sown, for it was then Rafinesque first saw the mounds, the rain-smoothed earthen monuments raised on the landscape by hundreds of generations of Native American builders. "They struck me with astonishment and induced me to study," Rafinesque says. He notes how swiftly the "earthy remains" were falling to the plow, and would be "obliterated ere long." There are a few places left in Kentucky, on family farms, where you can see the mounds as Rafinesque did, geometric land sculptures covered with grass, half in the field and half in the forest. He declared it "high time that these monuments should all be accurately surveyed" and undertook the work himself. But the book he produced, *The American Nations*, is an interminable pseudo-scholarly taffy pull of his dream theories on the origin of New World societies, which he contends sprang from a voyage of Mediterranean ur-colonizers, the "Atalantes." On and on, lineages of chiefs, names, dates, for thousands of years, information that would change everything had Rafinesque actually possessed it, had he not somehow himself been able to sit there and endure the tedium of inventing it.

Not content with farce he descended to forgery, cooking up an entire migration saga for the Lenape Indian tribe. He wrote of having received, in Kentucky, a set of "curiously carved" wooden sticks, the markings on which consumed his thoughts for years, until at last he completed his great decipherment! The sticks themselves had disappeared, tragically. But at least the translation survived. This was the famous *Walam Olum*, which obsessed the pharmaceutical tycoon Eli Lilly his whole adult life and is still taken for real in corners of the scholarly world, though the Lenape scholar David M. Oestreicher definitively revealed it as a hoax in 1994.

There was only one true writing system in the pre-Columbian Americas, the Mayan. As it happens, Rafinesque is today considered a "prime mover" in the eventual decipherment of the Mayan glyphs, making him the only thinker ever to have both successfully unlocked the secrets of one ancient language and at least half deviously attempted to counterfeit the existence of another. But it's the lovely and disorientingly modern poetry yielded up by the *Walam*

Olum's verses, when they are unburdened of scholarly expectation, that deserves honor. The *Walam Olum* is in fact a great mid-twentieth-century American poem, written in the 1820s or early 1830s, and at least half-seriously purporting to date from the dawn of time. It is not a translation but a divination, performed in a state of partial madness by someone for whom English was a fourth or fifth language:

> It freezes was there, it snows was there, it is cold was
>   there.
> To possess mild coldness and much game, they go
>   to the northerly plain, to hunt cattle they go.
> To be strong and to be rich the comers divided into
>   tillers and hunters. *Wikhi-chik, Elowi-chik.*
> The most strong, the most good, the most holy, the
>   hunters they are.
> And the hunters spread themselves, becoming
>   northerlings, easterlings, southerlings,
>   westerlings.

Rafinesque's virtues are often misplaced in this way. His two-volume *Medical Flora* is in all likelihood literally dangerous from a medical angle ("Dismal, indeed, must be the 'times,'" reads a sober contemporary review, "that can make an apothecary's muller of such a learned head"), but the work is filled, too, with sophisticated, rigorous folk anthropology. All along his estimated eight thousand miles of "botanical travels," Rafinesque consulted Indians, slaves, and poor whites on their practice of herbal and root cures—for snakebite, for cancer. We have yet to mention that his racial theories were as forward-looking as to seem futuristic. It has never been singled out for notice that Rafinesque was the first person ever to deny in print the very existence of race as a meaningful biological idea. "How idle have been the systems and disputes on these colors and on Negroes," he writes. "It is doubtful even what is a Negro! Since there are presumed Negroes of all colors and hues, with wooly or long and silky hair, ugly and handsome features, &c." He professed never to have "despised knowledge because imparted by an uncouth mouth." As a result he preserved much that is precious.

The point is, never listen to him about his own work. He didn't understand it. He never had time to understand it. His "great poem," *The World: Or, Instability,* is touchingly inept as poetry, but its long train of self-explanatory endnotes, predating *The Waste Land* by a hundred years, ranks among his finest writings. It's there he fantasizes about hot-air balloons with sails and steam power and shaped like "a boat or spindle, a fish or a bird." It's there he calls for an end to enclosures, a return to the commons. "I hate the sight of fences like the Indians!" he says. *Annals of Kentucky,* the rarest of his books, consists mostly of more Atalantes garbage, but its five-page time-lapse present-tense reenactment of the geological formation of the state of Kentucky is a prose diamond: "The briny ocean covers the whole land of Kentucky . . . By the operation of submarine volcanoes, the strate of coal, clay and amygdaloid are formed and intermixed . . . The Cumberland or Wasioto mountains emerge from the sea." It's Rafinesque the writer, among all the souls he contained, whom we need to meet. Like Conrad or Isak Dinesen, he made the subtle offness of his foreign inflection serve him in English, finding effects concealed from native speakers. Warning would-be field-workers, he wrote, "You may travel over an unhealthy region or in a sickly season, you may fall sick on the road and become helpless, unless you be very careful."

Reading this sentence, I remember that Josephine, the "perfid" Sicilian bride, was apparently the last woman with whom Rafinesque shared a bed for longer than an hour, though he outlasted that marriage by twenty-five years and was thirty-two when it ended. He had a strange body. His hips were wide, and he was heavily muscled, though squat. I think maybe naked he looked like Harvey Keitel in *The Piano*, but with a giant forehead, a forehead so large that people in Kentucky couldn't agree if he was "rather bald" or had "a full suit of hair." A reporter in Philadelphia during that first, earlier American trip had called him "grotesque." Audubon's wife and daughter, at least, had been sweet to him. He became an eccentric uncle in that family. Little misspellings—*drownded, unic, condamned*—give clues to the mustache-twirling stage Frenchness of his accent, which delighted the girls.

By the boat landing, Audubon noticed "some degree of impatience in his request to be allowed at once to see what I had." Accordingly, "I opened my portfolios and laid them before him."

Rafinesque gave criticisms, "which were of the greatest advantage to me," writes Audubon, "for, being well acquainted with books as well as with nature, he was well fitted to give me advice."

All Americans ought to read, in Audubon's *Ornithological Biography*, his chapter on their three-week idyll in Hendersonville, in 1818; it's our Gauguin and Van Gogh, with gentler madness. Audubon writes, "We strolled together in the garden." They talked and talked, or were silent. They walked in the woods or went river-shelling. Audubon even got Rafinesque to drink brandy, though only by scaring him into arrhythmia, leading him on a snipe hunt in a miles-thick canebrake where it got dark and stormed and a young bear brushed them, and the canes popped in the suffocating humidity like guns, and "the withered particles of leaves and bark attached to the cane stuck to our clothes." Like scales. Now they were the fishes! Audubon had hunted with Boone and chuckled at such adventures. Rafinesque had shot a bird once. He never got over the "cruelty." Audubon extended his flask. Wincing, Rafinesque drank, then "emptied his pockets of the fungi, lichens, and mosses which he had thrust into them" and "went on for thirty or forty yards with a better grace."

Safely home, they sat up over cold meat. "I listened to him with as much delight as Telemachus could have listened to Mentor," Audubon says. It was hot, and they put the window open; the candle drew bugs. We have, for our still life, Messrs. Rafinesque and Audubon at a table by an open window in the middle of the night in 1818, in Kentucky, a place whose name the inhabitants have for some reason always wanted to mean "dark and bloody ground" but that probably means "meadowland," and they are joking in a mélange of English and French about bugs on a night of summer weather all central Kentuckians know, of thunderstorms that have given onto an invigorating late humidity. Gazing down on the woods that surround these two like a starless ocean, you'd assume they were the loneliest people on earth, but in fact they're at rare ease. Inside the cone of their little flame, it's Paris. Audubon grabs a big beetle and bets it can carry a candlestick on its back. "I should like to see the experiment made, Mr. Audubon":

It was made, and the insect moved about, dragging its burden so as to make the candlestick change its position as if by magic, until coming upon the edge of the table, it dropped on the floor, took to wing, and made its escape.

Before dawn Audubon woke to uproar. Hurtling through Rafinesque's door, he found the smaller man leaping naked in the dark, holding the neck of Audubon's Stradivarius, which he'd bashed to splinters trying to stun small bats. These had come to eat bugs by his still-burning candle. Rafinesque was "convinced they belonged to 'a new species.'"

A few days later he vanished at evening without a word. He rejoined the ark. "We were perfectly reconciled to his oddities," Audubon says, "and hoped that his sojourn might be of long duration."

In ev'ry man we must behold a brother,
A fellow passenger on this sad sphere,
As such must hold him dear.

(From one of Rafinesque's poems.)

Even the hospitable, large-souled Audubon hadn't been able to resist a little fun at Rafinesque's expense—or in Rafinesque's presence, rather, since the latter remained his entire life indifferent to open mockery, minding only secret conspiracies. For a joke Audubon described imaginary fish to Rafinesque, which the latter in all innocence entered into the ichthyological record; these perplexed Ohio River researchers forever. But it was Rafinesque's peers in botany who picked on him worst. When he published a paper in the *Western Review* on the different kinds of lightning in

Kentucky (the state has fantastic lightning, including a high incidence of "ball lightning," which my grandfather saw as a boy), the joke among the savants was, *Have you heard? Rafinesque's found new species of lightning!* With him "all is new! New!" said John Torrey. "He has an opinion that there are no plants common to Europe and America."

Yet he saw much of what Darwin saw, could feel with his antennae the knowledge that would be Darwin's glory. This isn't making claims. Darwin himself acknowledges Rafinesque as a forerunner in *The Origin of Species*. He quoted a sentence from *New Flora and Botany of North-America*, albeit grudgingly. In a letter to a colleague, Darwin writes: "Poor naturalist as [Rafinesque] was, he has a good sentence about species and var[ietie]s. which I must quote in my Historical Sketch and I sadly want the date at once." The good sentence was this: "All species might have been varieties once, and many varieties are gradually becoming species by assuming constant and peculiar characters."

But in reality Darwin had little idea how far Rafinesque had gone. In a letter of 1832 to Torrey, Rafinesque wrote:

> The truth is that Species and perhaps Genera also, are forming in organized beings by gradual deviations of shapes, forms and organs, taking place in the lapse of time. There is a tendency to deviations and mutations through plants and animals of gradual steps at remote irregular periods. This is a part of the great universal law of perpetual mutability in every thing. Thus it is needless to dispute and differ about new Sp[ecies] and varieties. Every variety is a deviation which becomes a Sp. as soon as it is permanent by reproduction.

One reason the scope of Rafinesque's ideas in this area wasn't known to Darwin or anyone else for so long is that Rafinesque buried their boldest expression in his unreadable poetry. The lines dealing with evolution are in fact some of his least awful, as you feel him, for a second, stop versifying and start thinking: "Just like a tree, with many branches; most Of genera produce the various kinds Or species; varieties at first, like buds Unfolding, and becoming species, when By age, they may acquire the proper forms."

The proper forms—you see his needle start to twitch there. Also, "constant characters," in the sentence Darwin references. He got close. Often when he approaches this question you can watch him—with a sudden flourish of meaningless, euphonious adjectives—trace a broken silhouette around the answer, as when he talks about "the natural evolution of spontaneous vegetable life exerted in wisdom thro' ages" or about "fixed forms, and those that may vary to produce breeds or proles, until these assume the specific rank by important features, united to permanency, multiplicity of individuals or insulation in distinct climes." Distinct climes! He was almost there—but the interior of the silhouette remains forever a vista of fog.

That's what's terrifying but also heroic in Rafinesque, to know he could see that far, function at that outer-orbital a level intellectually, yet still wind up viciously hobbled by the safe-seeming assumptions of his day. We do well to draw a lesson of humility from this. It's the human condition to be confused. No other animal ever had an erroneous thought about nature. Who knows what our version of the six-thousand-year-old earth is. It's hiding somewhere in plain sight. In five hundred years there'll be two or three things we believed and went on about at great length with perfect assurance that will seem *hilarious* to them. Rafinesque, who sensed the presence of those voids with exquisite, defenseless nerves, nonetheless tumbled into them.

There are some lonely destinies, but Rafinesque's is up there, the destiny of geniuses lost in time, heralds of false dawns. His beautiful human brain was wrong for the nineteenth century. He was an eighteenth-century man. In fact, this is an essential feature of his charm, that he carries a gospel of newness, and is remembered as a thinker too far ahead of his time, but had about him, too, something fusty, something frock-coat-and-jabot. In one of our scant glimpses of his childhood we find him alone in the library, reading the *Spectacle de la Nature*, one of those anonymous or pseudonymous or otherwise clandestine Enlightenment pamphlets put out in Paris in the 1750s or '60s. It's a helpful detail. This is the milieu of Diderot's *Encyclopédie*, of total knowledge and all-enveloping *systèmes*. It's here that Rafinesque's mind is formed, and formed with the tenacity only intense early self-education can impart. He never attended a university, not for a day. He says obscurely, "I was to go to Switzerland, into a College . . . but this project was not fulfilled." Instead he was shuttled between aristocratic grandmothers who told him he was the smartest boy on earth and to go read. He taught himself Latin and Greek at fourteen not because a tutor demanded it but because he found himself needing them in order to follow the footnotes any further. His command of those languages, though he seldom had his books handy, was absolutely pure (there's a note in an old ornithological journal: a field researcher tried to tinker with one of Rafinesque's genus names, *Helmitherus* [warbler], on the basis that it was bad Greek, but one of the dons wrote in to overrule, pointing out that Rafinesque's nominative stem, though not well-known, had been preferred by Aristotle).

The years when Rafinesque should have been getting properly taught and trained, right around 1800, are when academic specialization as we know it was codifying itself. The million philosophical projects launched by the Enlightenment had generated the West's first overwhelming wave of data sets, especially in natural history. In order to know something thoroughly now you had to know much less. Rafinesque slept through the alarm on this shift in the matrix. He showed up still wanting to know it all, to be a synthesizer. He didn't see it was a time instead for clean, precise, empiricist gathering. His books, he quaintly announces, are henceforth to be thought of as volumes in a life's work, the *Annales de la Nature*. Deep down he is still in Grandmother's library. And then he goes to America, where the profusion of unclassified organisms that has helped to trigger these methodological and conceptual upheavals to begin with lies waiting. He might as well have on a banyan and turban when he says things like "The variety of sounds which [thunder] produces, can hardly be reduced to any descriptive enumeration: I mean however to attempt it at another time." The New World shattered him, and we have these magnificent shards. Rafinesque knew more, but knew it broken. His rivals knew less, but knew it more solidly.

He invents the word *malacology* (the study of mollusks). He invents the still-current word *Taino*, for the Caribbean islanders met by Columbus. He earns the title "father of American myriapodology" (study of many-legged bugs). He becomes the first person to understand dust, that much of it comes from the atmosphere.

In 1831 he writes to a philosophical club in New York proposing the establishment of a "Congress of Peaceful Nations." He then writes an open letter to the Cherokee, warning that they will soon be forcibly moved to the West, a decade before it happens.

In 1821, in Lexington, Kentucky, he had published and tried to pass off as an epigram of Ben Franklin's (it's not—I've looked everywhere) this exhortation: "Agricultural nations! Have no slaves among you; the earth is a free gift of God, and must be tilled by free hands."

And as subway-prophet crazy as can be his gibberish about the Atalantes, he was the only early researcher to work seriously on the Kentucky mounds who *never harmed them*. He did not excavate. He knew there were grave goods inside, but he felt that the most important thing was to describe the exterior as accurately as possible and then protect everything. He looked toward the day when "our pyramids and monuments will be visited like those of Egypt." This philosophy, had it been taken seriously, would have been more important than any archaeological idea to emerge from America in the nineteenth century. I mean that in all transparency. We can't go at most of the mounds with our ground-penetrating radar and carbon dating, because they were destroyed by people trying to prove the Indians are Hebrews. Rafinesque only wanted to look.

At Transylvania University, in Lexington, Kentucky, where he walked into a five-year roving professorship in the natural sciences after leaving Audubon's place, they wouldn't let him teach *materia medica*, because he wouldn't cut cadavers.

———

At Transy he wound up living with my great-great-great-great-great-grandparents Luke and Ann Usher (I'd been fascinated with him for years when I learned this). The Ushers were stewards at Transy, meaning they built a boardinghouse on campus where the school's out-of-town students lived. Rafinesque kept a room there during the first year of his appointment. One of his students left an admirably vivid account:

> He wore wide Dutch pantaloons of a peculiar pattern, and never wore suspenders. As he proceeded with a lecture, and warmed up to a subject, he became excited, threw off his coat, his vest worked up to make room for the surging bulk of flesh and the white shirt which sought an escape, and heedless alike of his personal appearance and the amusement he furnished—was oblivious to everything but his subject.

He became greatly fat in Lexington. One can probably blame my great-&c.-grandmother Ann for that. She herself was huge, and so was Luke ("of the Falstaffian model" is the phrase recorded). She's known to have physically forced plum pudding on people. Right after that year in Rafinesque's life, you start seeing the word *corpulent* in descriptions of him.

Perhaps on account of the family connection, I've long felt an intimate familiarity with the "room in College proper," where Rafinesque spent 1821–22. You can't read him and not feel it. In his writing it's the one place where you find him getting cozy, the moment when he looks around and notices that he inhabits a human dwelling. Since he's a naturalist and always making lists and notes, we know a lot about that space, which a graduate remembered as "a curiosity, filled with butterflies and bugs and all sorts of queer things." Letters from Governor DeWitt Clinton of New York and from Jefferson, with whom Rafinesque has renewed contact, lie oopsily conspicuous on the edge of the table. The least dreadful among the essays stacked and waiting to be corrected would be that of young Master Jefferson Davis, who when imprisoned by Lincoln in 1866 will ask his physician at Fortress Monroe to procure a few volumes of "conchology, geology, or botany," he desiring to commune with the interests of more innocent days. On the outside sill at Rafinesque's southwest window, nestled close over by the right jamb so the sun won't hit it, a metal thermometer made by Frederic Houriel of Paris silently transmits knowledge year-round. There is sound: "On the 11th were heard the first frogs . . . On the 25th the Black birds were already noisy." Vegetation we watch: "The grass begins to grow and was quite green . . . the catkins of lombardy poplars begin to appear." Then a "remarkably white frost happened on the morning of the 29th." An unrolled ink-drawn map of an Indian site strains to curl up on itself, but its edges are pinioned with fossil-rock paperweights on two opposing corners, a magnifying glass on the third, and on the fourth a perfectly smooth and homogenous lump of ash-gray limestone, which rests on its flat, fracture side.

Rafinesque hunches with a thick pencil over proofs for the first and only issue of the *Western Minerva*, the magazine he's started, which will get suppressed before it leaves the printer by what he describes to Jefferson as *"une cabale nouvelle del ignorance contre les lumières."* The existing copy is mainly a time capsule of Rafinesque's astonishing social obnoxiousness whenever he felt slighted, which is how he woke up in Lexington, a town that showed him more respect than any other on earth and gave him the only real job of his life, but where, as everywhere, he felt they ought to have followed him around with styli and tablets at the ready. Nonetheless he founded societies there and a botanical garden and gave open lectures on science. (People flocked to hear him do the one on "the history of the ants," in which he described them "as having lawyers, doctors, generals, and privates, and . . . great battles." Yet he scoffed at the citizens as "Squires and Sanchos." He went to their parties and snorted at the cloddish dancing, whining that everyone stood in little groups, so that "no one can shine to any advantage . . . since it is ten chances to one that the best bon-mot will only be heard by a couple of neighbors" (the eighteenth-century manners).

The *Minerva*, he believes, will spark an Enlightenment of the early West. He sits going over the proofs in the small hours of the morning. The vaguely menacing footsteps of the students past his door have ceased, and the only person likely to bother him is my grand-cookie, asking if he wants some coffee and corn cakes.

Rafinesque burned too many candles. The school actually complained at one point about how much they were paying Luke for them (the school that surely could have found Rafinesque a freestanding cabin somewhere).

He's tired, rubbing the "fine, black eyes." He comes to the end of the issue. There's a poem he's written, entitled "To Maria. Who asked me if I should like to Live in a Cottage." It's the only one of the poems he's signed "Constantine," rather than with some foppish nom de plume. The name Maria would have been understood by Lexington readers to signify Mary Holley, wife of Horace, the president of Transy. She presided over a parlor salon at which Rafinesque was ever present, though he couldn't stand the husband, his boss—and his rival, for, in Mary, Rafinesque had found his philosophical angel. She was a shockingly accomplished and sophisticated woman to be over the mountains at that date. In later life she wrote a history of Texas that's said to have been the single most important text in persuading people to migrate there before the Civil War. She made sure Rafinesque's hair got brushed and the mud from his caving expeditions washed from his clothes. He ate supper with the Holleys on many nights, no doubt refusing eye contact with Horace. It seems to have been one of those things. When Mary said, "Oh, I do adore you, Msr. Rafinesque," she meant that she loved his mind, whereas he heard something like, "Help me to escape this toad and free me to bear your genius heirs." At any rate they'd grown comfortable with this bandying of the word *love*, which is why he's permitted himself the cheek of dedicating these verses to her.

He sits up. He's caught an error in the last line, where it says, "We'll fell the joys of love and sing its power." That should be "feel." He makes the correction. You can actually see it there in his fat dark pencil on one of the two copies to survive the scuttling of the *Minerva*. But he slips. He misses an earlier, more serious error, in the poem's title, which reads, "For Maria, who asked me if I should like to Love in a Cottage." Doubtless she'd asked him if he would ever like to *live* in a cottage.

Suddenly the whole poem sounded different, or, rather, like what it really was. "Let us repair where purling streamlets roll," it goes on, "With mingling hearts, a tender bliss we'll share." Rafinesque's bowels must have sickened when he heard the next morning that a set of proofs had been leaked, and looked up to find the "sophisters, aristarchs, and moles" coming toward him. You can see plainly that his boldest note at the top of the poetry section is "I must see another proof." Not his fault this time. Still, he left himself open. From then on Rafinesque had only vicious things to say about Horace Holley and Transylvania, too.

In 1825 he went on a months-long journey to botanize and attend a meeting of the Academy of Natural Sciences in Philadelphia, where he was spotted and remembered as "rather corpulent." When he came back to Lexington, he found that Horace Holley—who, like most sensible persons there, assumed he was dead—had, in order "to evince his hatred against sciences and discoveries . . . broken open my rooms, given one to the students, and thrown all my effects, books and collections in a heap in the other."

Rafinesque slunk away, "leaving the College with curses on it and Holley." He notes with unappealing approval in his memoir that the curse must have worked, as "the College has been burnt in 1828 with all its contents."

In 1924 some bones believed to be Rafinesque's were moved from an unmarked grave in downtown Philadelphia back to Transylvania, where they were entombed in a cube-shaped concrete vault in Old Morrison Hall.

In January 1969 my mother began the second semester of her freshman year at Transy. That month Old Morrison burned to the ground, leaving untouched only the concrete cube, with its bronze plaque inside reading, HONOR TO WHOM HONOR IS OVERDUE.

In 1987 the foremost modern scholar of Rafinesque's works, Charles Boewe, proved to the satisfaction of most reasonable persons that the bones in Rafinesque's tomb are those of a sixty-two-year-old pauper named Mary Passamore, who died of consumption in 1847. The Philadelphia exhumers hadn't dug deep enough.

The Philadelphia years were a long decline punctuated by spasms of frantic, fruitless activity. He tried to start a Utopia in Illinois. He tried to get funding for a *Beagle*-style voyage to go around the world collecting specimens. Of course, he also, during these years, deciphered "dot-bar numeration," the counting system used in the Mayan glyphs, though his paper on that subject was ignored so utterly that a French abbé spent a chunk of his life recracking it forty years later, never having so much as heard of Rafinesque (who had also predicted, correctly, that the Mayan script would eventually be solved by connecting it with some language still spoken in a part of Mexico. One of his pathetic deathbed letters was to John Lloyd Stephens, the presidentially appointed Maya man, begging Stephens to throw him a bone and credit him for having realized this, about the living-language angle, years before Stephens himself. The latter took no action).

His letters get sadder and sadder. He's asking for money; at one point he's asking for bail money. He writes to Torrey, in a last, tantalizing statement on evolution: "My last work on Botany if I live [will contain] genealogical tables of the gradual deviations having formed one actual Sp[ecies]. If I can not perform this, give me credit for it, and do it yourself upon the plan that I trace."

He wrote to his daughter, Emilia, begging her to come to him. She wrote back these sweet, effusive letters that basically said, "Who are you?"

He wrote to the Cherokee Nation asking how his name should be pronounced in their language.

They replied to him. "La-hwi-ne-ski" was the answer.

Did he ever forget Mary Holley? Is she the woman he speaks of in a late poem?

> But when he found the lovely maid entwining
> The poet's wreath, a cruel fate decreed
> She should be torn from him.
> In solitude He wanders yet thro' life; but tries to soothe
> His lonely way, by culling mental blooms . . .

One must assume so. She's the only woman with whom we see the American Rafinesque having affectionate interaction of even the very, as he would put it, "wannest" variety. We know he kept in touch with her during the Philadelphia years, because she's included in a list of his botanical correspondents, her name given as "Mary Holley born Snowden." Who knows what they'd shared—some kind of mystical communion, surely. In his will, he left his immortal soul to "the Supreme Ruler of Millions of Worlds moving through space." Mary Holley, after drawing her last breath on her New Orleans deathbed, gasped, "I see worlds upon worlds rolling into space. Oh, it is wonderful!" (Those were better than Rafinesque's last words, "Time renders justice to all at last," which were either grouchy or untrue.)

He did not fear death, which came agonizingly from stomach cancer. Last in his list of misplaced virtues is this: his natural science makes a marvelous metaphysics. He was among the first to appreciate the implications of humanity's rediscovery of itself as an animal, as an actual physical projection over eons of the material universe. "Nature does not make leaps," had said Leibniz, one of Rafinesque's guides. If we are part of nature, then we are synonymous with it at the metaphysical level, every bit as much as the first all-but-inorganic animalcules that ever formed a chain of themselves in the blow hole of a primordial sea vent. There is no magic rod that comes down three hundred thousand years ago and divides our essence from the material world that produced us. This means that we cannot speak in essential terms of nature—neither of its brutality nor of its beauty—and hope to say anything true, if what we say isn't true of ourselves.

The importance of that proposition becomes clear only when it's reversed: What's true of us is true of nature. If we are conscious, as our species seems to have become, then nature is conscious. Nature became conscious in us, perhaps in order to observe itself. It may be holding us out and turning us around like a crab does its eyeball. Whatever the reason, that thing out there, with the black holes and the nebulae and whatnot, is conscious. One cannot look in the mirror and rationally deny this. It experiences love and desire, or thinks it does. The idea is enough to render the Judeo-Christian cosmos sort of quaint. As far as Rafinesque was concerned, it was just hard science. As for what this thing, this world, is— who knows. That part is mysterious. "She lives her life not as men or birds," said Rafinesque, "but as a world."

Mystery is not despair. The sheer awe inspired by Rafinesque's vision makes a sufficiently stable basis for ethics, philosophy, love, and the conclusion that a fleeting consciousness is superior to none, precisely because it suggests magnificent things we cannot know, and in the face of which we simply lack an excuse not to assume meaning.

Rafinesque perfected his variant of this honorable philosophy while botanizing in the literal backyards of my childhood, examining ruderal plants I've known all my life, and so I have appropriated it from him, with minor tweaks. It works perfectly as a religion. Others talk about God, and I feel we can sit together, that God is one of this thing's masks, or that this thing is God.

To quote Robert Penn Warren (who set part of his best novel at Transy in the nineteenth century), "Can you think of some ground on which that may be gainsaid?"

UNNAMED CAVES

Henry Louis Mencken famously called the American South a "Sahara of the Bozarts," the joke being that's what a Southerner hears when somebody says *beaux arts*. He was exaggerating, but even at the time, many Southerners conceded the point: the region has always produced its geniuses, but nobody ever referred to it as an incubator of civilization.

Which makes it stranger and more wonderful that over the last few decades, archaeologists in Tennessee—working for the most part in secrecy and silence—have been unearthing an elaborate tradition of prehistoric cave art, which dates back thousands of years. The pictures are found in dark-zone sites—places where the Native American people who made the artwork did so at personal risk, crawling meters or, in some cases, miles underground with cane torches—as opposed to sites in the "twilight zone," speleologists' jargon for the stretch, just beyond the entry chamber, that is exposed to diffuse sunlight. A pair of local hobby cavers, friends who worked for the U.S. Forest Service, found the first of these sites in 1979. They'd been exploring an old root cellar and wriggled up into a higher passage. The walls were covered in a thin layer of clay sediment left there during long-ago floods and maintained by the cave's unchanging temperature and humidity. The stuff was still soft. It looked at first as though someone had finger-painted all over, maybe a child—the men debated even saying anything. But the older of them was a student of local history. He knew some of those images from looking at drawings of pots and shell ornaments that emerged from the fields around there: bird-men, a dancing warrior figure, a snake with horns. Here were naturalistic animals, too: an owl and a turtle. Some of the pictures seemed to have been first made and then ritually mutilated in some way, stabbed or beaten with a stick.

That was the discovery of Mud Glyph Cave, which was reported all over the world and spawned a book and a *National Geographic* article. No one knew quite what to make of it at the time. The cave's "closest parallel," reported *The Christian Science Monitor*, "may be caves in the south of France which contain Ice Age art." A team of scholars converged on the site. The glyphs, they determined—by carbon-dating charcoal from half-burned slivers of cane—were roughly eight hundred years old and belonged to the Mississippian people, ancestors to many of today's Southeastern and Midwestern tribes. The imagery was classic Southeastern Ceremonial Complex (SECC), meaning it belonged to the vast but still dimly understood religious outbreak that swept the eastern part of North America around A.D. 1200. We know something about the art from that period, having seen all the objects taken from graves by looters and archaeologists over the years: effigy bowls and pipes and spooky-eyed, kneeling stone idols; carved gorgets worn by the elite. But these underground paintings were something new, an unknown mode of Mississippian cultural activity. The cave's perpetually damp walls had preserved, in the words of an iconographer who visited the site, an "artistic tradition which has left us few other traces."

That was written twenty-five years ago, and today there are more than seventy known dark-zone cave sites east of the Mississippi, with new ones turning up every year. A handful of the sites contain only some markings or cross-hatching (*lusus Indorum* was the antiquarians' term: the Indians' whimsy), but others are quite elaborate, much more so than Mud Glyph. Several are older, too. One of them, the oldest so far, was created around 4000 B.C. The sites go from Missouri over to Virginia, and from Wisconsin to Florida, but the bulk are in middle Tennessee, and of those a greater number exist on or near the Cumberland Plateau, which runs at a southwest slant down the eastern part of the state, like a great wall dividing the Appalachians from the interior.

That's what it was, for white settlers who wanted to cross it in wagons. If you read about Daniel Boone and the Cumberland Gap, and how excited everyone got in the eighteenth century to have found a natural pass (known, incidentally, to every self-respecting Indian guide) through the "Cumberland Mountains," those writers mean the plateau. Technically, it's not a mountain or a mountain chain, though it can look mountainous. A mountain is when you smash two tectonic plates together and the leading edges rise up into the sky like sumo wrestlers lifting up from the mat. A plateau, on the other hand, sits above the landscape because it has remained in place while everything else washed away. On the high plain of the Cumberland Plateau lies an exposed horizontal layer of erosion-resistant bedrock, a "conglomerate" (or pebbly) sandstone, which keeps the layers directly underneath from dissolving and flowing into the rivers, or at least holds back the process. It can do only so much. Fly above the plateau in a small plane, and you can see that it's a huge disintegrating block, calving house-size boulders as it's inwardly shattered by seasonal "frost-wedging" or carved away by streams that crash down through the porous strata. Water bursts from steep bluff faces: the sides of a plateau don't slope like a mountain's do, they shear away or tumble down at the edges. Those cliffs create a physical barrier for species, meaning you get different animals and vegetation on top and at the bottom. The German naturalist Alexander von Humboldt called that a requirement for a true plateau, this eco-segregation (Humboldt liked to chide his colleagues for playing fast and loose with the term *plateau*).

The Cumberland is a special kind of plateau; it's a karst plateau, and karst means caves. Really it means cave country, or what you get when there's plenty of exposed limestone and rain. The term *karst* is derived from the name of another plateau, the Kraška Planota in Slovenia. There geologists made the first studies of what they termed *Karstphänomen*, the unique and in some cases bizarre hydrologic features associated with karstic terrain: sinkholes, blind or pocket valleys, coves, and subterranean lakes. Among the most famous Karstphänomen is the so-called disappearing stream. You have a big rushing stream that runs along for a million years, then suddenly a hole is dissolved in its limestone bed, and the entire flow goes underground, into a cave system, never to return. It can happen in an instant: people have watched it happen. A classic disappeared stream, all but a ghost river, can be seen on the Cumberland Plateau; its eternally dry bed winds on through the forest like a white-cobbled highway.

The plateau is positively worm-eaten with caves. Pit caves, dome caves, big wide tourist caves, and caves that are just little cracks running back into the stone for a hundred feet—not long ago, explorers announced the discovery of Rumbling Falls Cave, a fifteen-mile (so far) system that includes a two-hundred-foot vertical drop and leads to a chamber they call the Rumble Room, in which you could build a small housing project. All that is inside the plateau and in the limestone that skirts its edges.

We were flying along the top of it in a white truck. The archaeologist Jan Simek, whom I'd just met in a parking lot, was driving (Jan as in Jan van Eyck, not Jan as in Brady). He's a professor at the University of Tennessee who, for the past fifteen years, has led the work on the Unnamed Caves, as they're called to protect their locations. We were headed to Eleventh Unnamed. It was a clear day in late winter, so late it had started to look and feel like earliest spring. Simek (pronounced SHIM-ick) is a thick-chested guy in his fifties— bushy dark hair mixed with iron gray, sportsman's shades. I'd expected a European from the name, but he grew up in California. His Czech-born father was a Hollywood character actor, Vasek Simek: he played Soviet premiers, Russian chess players, ambiguously "foreign" scientists. Jan looks like him. His manner is one of friendly sarcasm. He makes fun of my sleek black notebook and offers to get me a waterproof one like his, the kind geologists use.

Simek was unaware of the caves when he came to UT in 1984. Only a few sites had been uncovered at the time. His best-known work, the research that built his career, was all in France—not in the celebrated art caves, but at Neanderthal habitation sites. Simek had spent close to a decade working at Grotte XVI, a Paleolithic cave in the Dordogne—a wide-mouthed open cave that had accumulated tremendously deep cultural deposits, and where the stratigraphy was all twisted, owing to the complicated hydrologic history of the cave. You couldn't dig it like a normal place. A twenty-thousand-year-old artifact could show up below one that was thirty thousand years old. And when you hit those very deep strata, they're so compressed, so thin, you end up looking for *smearings* of dark soil: Neanderthal fire pits. "I really do soil chemistry," Simek said. His work at Grotte XVI has played a major role in the movement, over the last decade, to reha-bilitate the Neanderthal, showing that they were more like us than we'd suspected, smarter and socially more complex (indeed, they are us: we know now from DNA research con-ducted in Germany that most of us have Neanderthals in our family trees).

Simek had heard talk of Mud Glyph, however—the book on the cave, edited by his colleague Charles Faulkner, was coming out just as he arrived. When the task fell to him, as a new hire, of recruiting grad students for the TVA to use in its natural-resource surveys, he made a point of reminding them, before they went out, to check the walls of any caves they found. After years of doing this to no effect, some stu-dents burst into his office one evening, talking excitedly about a cave they'd seen, overlooking the Tennessee River, with a spider drawn on one of the walls inside. They com-peted to sketch it for him, how its body had hung upside down on the wall, with the eyes in front. Simek went to the shelf and pulled down a book. He spread it open to a picture of a Mississippian shell gorget with an all but identical spider in the center. "Did it look like this?" he asked.

That was First Unnamed Cave, "still my heart cave," Simek says. When I visited it with him he showed me the spider. Also a strange, humanish figure, with its arms thrown back above its head and long flowing hair. First Unnamed happens to be the youngest of the Unnamed Caves. Its images date from around 1540. The Spanish had been in Florida for a few decades already, slaving. Epidemics were moving across the Southeast in great shattering waves. De Soto and his men came very near that cave in their travels, just at that time. The world of the people who made those glyphs, the Late Mississippian, was already coming apart.

We turned onto a side road, then onto another, more overgrown one, then started hairpinning down into a valley. Only at the bottom, climbing out and gazing around, did I get a sense of what we'd descended into—it looked as if a giant had taken an ax and planted the blade a mile deep in the ground, then ripped it away. The forested walls went up, up, up on all sides. We started walking across the little narrow patchwork fields, the farm of the people who owned and protected this place. Jan had called them to say we were coming. Overhead was a wedge of blue sky, with storm clouds starting to mass at one end. Thunder filled the coves.

We approached a grotto. A curving, amphitheater-like hillside went down to a basin. It was Edenic. "No diver has ever been able to get to the bottom of that thing," Jan said, indicating the blue-black pool of water. Frogs plashed into it at the sound or sight of us. We stepped sideways, following a half-foot-wide path through ferns and violet phlox, little white tube-shaped flowers whose name I didn't know.

Following a ledge around the pool, we reached the

entrance. Jan struggled with the lock on the gate. It looked like a major piece of metal. I wondered if they weren't overdoing it—that was before I'd heard all the stories of what some Tennesseans will do to get into caves they've been told not to enter, using dynamite, blowtorches, hitching their trucks to cave gates and attempting to pull them out of hillsides whole. Jan sent me back to the truck for motor oil, to lubricate the lock. I went gladly, jogging no faster than I had to back through that sanctuary, my pristine white caving helmet bouncing on my hip.

There survives a record of the first whites ever to see this place. In 1905 a local inhabitant came upon the journal of his great-grandfather, one of the original party who'd settled the valley in the 1790s, and he wrote it up for the paper. They'd journeyed from Maryland, men and women and children, with hopes of forming a tiny Utopia here, a community that would have its own laws. Their leader was a man named Greenberry—Greenberry Wilson. They brought a handful of slaves, who had musical instruments, and every now and then, supposedly, Greenberry would call a tune. "Old Cato gives the wink and the melody of old Zip Coon swells up on the forest air. The wild beasts listen at a distance, the dusky Indian maid approaches and looks upon her white sisters' enjoyment with envious eyes." The descriptions are fanciful like that. It's not clear to what extent you can trust them as transcriptions. The great-grandson seems to have been a drinker. He tells the same stories in wildly different ways, in the same newspaper, weeks apart. He's clearly mixing details from the old journal with his own dreamings. I think at one point he admits he's doing that, then at another tries to conceal it. The reason we know there was an eighteenth-century journal at all, that this descendant didn't invent the whole thing, is that he has the settlers say the cave was full of mummies. There's no other way he could have known that in 1905.

> We prepare a good torch light and pass around to the right
> of the pond of water on a ledge or table of rock, there we
> enter a hall way ten or twelve feet wide, we travel this for
> fifty or sixty feet, and the hall begins to expand . . . Here
> jutting from the walls are tables or shelves covered with
> skeletons of vast proportions belonging to some passed age
> of the world.

The burials are still in there, covered with sediment that got washed through the karst when farmers started clearing the uplands around 1800. UT excavators found them out on the ledges, right where the journals said, silted over. The archaeologists left them alone, once they saw the bones peeking through the mud. All their jewelry and other items for the afterworld had been stolen, probably—the little band of settlers had included a few eager looters. When they got done seeing the cave that day, they tore open the Indian mound two miles farther down the valley. The "party began in the center of the mound" and "secured many relics."

At that time the bottoms of these coves were filled with stone-box graves. You can read about them in the little-known *Travels* of George Featherstonhaugh. He was a government geologist who rode right through there in the 1830s. He notes the mounds ransacked by the settlers' party forty years before, and describes them as "almost obliterated by time." Mostly, though, what he talks about is how the farmers were obsessed with the hundreds of stone-box graves in their fields. They competed to see who could open the most and find the best trinkets inside. Little coffins made of limestone slabs. None was over two feet long. So, the Indians were exposing and desiccating the bodies first, perhaps, then flexing them and burying them in a ritual way. The farmers were sure they represented an unknown pygmy race. Each burial had one pot, a single earthen pot, under its head. Featherstonhaugh decided to open a stone-box grave himself. He used his knife to pry off the limestone lid. Inside was the skeleton of a small Mississippian child. Lying next to it were a snail shell and a deer's rib.

Tearing open mounds is what people did in America for the first few hundred years of white occupation. This makes it hard for us to imagine a landscape full of them. But the Eastern Native American societies had been building them for five millennia, beginning with the Poverty Point culture in Louisiana, which some think predates even the monumental architecture of South America. Then you had the Adena, the Woodland, and the Mississippian, all mound-building cultures. Some were straight burial mounds, dirt heaped over the corpse of someone important or beloved; others were symbolic, shaped like animals, such as the lovely and strikingly large bird- and snake-shaped mounds in Ohio and Kentucky. Finally, there were the giant flat-topped temple mounds of the Mississippian people, whose purpose remains a mystery. A mere fraction of these escaped the depredations of white looters.

The first thing the Pilgrims did was loot a mound. Myles Standish led a little group of them ashore. They followed a sand path. They saw a grave mound. It had a pot buried at one end and an object like "a mortar whelmed" (that is, upside down) on top. They discussed and decided to dig it. They pulled out a bow and some rotted arrows. Then they covered it up and moved on, "because we thought it would be odious unto them to ransack their sepulchers."

Precious few of their descendants bothered with those scruples. On top of old-fashioned pioneer looting, such as the incident recounted in the journal, you had commercial mound-diggers in the nineteenth century (traveling on houseboats through the South, shoveling out pots and selling them in classified ads), followed by the preprofessional antiquarians who tore open untold mounds in the Midwest, leading to the Great Pyramid–level digs carried on under New Deal auspices in the thirties and forties. The sheer mass of material unearthed by those last excavations led to the first serious codification of Mississippian art and the birth of the Southern Cult as an idea. Two scholars, Antonio Waring and Preston Holder, noticed the profusion of certain images all over the South, and argued that these represented an evangelical movement, built on the worship of unknown gods.

Gate open, we switched on our headlamps. The same silty runoff made it harder now to get into the cave. We couldn't simply "enter a hall way" like they did in the 1790s. Instead we squeezed through on our bellies. The mud had a melted Hershey's quality. It oozed through the zipper in my dollar-store coveralls. The squeeze got tight enough that, as I wriggled on my stomach, the ceiling was scraping my back. Jan said they'd been forced to dig a couple of people out.

At last we came through and could stand, or stoop. I turned my head to move the beam up and down the wall: a light brown cave. Jan had a bigger, more powerful, battery-powered light. He flashed it around. "Stoke marks," he said, nodding at a spot on the wall. His line of sight led to a cluster of black dots, like a swarm of black flies that had been smashed all at once into the stone. You could find them throughout the cave. They marked places, Simek said, where the ancient cavers had "ashed" their river-cane torches. The longer you went without doing that, the smokier it got.

He stopped and waited for me to catch up. He was facing the wall. "First image," he said, tightening his beam. "Double woodpeckers." Faint white lines etched into the limestone. The birds were instantly recognizable. One on top of the other. A conspicuous percentage of the caves, Simek said, had birds for their opening images.

"What does that mean?" I asked.

"We don't know," he said.

I learned that this was his default answer to the question *What does it mean?* He might then go on to give you a plausible and interesting theory, but only after saying, "We don't know." It wasn't grumpiness—it was a theoretical stance.

Woodpeckers could be related to war, he said. In other Native American myths they carry the souls of the dead to the afterworld.

We advanced. There were pips—a small brown kind of bat—hanging on the wall, wrapped in themselves. Condensation droplets on their wings shone in our lights and made the little creatures look jewel-encrusted. Jan, kneeling down to peer at something lower on the wall, got one on his back. He asked me to brush it off. I took my helmet and tried to suggest it away—the bat detached and flew into the darkness.

Jan went a few yards and then lay down on his back on a sort of embankment in the cave. I did likewise. We were both looking up. He scanned his light along a series of pictures. It felt instinctively correct to call it a panel—it had sequence, it was telling some kind of story. There was an ax or a tomahawk with a human face and a crested topknot, like a Mohawk (the same topknot we'd just seen on the woodpeckers). Next to the ax perched a warrior eagle, with its wings spread, brandishing swords. And last a picture of a crown mace, a thing shaped like an elongated bishop in chess, meant to represent a symbolic weapon, possibly held by the chiefly elite during public rituals. It's a "type artifact" of the Mississippian sphere, meaning that, wherever you find it, you have the Southeastern Ceremonial Complex, or, as it used to be called (and still is by archaeologists when they think no one's listening), the Southern Death Cult. In this case the object appeared to be morphing into a bird of prey. What did it mean?

"We don't know," Simek said. "What it is clearly about is transformation."

Everything in it was turning into everything else.

When it comes to meaning, not everyone is as skeptical as Simek. Over the past decade a group of scholars, organized by the anthropologist F. Kent Reilly in Texas, have been using a combination of historical records—nineteenth-century ethnography, mainly—to work their way back into the Mississippian worldview, with its macabre warrior gods and monsters and belief in a three-part cosmos: the Upper World, This World, the Lower World. The SECC Working Group, as they are called, argues that more of the Mississippian culture survived into the historic period than has been allowed (Europeans met them, after all: the embers of Mississippian society weren't extinguished until the French sold the last Great Sun, chief of the Natchez, into slavery in 1731). Reilly and his colleagues have modeled the group explicitly on the

Maya Hieroglyphic Workshop at the University of Texas, an epigraphers' seminar that helped decipher the Mayan glyphs, and so opened Mayan society (slightly) to our comprehension.

In the North American case, however, we have no language to crack. Our most technically advanced Native American society, the High Mississippian—a culture that built mounds nearly equal in grandeur to the stone ruins in Mexico, but of earth, so they faded—left us nothing to read. That has always driven scholars of North American prehistory a little bit crazy. More than one crackpot "Mound Builder" theory revolved around a mysterious writing tablet that surfaced in an Indian mound, covered in Hebrew or Phoenician letters. There's even one nineteenth-century thinker, the cracked Kentucky genius Constantine Rafinesque, who made real and universally recognized strides toward decoding the Mayan language *and* forged an otherwise nonexistent North American written language, the Lenape.

I met Kent Reilly in Chicago several years ago. He gave me a tour of the "Hero, Hawk, and Open Hand" exhibit at the Art Institute. It was the first truly representative display of Eastern Native American art ever staged. It included the major pieces—large statuary, mica cutouts, human face pots from Arkansas—but even someone knowledgeable in the field might have been stunned by some of the lesser-known artifacts: the effigy of a human thumb, taken from a two-thousand-year-old Hopewell site, or the so-called Frog Vessel, a red Mississippian bowl that is crawling with little naturalistic green frogs. How many Middle Americans knew that the societies under their feet had reached these levels of expression?

Reilly described some of the group's achievements. Using

intense motif analysis, two of its members identified an exotic-looking geometrical shape, which appears on various Mississippian objects, as a butterfly. They matched the number of segmented dots on its uncoiling body—which you can see if you stare—to an actual species. Reexamining gorgets from the Etowah mound in Georgia, they noticed that the head on a certain human-headed serpent appeared to be the same head that a falcon-warrior was holding on another gorget. "We think we may have identified a new deity complex—based purely on artwork," Reilly said.

Simek doesn't go in for that talk. He likes data. He likes "two hundred meters into the cave we found a pictograph of a dog, charcoal, oriented vertically," and so forth. He doesn't want to talk about whether the dog was leading dead souls along the spirit path—although dogs did that in more than one Southeastern religion. He doesn't like the "maybe" place where that leaves you. The societies investigated by those ethnographers had undergone immense shocks and disruptions since the Mississippian period, most obviously with the European Encounter, but even before that. High Mississippian culture fell apart just *before* the Spanish reached Florida, not just after as you'd expect, given the diseases and the massacres—it's a riddle of American archaeology. Simek simply didn't feel we could get back through the static of all that with anything like a scientific certainty.

"Corn, beans, and squash," said Reilly, when I ran Simek's criticisms by him. He was referring to the tedium of anthropology-lab dry data. Meaning, as I took it: if they want to stick to the boring stuff, let them.

This was not boring, though, whatever we were seeing. I lay there just staring at the panel, in the cave's cool atmosphere, which you hold in your skin as a physical memory if

229

you grew up in karst country like I did, southern Indiana, childhood trips to Wyandotte Cave, when they'd cut out the lights—"That is total darkness, kids"—and have you put your hand in front of your face, to make you see that you couldn't see it.

"My colleagues argue about, 'What is the SECC? What does it mean?'" Simek said. "I bring them here. I mean, look at these things. This is the Southern Cult."

We moved forward. The next pictograph, Simek said, was an image that appears in several of the Unnamed Caves: the gruesome Toothy Mouth. A round, severed head with gore spilling out of the neck. Weeping eyes. A big pumpkin grin, probably meant to suggest the receded gums of decomposition. Simek said they tend to see these wherever there are burials. They had found one even in a Woodland cave— that's the period, preceding the Mississippian, about which we know even less. But for at least a couple of thousand years, this picture on a cave wall in this country meant "bodies buried here."

Simek had one graduate student who was Cherokee. A good archaeologist, Russ Townsend—he's now the "tribal historic preservation officer" for the Eastern Band of Cherokee Indians. Townsend has worked with Jan on plenty of projects, but he has never gone into the caves. I asked him about it. "The Cherokee interpretation is that caves are not to be entered into lightly," he said, "that these must have been bad people to go that deep. That's where they took bad people to leave them. So they can lie on rock and not on the ground. It makes a lot of Cherokee uneasy. The lower world is where everything is mixed up and chaotic and bad. You wouldn't want to go to that place, where the connection between our world and the otherworld is that tenuous."

We entered a large hall. The ceiling was very tall, it looked a hundred feet high. It was smooth and pale gray. Simek shone his lamp up and arced it around slowly. "What do you see?" he said.

"Are those mud dauber nests?" I asked. That's what they looked like to me.

"The ceiling," he said, "is studded with three hundred globs of clay."

I stared up with open mouth. I didn't have a good question for that one.

"We said the same thing," he said. "What were they doing?" So a researcher had climbed up and removed one of the globs and taken it back to the lab at UT. They sliced it open. Inside was the charred nubbin of a piece of river cane, like a cigarette filter. "We got a piece of cane about that big," Jan said, indicating his little finger. The Indians had jammed burning stalks of river cane into balls of clay and hurled them at the ceiling. "They lit up this place like a birthday cake, man!" he said.

"Was it some kind of ceremony or something?"

"Who knows!" he said. "Maybe they were hunting bats."

"What were they doing here?" I asked, as if asking no one.

"Minimally," he said, "making art, burying their dead, lighting it up like a Christmas tree. Maybe hunting bats."

At the back of the cave we ascended a mud slope. There were two bare footprints side by side. Simek said they had shown casts of these to an orthopedic surgeon, without telling him what they were. The doctor said, "That person didn't wear shoes." The toes were splayed.

At the top of the mud bank we saw a final image, the same as the first, but only one woodpecker this time. A charcoal pictograph covered in a transparent flowstone veneer, as if laminated. That was how old these things were. The stone had flowed over the bird, encasing it. This woodpecker was upright, as if working on a tree. Woodpeckers at the beginning, and a woodpecker here. What did it mean?

"End of book," he said.

Jan didn't come along personally on the next cave trip he arranged for me—a long, wet, difficult cave. He'd done it enough times already. It was to see one of the oldest sites, from the late Archaic, about four thousand years old.

I'd come to know some of the other people involved with the Unnamed Caves, a squad of high-level cave freaks formed by Simek in the nineties under the moniker CART (Cave Archaeological Research Team). There's a cave-burials expert, there's a *National Geographic* cave photographer, there's a scholar of historic cave use (saltpeter mining and "cave dancing").

The hero of CART is Alan Cressler, a tall, thin, bald guy who works for the U.S. Geological Survey in Georgia, super-fit despite many injuries. His arms and legs are hairless—did he shave himself, to move through the caves more easily? It seems to have happened evolutionarily. He's an "exploration" caver, as opposed to a "sport" caver. He likes finding virgin passages, pushing leads. He's also known to be an expert on Southeastern ferns. When I asked him about this, he said, "I've always had the ability to train myself to find stuff. For a long time, I was mainly into ferns. I'd be driving down the highway going fifty miles an hour, past this wall of green stuff, typing ferns as I went. I can see an arrowhead in a whole sea of gravel."

Once Cressler joined CART the rate of discovery soared. He is personally responsible for finding more than a third of the seventy-some Unnamed Caves. He can't explore as aggressively anymore, so he goes after the art and photographs it. There are a couple of sites that Jan has never seen and may never see—the caving is too difficult. Cressler brings back pictures.

That day we followed one of Jan's former graduate students, Jay Franklin, and a few of Franklin's undergrads. Everybody had on a big poncho but was getting soaked anyway. Franklin spoke in a slow, considered way as we walked, loud enough for the group to hear. His research focus is on the archaeology of the plateau. He explained that for a long time there had been a misconception among Southern archaeologists that the plateau was a no-man's-land. This was because the Native Americans didn't tend to establish permanent villages there. They didn't leave behind any of the good artifacts, "the stuff you can send off to the Smithsonian." What Franklin had learned, however, was that they used the plateau extensively, traveling up and down it, getting resources from it, exploring its caves.

Jan had said there even existed evidence that the plateau itself was a sacred space to the Southeastern people, a pilgrimage site. A colleague had found in the lab and analyzed an old ceramic assemblage, collected in the 1970s at an open-air rock-art site, "a little shelter at the very top of the plateau, facing the setting sun to the west." The pottery styles, they noticed, were strangely diverse. "It came from all over the place." Meanwhile, at the hunting camps, the pottery came up fairly homogenous. "The rock-art sites," Jan said, "were clearly getting visited according to a different plan." And the plateau was covered in them.

The mouth of Third Unnamed hung open maybe thirty feet above the river, which was angry, brown, and already rising up the trunks of the closest trees (mere hours, it turned out, from breaking its banks). But we'd be safe. You could squat in the mouth of the cave, dry and comfortable, and by turning your head look up and down the river, remaining unseen. There was something about the little vestibule, the density of the dirt in the floor, the contour of it, I want to say, that let you sense how long people had been crouching here.

Franklin started into the cave and we fell in behind. The entrance narrowed quickly. We passed a waterfall, a wildly twisting rope of white water in the middle of the cave, plummeting into who knew what hidden levels. This was a wild cave, no stairs or handrails; you could touch the icy water.

We halted. Franklin turned to address us. We had reached the tricky spot, he said, a place where the tunnel floor fell away. We needed to watch him; he would show us how to get across. He worked his body up off the ground and positioned it horizontally between the walls of the cave—sideways— with his feet against one wall and his shoulders against the other, thrusting his muscles to fix himself there. Once you were pressure-set in the passage like that, you started sidling your body to the right. That's how you'd pass over the sixty-foot drop in the floor. It was called a chimneyed traverse. The students were doing it easily, giggling about it. And it wasn't a hard thing to do, technically speaking. Franklin had explained the physics. Your legs are so much stronger than what was required to keep you flexed between those surfaces. In order to fall, you'd have to do an insane thing and let them go slack. Even so, my legs were quivering when I hit the other side. I stepped on a loose rock, and it made a machine gun sound.

There were the by-now-familiar stoke marks all around us, those constellations of black daubs that were like pixelated shadows of the Indians' movement through the tunnels. And in this cave you could really feel them with you physically, just in front of you. Thick smoke of their torches flowing along the ceiling. Caving in these prehistorically rich contexts has that effect. It's something about the focused containment of the space, its physical tightness—you're constantly finding yourself doing things in just the way they would have done it. You know they had to slide their backs along the rock like this. They had to step there; they had to crouch down here.

Franklin stopped again. We piled up behind him. We were in the last chamber of the cave, where the art is: a long, low-ceilinged room with a bunch of dark dormers along the edges, places resistant to your lamp.

Franklin led us around like a docent with his fluorescent wand, showing us the various petroglyphs. A geometric diamond pattern. A thing that was possibly some kind of eye, with one set of long lashes. A creature with a pointy head and pointy ears, its tail hanging down, arms and legs extended. They called it "Possum Boy." There was a sun symbol. A friend of Patty Jo Watson's—Watson is the most prominent cave archaeologist in the East; if you've ever seen a woman on cable talking about dissecting paleo-feces in Kentucky, you've seen Patty Jo Watson—had been lying on her back in this room, examining the ceiling with her headlamp, when she shouted, "The sun! The sun!" Everyone thought she'd found another opening and got excited, thinking now they wouldn't have to hike back out.

Franklin progressed through the art quickly. It wasn't his interest. He was a lithics person—stone tools. When he'd checked off all the glyphs, he led us into a corner, where he got down on his knees. We gathered behind him in a semi-circle and shone our lights onto the ground in front of him. Big blobs of black chert lay all around—chert is a pure form of flint, the gray glassy stone from which most arrowheads are made. Both flint and chert occur by a chemical process inside limestone. The rock had extruded these balls of first-rate chert onto the ground. They may have been the reason why the ancient miners had come this far into the cave, had risked their lives—to get this stuff for their weapons and tools. And yet Franklin said there was equally good flint available on the surface. A riddle of the place was why they were coming in here at all.

Franklin grew more alive, showing us how they'd broken open these rock balls to get at the good chert inside. It was remarkable to watch his hands as he reconstructed the nod-ules, running nimbly through the "reduction sequence" in reverse; where the Indians had cracked it apart, he put it back together. All the pieces were lying there for him as they'd been dropped four thousand years ago—it was like watching one of those kids who can solve a Rubik's Cube very fast. And suddenly Franklin was holding the complete ostrich egg of dark stone in his hand, as though he had healed it.

The Indians had known they were on the clock, he told us. They had to plan these trips: They built fires in the cave, which meant bringing in wood on their backs. They carried hammer stones to pound with. "They couldn't get trapped back here," Franklin said. The way he could tell was how they had moved so quickly through the chert, discarding even some good pieces. They'd break one open. When they didn't immediately like the quality, they cast it aside and started another one. And yet they'd found time to draw those pictures.

Before we left the "Glyph Chamber"—Franklin called it the "Work Chamber"—he took us down to the far end of it, where he let us gawk at some four-thousand-year-old footprints. Left, right, left—a little fossilized sequence of movements. You half expected to get to the last one and find the heel of the foot leaving it with a sucking sound. Each toe mark was distinct. This footprint had been here for three thousand years already when the other one I'd seen—the one with the splayed toes—was left in the mud. There is, of course, nothing new about the New World. The Indians had their own prehistory. They used to pick up spearheads ten thousand years old and reshape them; a few of those have been found in graves. They had their own theories on who built the mounds.

In Simek's office one day, he brought down a couple of matching brown nineteenth-century-looking volumes. This was Garrick Mallery's *Picture Writing of the American Indians*, first edition, a treasure of his rock-art library. He turned to a particular run of pages. Mallery didn't pay all that much attention to the East. None of the early writers on American rock art did. They liked the huge vivid panels out in the Western canyons. The cliff cities, in their ideal desert conditions, are there; you can visit them. Our cities are invisible.

There were, however, a few famous Eastern sites. The

Dighton Rock was the best-known. Cotton Mather wrote about it; Bishop Berkeley went to see it. It's a big whale-shaped boulder from the Taunton River near Berkley, Massachusetts, covered in twisty Native American petroglyphs. Jan showed me the pages in Mallery's book—I'd seen them in my paperback reprint, but these plates were glossy with rich blacks—on which the author had quite ingeniously reproduced more than two hundred years of renderings of this rock. He cropped them all, so that they were the same length and width, and then ran them down the pages in a row, chronologically. It was a historical portal; you could slip into it and get behind the eyes of the American mind for a minute. You could watch it change: in the beginning, the various artists had been trying to make the markings look like "hieroglyphic" writing they knew—Egyptian, Norse, or whatever it was. Or they turned them into anachronistic modern things, a sailboat or a pilgrim. Only as the decades and centuries flipbook by do the lines untangle themselves, and you start to see human shapes, quadrupeds. Still we are far from any meaning. In fact, that's what has taken place. The eye lets go of the desire for meaning; the pictures emerge. Simek was showing me Mallery's pages by way of saying, It's dangerous to read something when you can't really read it. And we can't.

Try to see it. That's hard enough.

We went west from Knoxville, toward the plateau. The fields in middle Tennessee in October were chilly and green, as if under frosted glass. We ate fast-food biscuits while Simek talked about our destination, Twelfth Unnamed Cave. "This one's really splendid," he said. There were more than three hundred images, some so tiny you had to squint.

It wasn't just this site. There were a handful of caves (now there are more) in that area—Twelfth was one—that appear similar to one another in style but unlike anything else the researchers had seen in the caves. Unlike anything anyone had seen. They were neither Woodland nor Mississippian in any recognizable way, though their dates (from around 1160, in this case) put them right at the Woodland/Mississippian threshold. Jan suspected these particular caves were survivals of some localized, regional Woodland culture, from before it had been swept away or absorbed by the spread of the Death Cult.

We drove bumping through a gate and straight onto another farm, another site that had been protected by discreet landowners. We geared up and walked across a stubbled field, adjusting our steps to miss clusters of cattle crap and white mushrooms. After a few hundred yards we started to trend downward, gently but noticeably. We were entering an ancient "sink," a place where a chamber in the limestone had broken through and left a depression. At the center of this green bowl was a more severe pit, like a crater. Trees grew around it. We clambered down over rubble.

Jan saw muddy footprints. "Whose are these?" he asked in surprise.

A floor cavity just inside the cave mouth: "That's fresh," he said. "That's pot-diggers."

There was a cola can on a rock above the pits. It was still warm. Jan picked it up and sniffed it, said, "Kerosene." They had heard his truck. They'd just run off.

There's a remarkable FBI wiretap transcript that was obtained in the 1990s. I got a copy of it from a former assistant U.S. attorney in East Tennessee, Guy Blackwell, who described the case as the strangest he'd ever worked. Some good old boys saw steam coming out of a hole in a hillside one morning (new caves are often discovered this way). They crawled inside and found what Quentin Bass, the Forest Service archaeologist for that area, described (on the basis of having seen it only after it had been destroyed) as "the closest thing to an actual secret Indian treasure cave you could ever want to see." Lake Hole Cave: people who work on Southeastern prehistory know about it. It was a perfectly intact late-Woodland burial cave. There were well over a hundred skeletons in it, generations. The entryways into the mortuary passages had been deliberately blocked with huge stones, like "Jesus Christ's tomb or something," said one of the looters who helped pry them loose. They spent weeks in there; they had a whole bucket system for moving the stuff outside. One of them was a fairly prominent local person, a rich guy with an artifact addiction. (Diggers, if they're good, usually end up working for "a rich guy"—"What can you tell me about him?" you'll say; "He's rich as hell," they'll say.)

The Feds had just busted another person from the same county, a tall half-Cherokee named Bob, for possession of looted artifacts (hundreds of thousands of dollars' worth, it was rumored). They convinced Bob to wear a wire on the Lake Hole case, getting one of the diggers to talk in exchange for a recommendation of leniency—the locals all knew Bob was into this stuff and would trust him.

He drove to the house of a man named Newell, and they sat in the living room together. Mostly what you pick up on is Newell's awe at what they had found, and what they had seen. He'd spent many nights in that cave, stoned (the Feds found a fat sack next to one of the pits), unearthing two-thousand-year-old relics that he'd been dreaming of finding since boyhood.

It's moving—and at the same time terrible, given that all or most of these objects were lost, thrown into the river when the diggers got wind of an impending bust—to read the little dialogue from the sofa, artifacts spread out on the coffee table:

BOB: I was going to see you and see if [the rich guy] wanted to sell that pipe.

NEWELL: He might.

BOB: I was wanting to look at it.

NEWELL: I know one thing, it's nothing that I've seen before. It's nothing like I've seen before.

BOB: But what's it look like, can you draw or describe it . . .

NEWELL: She's a, I ain't artist . . . OK we'll start here. Now she's got a long up here, up here she going up like 'at. Cross like 'at, back down here. And she's got a great big stem, comes back just like this right here . . .

BOB: So it's, it's—

NEWELL: It's got wings here, but it's made out of the same material. The damn stuff is strange.

BOB: What is it?

NEWELL: We don't know. It's clay, but it's got something that has been ground and put on the outside of it . . .

BOB: Shit.

NEWELL: . . . I say hell I've hunted all my life and seen stuff in Hopewell Mountains and Ohio Valley for seventeen long years, they're the biggest museums in Columbus and ah, Pennsylvania, Pittsburgh, all of them but I have never seen material like to coal black . . .

In another place they talk about a turtle—that's all they say, "that turtle . . . that turtle," Bob didn't want to spend all his tax-return money now, and meanwhile somebody else buys that turtle. Newell showed him a shell gorget, with an elaborate rattlesnake design:

BOB: Whew.
NEWELL: It's southern cult, Death Cult.
BOB: Yeah, I'd like to see one of those wood peckers . . .
NEWELL: It'd be rare.

That's what I mean about the *level* of erasure. There have been countless Lake Hole Caves. And it comes in waves. The Depression was bad. At the same time those giant New Deal excavations were happening, local people who'd noticed all the interest started pot-digging like mad. The 1970s were bad. Hippie-fueled interest in Native American culture drove up the prices for artifacts (there's a place in the Lake Hole wiretap where Bob says, "I'd like to see some of that stuff like what they used to find in the seventies"). That decade marks the moment when pot-digging and recreational caving intersected culturally. Places were reached that hadn't been accessible before. Markets expanded in Germany and Japan, where many people are fanatical about Native American history.

A lot of major sites we know about only because of looter leads and accounts. The Spiro Mound, in Oklahoma, for instance, at the western edge of the Death Cult sphere. Spiro has provided probably more material and iconographic grist to the mill of the SECC working group than any other site, and there are major components of those mounds that we know about exclusively from interviews with the looters. It wasn't even an anthropologist who interviewed them, it was a banker from Missouri, Henry Hamilton. He visited the site and sussed out what was going on there. Six local men had actually incorporated themselves—they declared themselves a mining company—and were just going at this mound complex night and day, bringing out the material in wheelbarrows. No notes, no photographs. They found an agent, who moved the pieces all over the country. Many, it was said, were sold in France. Hamilton realized, from listening to the men, that they had seen remarkable things, which if physically irrecoverable could at least be described. He got four of the diggers to talk to him. They told how they had tunneled into the center of the largest mound, and there found an inner chamber, constructed of logs. The logs the men took outside and burned for fuel. But the chamber had been empty and dry. Cool air rushed into their faces when they breached it. Inside there were altars, with beads and female effigies on them. Conch shells lay in a pattern on the floor along the walls. That little room, a late Mississippian mortuary tomb, is a unique picture, given to us by looters, by the men who destroyed it. They invited Hamilton to crawl through the tunnel himself and see what was left, but when he saw it wasn't supported in any way, he declined.

I once visited an archaeologist in Kentucky, a tall, laid-back, deceptively sharp guy named Tom Des Jean, who's the cultural resource specialist ("I go by that instead of archaeologist," he said, "'cause when they're slicing jobs it makes you harder to fire") at the Big South Fork state park, which straddles Tennessee and Kentucky, on the plateau. Des Jean actually got to know some looters, through his constant confrontations with them on park land. When they realized he didn't want to prosecute them, just discourage them, a few invited him home to view their collections. He was repeatedly stunned by what he saw—pieces that, even robbed of provenance and context, impinged on the story of plateau archaeology purely by their existence. He realized that he had to establish a kind of détente with the looters; there was too much to be lost through snobbery. "You've got all these people who are finding all this amazing stuff," he said. "And they're scared to tell anybody about it, because they don't want to get busted. But who's the loser?" Des Jean started writing about their collections, bringing them in on the digs as consultants. Possibly as a result, digging is down in the park, and more sites are being reported. He gave me an interesting paper that a colleague had written on how to extract site information from looted artifacts, using soil analysis.

Des Jean explained to me that a whole folk culture of rock-shelter digging existed in the caves on either side of the park. They called it sifting (there was a place called Sifter's Hill by the check-in area, he said). He had put together that it was related to hunting. "The game eat a lot in the morning," he said. "They'll be out foraging, and then they'll be sated, and won't come out again till dusk, so during that time, you're out in the woods. What do you do? You go dig for airyheads." He told me about a family who liked to dig together at night, hooking up lights to the battery in their army Jeep (the influx of Jeeps into the country after the war spurred looting, according to Des Jean). The son of this family, the most zealous digger among them, once remarked to Des Jean that in his opinion, the ringing of dirt in a sifting box was as sweet as music. Des Jean actually took me to meet this man at his home. On the road he told me the tale of Walnut Rockhouse, the family's favored site. They had looted it pretty regularly for a decade. "If they'd only left it alone," Des Jean said, "people would be studying it in grad school." They got into some ancient layers, unusually intact, Early Archaic, almost Paleo-Indian. One burial they removed, Des Jean said, looked to be at least eight thousand years old, possibly older, based on what he was able to gather deductively through the son's collection.

The son met us at the door of a modest wooden house on a piece of marginal rural property. He introduced us to his mules and to his all-but-mule-size dog. He was hale and hearty. He had gray hair but a sort of boyish haircut. He wore glasses and spoke very loudly. He talked all the time. Sort of talked over you but not in a rude way, more like he was hard of hearing. In the older photographs of him that I saw, he had a beard, including in one photograph in which he stood plunged into the water of a pond, twenty below, with his motorcycle parked next to him on the ice. "I couldn't even get anybody to come with me and take the picture," he said. "I had to take it myself." He wasn't so wild and crazy now; he'd hurt his back in a motorcycle accident—sold off a lot of artifacts, in fact, to pay the bills on that—but he still seemed happy and proud to open his giant gun safe for us and show us some things he hadn't been able to part with. Des Jean had assured him that I didn't intend to use his name, so he immediately started talking about burials—that was what excited him. Des Jean had said earlier that within the culture of Appalachian looting there's a smaller culture of prehistoric bone fetish. He told me the story of a man in nearby Huntsville, Tennessee, who had lain down, Des Jean said, "next to a fully rearticulated skeleton of a woman estimated to be about twenty-four years of age—she's a Late Woodland burial, which makes her about twelve hundred years old, thereabouts—and his wife took pictures of him with the skeleton, and they were handing them out to people. Some-one filed a complaint with the sheriff. As the guy was being put into the back of the car in cuffs, he was yelling, 'Do I get back my bones?'"

"I pulled this off a burial," the son said, peeking at my eyes in readiness for my reaction. "There was an infant and two grown-ups." He put it into my hand, a necklace of conch beads. Each was taken from the inside of a conch shell, where the spiral is thick enough to make a bead. "You can see where the body's corroded 'em," he said. His mother had the muscle-shell burial necklaces at her place.

As I sat in his living room, on the couch, he jogged in suddenly and rolled a chunkey stone at me across the carpet. It was gorgeous. (Chunkey was a game—a little like a run-ning version of curling, in which people sometimes got killed—played all over the prehistoric and even historic South-east; it had ritual aspects; it was connected to war.)

"They would play with that," the son said.

He put another weird-looking dark rock in my hand. "Now look at that," he said. "I found that in a burial. That's a meteorite. You can't cut it with a hacksaw."

He showed me a paper-thin ceremonial point. "Can you believe he could get it that thin?" he says. At one point he was pulling points out of an underwear drawer while Des Jean and I stood there in his unfinished guest bedroom lis-tening. He said that on one day, "my greatest day," he'd pulled out fifty-seven pieces "in a single day of sifting. And I don't consider something that's broken or cracked a piece."

He said, "Once you hit that ash it's easier than digging sand."

He said, "My *former* nephew by marriage broke into my

house, took the points he wanted off of a display mount, and traded 'em for dope." We were looking at the remnants of what the man had dug in his time.

The whole time we were talking, there was a very conspicuous thing on top of the TV; it was covered in a big sheet of green tissue paper. The son kept eyeing it, daring me to ask about it. Finally I did. He brought it over—a female skull that he believed to be twelve thousand years old. (It was the one Des Jean thought dated closer to eight or nine thousand.) He presented it to me. He showed me where her teeth are ground almost to nothing "from chewing hides."

He talked about local people who were "buying and selling." He added, "I'd never sell my collection for any price. I didn't dig it to sell."

He talked about a "fella who has a mechanic shop, who'll do service for you, and you can pay him in relics. You need new brake shoes and you don't have any money? Lay out some points, some relics. He'll give you your brake shoes."

I asked if he was still digging. Sometimes, he said. Not as fast and effectively as before. He liked to go out and "collect" around ten or eleven at night. I asked why. He said, "'Cause I work. 'Cause I'm not on welfare. I oughta go on welfare. Then I could dig all the time." He talked about people jumping his claims. Said that at night when he's done he empties out the trench and casts it all into the woods. A lot of times the next day he'll come back and the trench is full. Somebody's come in and dug behind him.

He said that of all the people in his family, only his father, who was a quarter Cherokee, wanted nothing to do with sifting. "What do I wanna be scratching around in some cave for?" the old man had asked.

On the way out he showed us a letter he got from Ronald Reagan, saying how interested Reagan had been to learn about his passion for artifact collecting.

We entered the twilight zone; the sunlit world was now a gaping hole at our backs. Jan switched on the magic wand. He was different in this cave; he didn't talk much. When I asked him about it later, he said he'd made more mistakes in that cave than anywhere he'd ever worked, because for the first hour and a half he was totally freaked out. I let my eyes adjust to the wand light. I had been in four or five Unnamed Caves by then and was learning to look at cave walls differently, more patiently. I never got very good at it, but I could see what others had found.

It was easy to see what had so impressed Simek about this place. You could look through any number of coffee-table books on prehistoric Native American art from the Southeast and see absolutely nothing that looked like these pictures. We saw birds, yes, but this seemed to be a sort of box bird— its square body was feathered. Now there were more of them.

A sun glyph, just as the sunlight disappeared.

Moving in, the creatures were changing. These weren't birds, but they were related to the birds; they seemed to emerge out of them; they were other box beings of some kind.

Now we saw box persons in juxtaposition to more natural-looking humans. Once again the glyphs were exchanging imagery, echoing and rhyming with one another.

The tunnels got lower, narrower. Our faces were inches from the cave walls. We encountered weird paddle-handed creatures with long wavy arms.

I began to feel that I was inside a hallucination, not that I was hallucinating myself—I was working very hard, in that cramped space, to write down Jan's few cryptic remarks—but that I was experiencing someone else's dream, which had been engineered for me, or rather not for me but for some other, very different people to progress through. It may have been shamanic. There's a spring in that cave, Simek said, that can start to sound like voices, after you've been in there for a while.

"It's composed like a mural," he said. He thought it might be an origin myth, or a way of indoctrinating the young into the religion of the tribe. I looked at him. For once he seemed as overwhelmed as I generally felt in the Unnamed Caves. He was still saying, "We don't know," but now it was coming at the end rather than the beginning of his riffs.

At one place in the tunnel, there was a birthing scene. "A triptych," Simek said. Box person on the left, with a square head and long alien arms. She has concentric circles in her belly. Distended labia. Appearing to deliver a tiny human being. She's holding hands with a more conventional anthropomorphic figure.

Not far off the floor, in a close tunnel, a dancing man with some kind of head regalia and a huge erect penis.

And now we arrived at the panel of birds. Tiny birds, each about the size of a silver dollar. Turkey. Hawk. At least one small songbird. Very finely etched into the limestone with a flint tool. Another cave that began and ended in birds.

Back outside and resting before the hike back to the truck, Simek said, "Think about it. What was there none of in that cave?"

I had no answer. Hadn't there been everything in that cave?

"Out of more than three hundred images, there wasn't a

single weapon anywhere," he said. "We have here an early Mississippian art in which there are no images of violence, where the birds are pure birds, not linked to war—they're in flight. Even the human figures are not obviously warriors."

Also there had been women and sex in that cave. I thought about it. No women and sex in any of the other caves.

"The old-time religion," Jan said.

Since I stopped following Simek and the CART crew, they've found several more sites on or next to the plateau that seem to contain imagery from this previously unknown tradition. Some of them are even further out, stylistically. One is full of those little naturalistic birds, hundreds of petroglyphs, turkey-cocks flying everywhere. In another cave they found, carved into a ceiling, a humanlike figure. His torso is a bent rectangle with Xs inside. His arms are scarecrowy and come off at ninety-degree angles. He has a round head with rabbit ears sticking out of it. His feet have long flowy toes, vaguely reminiscent of the paddle hands back at Twelfth Unnamed. The sun is coming out of his belly. "That's the most succinct way to say it," Jan told me. "The sun is coming out of his belly."

As years went by, Jan's statements about the artwork's possible meaning began to change. So many sites had come to light, so to speak—there were so many data points now—that some speculative stabs could be made. He wasn't going all the way out into SECC Working Group territory. Anyway that wasn't an option. There are no extant myths for those Woodland people, not even indirect sources. We will never know the names or characters of their gods. But what Jan and his colleagues were seeing was something deeper, something antecedent to myth, namely a spiritualized vision of the landscape. Both the caves and the aboveground sites "identified places of power, where they tied themselves spiritually to the land," and the sites were connected. In this discovery, Simek unexpectedly overlapped with one of the very first observers of Tennessee antiquities, Judge John Haywood, who had written, in his 1823 *Natural and Aboriginal History*, of a "connexion between the mounds, the charcoal and ashes, the paintings, and the caves."

One night on the phone Jan said they'd found a site—it was just outside Knoxville, not far from his house—with a hunting scene in it, a charcoal dark-zone pictograph of a man hunting a deer. They extracted a microflake of carbon. The date came back: six thousand years old. They didn't believe it. Sometimes the organic material left over in the limestone, the proof of its biological origins (limestone is essentially prehistoric shell), will leach out and contaminate the samples. They tested the stone. No such material.

The weapon the man in the picture is holding may be a spear. But when you throw a spear, you keep your nonthrowing arm in the air. This person has his off-arm down at his side. That's what you do when you throw an atlatl, the spear-flinging weapon that preceded the bow and arrow.

There survive, as far as I can determine, no other images of people using atlatls, anywhere in the world, New or Old. This would be the only one. A weapon that kept our species in meat for thirty thousand years and has something to do with our dominance on the planet. The hunter who holds it is just releasing the missile from its shaft.

Two thousand years ago a Woodland explorer, a contemporary of the artists who made those intricate panels of birds, might have passed this little picture—farther from his own time even than he is from ours—and wondered who made it, or what it meant.

UNKNOWN BARDS

Late in 1998 or early in '99—during the winter that strad-
dled the two—I spent a night on and off the telephone with
a person named John Fahey. I was a junior editor at the *Oxford American* magazine, which at that time had its offices
in Oxford, Mississippi; Fahey, then almost sixty and living
in room 5 of a welfare motel outside Portland, Oregon, was
himself, whatever that was: a channeler of some kind, certainly; a "pioneer" (as he once described his great hero, Charley Patton) "in the externalization through music of strange,
weird, even ghastly emotional states." He composed instru-
mental guitar collages from snatches of other, older songs.
At their finest these could become harmonic chambers in
which different dead styles spoke to one another. My father
had told me stories of seeing him in Memphis in '69. Fahey
trotted out his "Blind Joe Death" routine at the fabled blues
festival that summer, appearing to inhabit, as he approached
the stage in dark glasses, the form of an aged sharecropper,

...ng and being led by the arm. He meant it as a post-modern prank at the expense of the all-white, authenticity-obsessed country-blues cognoscenti, and was at the time uniquely qualified to pull it. Five years earlier he'd helped lead one of the little bands of enthusiasts, a special-ops branch of the folk revival, who staged barnstorming road trips through the South in search of surviving notables from the prewar country blues or "folk blues" recording period (roughly 1925 to 1939).

Fahey was someone whose destiny followed the track of a deep inner flaw, like a twisted apple. He grew up comfortable in Washington, D.C., fixated from an early age on old guitar playing, fingerpicking. After college he went west to study philosophy at Berkeley, then transferred at a deciding moment to UCLA's folklore program, a degree from which equipped him nicely to do what he wanted: hunt for old bluesmen. He took part personally in the tracking down and dragging back before the public glare of both Booker T. Washington "Bukka" White and, in a crowning moment, Nehemiah Curtis "Skip" James, the dark prince of the country blues, a thin black man with pale eyes and an alien falsetto who in 1931 recorded a batch of songs so sad and unsettling it's said that people paid him on street corners not to sing. Fahey and two associates found him in a charity hospital in Tunica, Mississippi, in 1964, dying with cruel slowness of stomach cancer. We know you're a genius, they told him. People are ready now. Play for us.

"I don't know," he supposedly answered. "Skippy tired."

I'd been told to get hold of Fahey on a fact-checking matter. The magazine was running a piece about Geeshie Wiley (or Geechie, or Gitchie, and in any case that was likely only a nickname or stage moniker, signifying that she had Gullah blood, or that her skin and hair were red tinted). She's perhaps the one contemporary of James's who ever equaled him in the scary beauty department, his spiritual bride. All we know about Wiley is what we don't know about her: where she was born, or when; what she looked like, where she lived, where she's buried. She had a playing partner named Elvie Thomas concerning whom even less is known (about Elvie there are no rumors, even). Musicians who claimed to have seen Geeshie Wiley in Jackson, Mississippi, offered sketchy details to researchers over the years: that she could have been from Natchez, Mississippi (and was maybe part Indian), that she sang with a medicine show. In a sadistic tease on the part of fate, the Mississippi blues scholar and champion record collector Gayle Dean Wardlow (he who found Robert Johnson's death certificate) did an interview in the late sixties with a white man named H. C. Speir, a one-time music store owner from Jackson who moonlighted as a talent scout for prewar labels dabbling in so-called race records (meaning simply music marketed to blacks). This Speir almost certainly met Wiley around 1930 and told his contacts at the Paramount company in Grafton, Wisconsin, about her—he may even have taken the train trip north with her and Elvie, as he was known to have done with other of his "finds"—but although at least two of Wiley and Thomas's six surviving songs (or "sides," in the favored jargon) had been rediscovered by collectors when Wardlow made his '69 visit to Speir's house, they were not yet accessible outside a clique of two or three aficionados in the East. Wardlow didn't know to ask about her, in other words, although he was closer to her at that moment than anyone would ever get again, sitting half a mile from where she'd sung, talking with a man who'd seen her face and watched her tune her guitar.

255

Not many ciphers have left as large and beguiling a presence as Geeshie Wiley's. Three of the six songs Wiley and Elvie Thomas recorded are among the greatest country-blues performances ever etched into shellac, and one of them, "Last Kind Words Blues," is an essential work of American art, sans qualifiers, a blues that isn't a blues, that is something other, but is at the same time a perfect blues, a pinnacle.

People have argued that the song represents a lone survival of an older, already vanishing, minstrel style; others that it was a one-off spoor, an ephemeral hybrid that originated and died with Wiley and Thomas, their attempt to play a tune they'd heard by a fire somewhere. The verses don't follow the AAB repeating pattern common to the blues, and the keening melody isn't like any other recorded example from that or any period. Likewise with the song's chords: "Last Kind Words Blues" opens with a big, plonking, menacing E but quickly withdraws into A minor and hovers there awhile (the early blues was almost never played in a minor key). The serpentine dual guitar interplay is no less startling, with little sliding lead parts, presumably Elvie's, moving in and out of counterpoint. At times it sounds like four hands obeying a single mind and conjures scenes of endless practicing, the vast boredoms of the medicine-show world. The words begin,

> The last kind words I heard my daddy say,
> Lord, the last kind words I heard my daddy say,
>
> "If I die, if I die, in the German War,
> I want you to send my money,
> Send it to my mother-in-law.

"If I get killed, if I get killed,
Please don't bury my soul.
I cry, just leave me out, let the buzzards eat me whole."

The subsequent verse had a couple of unintelligible words in it, whether from mumbling on Wiley's part or from the heavily crackling static that comes along with deteriorated 78 rpm discs. One could hear her saying pretty clearly, "When you see me coming, look 'cross the rich man's field," after which it sounded like she might be saying, "If I don't bring you flowers / I'll bring you [a boutonniere?]." That verged on nonsense; more to the point, it seemed nonidiomatic. But the writer of the piece I was fact-checking needed to quote the line, and my job was to work it out, or prove to the satisfaction of my bosses that this couldn't be done. It was Ed Komara, in those days keeper of the sacred B.B. King Blues Archive at Ole Miss, who suggested contacting Fahey. Actually, what I think he said was, "John Fahey knows shit like that."

A front-desk attendant agreed to put a call through to Fahey's room. From subsequent reading, I gather that at this time Fahey was making the weekly rent by scavenging and reselling rare classical music LPs, for which he must have developed an extraordinary eye, the profit margins being almost imperceptible. I pictured him prone on the bed, gray bearded and possibly naked, his overabundant corpus spread out like something that got up only to eat: that's how interviewers discovered him, in the few profiles I'd read. He was hampered at this point by decades of addiction and the bad heart that would kill him two years later, but even before all that he'd been famously cranky, so it was strange to find him ramblingly familiar from the moment he picked up the phone. A friend of his to whom I later described this conversation said, "Of course he was nice; you didn't want to talk about him."

Fahey asked for fifteen minutes to get his "beatbox" hooked up and locate the tape with the song on it. I called him back at the appointed time.

"Man," he said, "I can't tell what she's saying there. It's definitely not 'boutonniere.'"

"No guesses?"

"Nah."

We switched to another mystery word, a couple of verses on: Wiley sings, "My mother told me, just before she died / Lord, [precious?] daughter, don't you be so wild." "Shit, I don't have any fucking idea," Fahey said. "It doesn't really matter, anyway. They always just said any old shit."

That seemed to be the end of our experiment. Fahey said, "Give me about an hour. I'm going to spend some time with it."

I took the tape the magazine had loaned me and went to my car. Outside it was bleak north Mississippi cold, with the wind unchecked by the slight undulations of flatness they call hills down there; it formed little pockets of frozen air in your clothes that zapped you if you shifted your weight. I turned the bass all the way down on the car's stereo and the treble all the way up, trying to isolate the frequency of Wiley's voice, and drove around town for the better part of an hour, going the speed limit. The problem words refused to give themselves up, but as the tape ran, the song itself emerged around them, in spite of them, and I heard it for the first time.

"Last Kind Words Blues" is about a ghost lover. When

Wiley says "kind," as in, "The last kind words I heard my daddy say" she doesn't mean it like we do; she doesn't mean "nice"; she means the word in its older sense of natural (with the implication that everything her "daddy" says afterward is unnatural, is preternatural). Southern idiom has retained that usage, in phrases involving the word *kindly*, as in "I thank you kindly," which, and the *OED* bears this out, represents a clinging vestige of the primary, archaic meaning: not "I thank you politely and sweetly" but "I thank you in a way that's appropriate to your deed." There's nothing "kind," in the everyday way, about the cold instructions her man gives for the disposal of his remains. That's what I mean about the blues hewing to idiom. It doesn't make mistakes like that.

Her old man has died, as he seems to have expected: the first three verses establish that, in tone if not in utterance. Now the song moves into a no-man's-land. She's lost. Her mother warned her about men, remember, "just before she died." The daughter didn't listen, and now it's too late. She wanders.

I went to the depot, I looked up at the sun,
Cried, "Some train don't come,
Gon' be some walking done."

Where does she have to get to so badly she can't wait for another train? There's a clue, because she's still talking to him, or he to her, one isn't sure. "When you see me coming, look 'cross the rich man's field," if I don't bring you something, I'll bring you something else, at least that much was clear, and part of an old story: if I don't bring you silver, I'll bring you gold, et cetera.

Only then, in the song's third and last movement, does it become truly strange.

> The Mississippi River, you know it's deep and wide,
> I can stand right here,
> See my baby from the other side.

This is one of the countless stock, or "floating," verses in the country blues, and players passed them around like gossip, much of the art to the music's poetry lying in arrangement rather than invention, in an almost haiku approach, by which drama and even narrative could be generated through sheer purity of image and intensity of juxtaposition. What has Wiley done with these lines? Normally they run, "I can see my baby [or my "brownie"] / from this other side." But there's something spooky happening to the spatial relationships. If I'm standing right here, how am I seeing you from the other side? The preposition is off. Unless I'm slipping out of my body, of course, and joining you on the other side. Wiley closes off the song as if to confirm these suspicions:

> What you do to me, baby,
> it never gets out of me.
> I believe I'll see ya,
> After I cross the deep blue sea.

It's one of the oldest death metaphors and must have been ready to hand, thanks to Wiley's nonsecular prewar peers. "Precious Jesus, gently guide me," goes a 1926 gospel chorus, "o'er that ocean dark and wide." Done gone over. That meant dead. Not up, over.

Greil Marcus, the writer of the piece I was fact-checking,

mentioned the extraordinary "tenderness" of the "What you do to me, baby" line. It can't be denied. There's a tremendous weariness, too. "It never gets out of me," and part of her wishes it would, this long disease, your memory. ("The blues is a low down achin' heart disease," sang Robert Johnson, echoing Kokomo Arnold echoing Clara Smith echoing a 1913 sheet music number written by a white minstrel performer and titled "Nigger Blues.") There's nothing to look forward to but the reunion death may bring. That's the narrow, haunted cosmos of the song, which one hears as a kind of reverberation, and which keeps people up at night.

I was having an intense time of it in the old Toyota. But when I got back on the phone with Fahey, he was almost giddy. He'd scored one: blessèd. That's what her mother told her, "Lord, blessèd daughter, don't you be so wild." I cued up to the line. It seemed self-evident now, impossible to miss. I complimented Fahey's ear. He cough-talked his way through a rant about how "they didn't care about the words" and "were all illiterate anyway."

This reflexive swerving between ecstatic appreciation and an urge to minimize the aesthetic significance of the country blues was, I later came to see, a pattern in Fahey's career—the Blind Joe Death bit had been part of it. It's possible he feared giving in to the almost demonic force this music has exerted over so many, or worried he'd done so already. I'm fairly certain his irony meter hovered close to zero when he titled his 2000 book of short stories *How Bluegrass Music Destroyed My Life*. More than that, though, the ability to flick at will into a dismissive mode was a way to maintain a sense of expert status, of standing apart. You'll find the same tendency in most of the other major blues wonks: when the music was all but unknown, they hailed it as great, invincible American art; when people (like the Rolling Stones) caught on and started blabbering about it, they rushed to remind everyone it was just a bunch of dance music for drunken field hands. Fahey had reached the point where he could occupy both extremes in the same sentence.

He'd gotten as far as I had with the "boutonnière," which remained the matter at hand, so we adjourned again. Came back, broke off. This went on for a couple of hours. I couldn't believe he was being so patient, really. Then at one point, back in the car, after many more rewindings, some fibers at the edge of my innermost ear registered a faint "L" near the beginning of that last word: *boLtered?* A scan through the OED led to *bolt*, then to *bolted*, and at last to this 1398 citation from John de Trevisa's English translation of Bartholomeus Anglicus's ca. 1240 Latin encyclopedia, *De proprietatibus rerum* (On the Order of Things): "The floure of the mele, whan it is bultid and departid from the bran."

Wiley wasn't saying "flowers"; she was saying "flour." The rich man's flour, which she loves you enough to steal for you. If she can't get it, she'll get bolted, or very finely sifted, meal.

> When you see me coming, look 'cross the rich man's
>   field.
> If I don't bring you flour,
> I'll bring you bolted meal.

Fahey was skeptical. "I never heard of that," he said. But later, after saying goodbye for what seemed the last time, he called back with a changed mind. He'd rung up people in the interim. (It would be fun to know whom—you'd be tracing a very precious little neural pathway in the fin de siècle

American mind.) One of his sources told him it was a War thing: when they ran out of flour, they started bolted cornmeal. "Hey," he said, "maybe we'll put you in liner notes, if we can get this new thing together."

The new thing was still in development when he died. On the phone we'd gone on to talk about Revenant, the self-described "raw musics" label he'd cofounded in 1996 with a Texas lawyer named Dean Blackwood. Revenant releases are like Constructivist design projects in their attention to graphic detail, with liner notes that become de facto transcripts of scholarly colloquia. Fahey and Blackwood had thought up a new release, which would be all about prewar "phantoms" like Wiley and Thomas (and feature new, superior transfers of the pair's six sides). The collection's only delimiting criteria would be that nothing biographical could be known regarding any of the artists involved, and that every recording must be phenomenal, in a sense almost strict: something that happened once in front of a microphone and can never be imitated, merely reexperienced. They had been dreaming this project for years, refining lists. And I'd contributed a speck of knowledge, a little ant's mouthful of knowledge.

Almost six years passed, during which Fahey died in the hospital from complications following multiple bypass surgery. I assumed with other people that he'd taken the phantoms project with him, but in October 2005, with no fanfare and after rumors of Revenant's having closed shop, it materialized, two discs and a total of fifty songs with the subtitle *Pre-War Revenants (1897–1939)*.

Anyone with an interest in American culture should find a way to hear this record. It's probably the most important archival release of its kind since Harry Smith's seminal *Anthology of American Folk Music* in 1952, and for the same reason: it represents less a scholarly effort to preserve and disseminate obscure recordings, indispensable as those undertakings are, than the charting of a deeply informed aesthetic sensibility, which for all its torment was passionately in communion with these songs and the nuances of their artistry for a lifetime. Listening to this collection, you enter the keeping of a kind of Virgil.

To do it right entailed remastering everything fresh from 78s, which in turn meant coaxing out a transnational rabbit's warren of the so-called serious collectors, a community widespread but dysfunctionally tight-knit, as by process of consolidation the major collections have come into the keeping of fewer and fewer hands over the years. "The serious blues people are less than ten," one who contributed to *Pre-War Revenants* told me. "Country, seven. Jazz, maybe fifteen. Most are to one degree or another sociopathic." Mainly what they do is nurse decades-old grudges. A terrifically complicated bunch of people, but, for reasons perhaps not totally scrutable even to themselves, they have protected this music from time and indifference. The collectors were first of all the finders. Those trips to locate old blues guys started out as trips to canvass records. Gayle Dean Wardlow became a pest-control man at one point, in order to have a legitimate excuse to be walking around in black neighborhoods beating on doors. "Need your house sprayed?" Nah. "Got any weird old records in the attic?"

Something like 60 percent of the sides on *Pre-War Revenants* are "SCOs," single copy only. These songs are flashbulbs going off in immense darknesses. Blues Birdhead, Bayless Rose, Pigmeat Terry, singers that only the farthest-gone of the old-music freaks have heard. "I got the mean Bo-Lita blues," sings the unknown Kid Brown ("Bo-Lita" was a poorly understood Mexican game of chance that swept the South like a hayfire about a hundred years ago and wiped out a bunch of shoebox fortunes). There's a guy named Tommy Settlers, who sings out of his throat in some way. I can't describe it. He may have been a freak-show act. His "Big Bed Bug" and "Shaking Weed Blues" are all there is of whatever he was, yet he was a master. Mattie May Thomas's astonishing "Workhouse Blues" was recorded a cappella in the sewing room at a women's prison:

> I wrassle with the hounds, black man,
> Hounds of hell all day.
> I squeeze them so tight,
> Until they fade away.

In what is surely a trustworthy mark of obscurantist credibility, one of the sides on *Pre-War Revenants* was discovered at a flea market in Nashville by the very person who engineered the collection, Chris King, the guy who actually signs for delivery of the reinforced wooden boxes, put together with drywall screws and capable of withstanding an auto collision, in which most 78s arrive for projects like this. The collectors trust King; he's a major collector himself (owner, as it happens, of the second-best of three known copies of "Last Kind Words Blues") and an acknowledged savant when it comes to excavating sonic information from the wrecked grooves of prewar disc recordings. I called him, looking for details of how this project had finally come to life. Like Fahey, King graduated college with degrees in religion and philosophy; he knows how to wax expansive about what he does. He described "junking" that rare 78 in Nashville, the Two Poor Boys' "Old Hen Cackle," which lay atop a stack of 45s on a table in the open sun. It was brown. In the heat it had warped, he said, "into the shape of a soup bowl." At the bottom of the bowl he could read PERFECT, a short-lived hillbilly label. "Brown Perfects" are precious. He took it home and placed it outside between two panes of clear glass—collectors' wisdom, handed down—and allowed the heat of the sun and the slight pressure of the glass's weight slowly to press it flat again, to where he could play it.

Sometimes, King told me, he can tell things about the record's life from how the sound has worn away. The copy of Geeshie Wiley's "Eagles on a Half" (there's only one copy) that he worked with for *Pre-War Revenants* had, he realized, been "dug out" by an improvised stylus of some kind—"they used anything, sewing needles"—in such a manner that you could tell the phonograph it spun on, or else the floor underneath the phonograph, was tilted forward and to the right. Suddenly you have a room, dancing, boards with a lot of give, people laughing. It's a nasty, sexy song: "I said, squat low, papa, let your mama see / I wanna see that old business keeps on worrying me." King tilted his machine back and to the left. He encountered undestroyed signal and got a newly vibrant version.

Strangest of the songs is the very oldest, "Poor Mourner" by the duo Cousins & DeMoss, who may or may not have been Sam Cousin and Ed DeMoss, semifamous late-nineteenth-century minstrel singers—if so, then the former is the only artist included on *Pre-War Revenants* of whom an image has survived: a grainy photograph of his strong, square face appeared in the Indianapolis *Freeman* in 1889. These two performed "Poor Mourner" for the Berliner Company in 1897. (Emile Berliner had recently patented disc, as opposed to cylinder, recording; discs were easier to duplicate.)

Dual banjos burst forth with a frenetic rag figure, and it seems you're on familiar if excitable ground. But somewhere between the third and fourth measure of the first bar, the second banjo pulls up, as if with a halt leg, and begins putting forward a drone on top of the first, which twangs away for a second as if it hadn't been warned about the immediate mood change. Then the instruments grind down together, the key swerves minor, and without your being able to pinpoint what happened or when, you find yourself in a totally different, darker sphere. The effect is the sonic equivalent of film getting jammed in an old projector, the stuck frame melting, colors bleeding. It all takes place in precisely five seconds. It is unaccountable. Chris King said, "That is not a function of some weird thing I couldn't fix." I asked if maybe the old machines ran slightly faster at the start. He reminded me that the song didn't start with music; it started with a high voice shouting, "As sung by Cousins and DeMoss!"

When this song comes on I invariably flash on my great-grandmother Elizabeth Baynham, born in that same year, 1897. I touched that year. There is no degree of remove between me and it. I barely remember her as a blind, legless figure in a wheelchair and afghan who waited for us in the hallway outside her room. Knowing that this song was part of the fabric of the world she came into lets me know I understand nothing about that period, that very end of the nineteenth century. We live in such constant nearness to the abyss of past time that the moment is endlessly sucked into. The Russian writer Viktor Shklovsky said that art exists "to make the stone stony." These recordings let us feel something of the timeyness of time, its sudden irrevocability.

If *Pre-War Revenants* marks the apotheosis of the baroque aestheticization of early black Southern music by white men—which has brought you this essay, among others—it's only proper that the collection appear now, as we're finally witnessing the dawn of a new transparency in blues writing: the scholarship of blues scholarship. Two good books in this vein have been published in the past few years: Elijah Wald's *Escaping the Delta: Robert Johnson and the Invention of the Blues* and Marybeth Hamilton's *In Search of the Blues* (subtitled, in the American edition, *The White Invention of Black Music*). Both are engaging and do solid, necessary work. I approached them with something like defensiveness, expecting to be implicated, inevitably, in the creepy racial unease that shadows the country-blues discourse, which has always involved, with a couple of notable examples (Zora Neale Hurston and Dorothy Scarborough), white guys talking to one another about black music, and about a particular period in the music, one that living black American artists mostly consider quaint.

Both new books replace hoary myths with researched histories of far greater interest. Both seek to deconstruct the legend of the "Delta bluesman," with his crossroads and hellhounds and death by poison, his primal expression of existential isolation. Both end up complicating that picture instead. Wald takes away the legend of Robert Johnson's "inexplicable" technical ability, for which, rivals whispered, he'd sold his soul, and gives us instead Johnson the self-aware technician and student of other people's records, including those of

Skip James, from whom Johnson lifted the beautiful phrase "dry long so," meaning indifferently, or for the hell of it. I don't think the reviews of *Escaping the Delta* that appeared at the time of its publication went far enough in describing its genius. Partly this owed to the book's marketing, which involved a vague suggestion that Robert Johnson would therein be exposed or even debunked as a mere pop imitator. What *Escaping the Delta* really does is introduce us to a higher level of appreciation for Johnson's methods.

Wald places you in Johnson's head for the San Antonio and Dallas sessions, and takes you song by song, in an extremely rigorous way (he's another lifelong student of the music); he shows you what Johnson decided to play and when and puts forward convincing reasons why, explaining what sources Johnson was combining, how he changed them, honored them. Wald's especially good at comparing the alternate takes, letting us hear the minutiae of Johnson's rhythmic and chordal modifications. These become windows onto the intensity of his craftsmanship. By picking up certain threads, you can track his moves. Blind Lemon Jefferson sang, "The train left the depot with the red and blue light behind / Well, the blue light's the blues, the red light's the worried mind." That was a good verse. That was snappy. Eddie and Oscar, a polished, almost formal country-blues duo out of North Carolina (Eddie was white, Oscar was black), had already copied that. Johnson probably heard it from them. But when he went,

> When the train, it left the station, with two lights on
> behind,
> Ah, when the train left the station, with two lights on
> behind,

> Well, the blue light was my blues, and the red light was
>   my mind.
> All my love's in vain

—that was something else. Johnson knew it was something else. He knew how good it was, knew the difference between saying "the red light's the worried mind" and saying "the red light was my mind." After all, he's the same person who wrote the couplet "From Memphis to Norfolk is a thirty-six hours' ride. / A man is like a prisoner, and he's never satisfied." Part of hearing the blues is taking away the sociological filter, which with good but misguided intentions we allow to develop before our senses, and hearing the self-consciousness of the early bluesmen, hearing that, as Samuel Charters put it in the liner notes to Henry Townsend's *Tired of Bein' Mistreated* (1962), the "blues singer feels himself as a creative individual within the limits of the blues style."

It's a remarkable thought-movie Wald creates for a hundred pages or so. If the jacket copy primed me to come away disabused of my awe for Johnson's musicianship, instead it was doubled. Everything Johnson touched he made subtler, sadder. He took the mostly comical ravings of Peetie Wheatstraw, the Devil's Son-in-Law, and smoothed them into Robert Johnson's devil, the melancholy devil who walks like a man and looks like a man and is much less easily laughed off.

Whereas Wald wants to educate our response to the country blues away from nostalgia and toward a more mature valuation, by persuading us that all folk was once somebody's pop, Marybeth Hamilton, an American cultural historian who teaches in England, looks back instead at that old sense of aura, asking where it came from, what it was made of. *In Search of the Blues* traces white fascination with the country blues to its roots in the mind of one James McKune, a weedy, closeted, alcoholic *New York Times* rewrite man turned drifter who kept his crates of 78s under his bunk at a YMCA in Brooklyn. Until now his tale has been known only to readers of the 78 *Quarterly*. McKune came from North Carolina and in 1971 died squalidly after a sexual transaction gone wrong. In the early forties he was among the first to break from the world of hard-core New Orleans jazz collecting, which had developed in Ivy League dorms and was byzantine with specialisms by the late thirties. Hamilton proves deft on the progression of McKune's taste. He started out an obsessive for commercial ethnographic material, such as regional dance songs from Spain on the Columbia label. He was interested, in other words, in culturally precious things that had been accidentally snagged and preserved by stray cogs of the anarchic capitalist threshing machine.

One of McKune's few fellow travelers in this backwater of the collecting world was Harry Smith, who would go on in 1952 to create the *Anthology of American Folk Music*. Smith urged McKune to send to the Library of Congress for a curious index, compiled by Alan Lomax during his field recording days and held in manuscript there, of "American Folk Songs on Commercial Records." That list is the real DNA of the country blues as a genre. Hamilton writes:

> What [McKune] read there confounded everything he had ever assumed about race records. The dizzying variety of musical styles, the sheer oddity of the song titles . . . Most intriguing of all were Lomax's mentions of blues recordings [that] promised something undiluted and raw.

A strangeness to notice here is that McKune's discovery happened in 1942. Robert Johnson, described on Lomax's list with the notes "individual composition v[ery] fine, touches of voodoo," had been alive and recording just four years earlier. Already he existed for McKune as he exists for us, when we approach him through the myth, at an archaeological remove. The country blues has its decade or so and then is obliterated with a startling suddenness, by the Depression, World War II, and the energy of the Chicago sound. In 1938, John Hammond, an early promoter of American folk music (later to become Bob Dylan's first producer), organized a concert called "From Spirituals to Swing." He intended it as a statement on the aesthetic legitimacy of African American music. Hammond sent off a cablegram inviting Robert Johnson to come north and be in the show, to perform at Carnegie Hall. It's a curious hinge moment in blues historiography—the second act, which would lead north and then to the festivals, reaches out to the first, which is disappearing with the onset of war, and tries to recognize a continuity. But Johnson had just died, at twenty-seven, either of poison or of congenital syphilis. He was employed to pick cotton at the time. At the concert they wheeled a phonograph onto the stage and played two of his records in the stillness. (Even the mediation we think of as being so postmodern, the ghostliness surrounding the recordings themselves as material objects, is present at the very beginning.)

McKune undertook to search out these records, to know them. Hamilton says he once rode a bus 250 miles from Brooklyn to the D.C. suburbs to hear Dick Spottswood's recently turned-up copy of Skip James's "Hard Time Killin' Floor Blues." He walked in, sat down, heard the record, and walked back out. Those who knew him recall his listening "silently. In awe." James sings: "People are drifting from door to door, / Can't find no heaven, I don't care where they go."

Spottswood was one in a circle of adepts who gathered around McKune in the late forties and fifties. They went on to become the Blues Mafia, the serious collectors. They didn't really *gather* around McKune—he lived at the YMCA—but he visited their gatherings and became a *chef du salon*, according to Spottswood (this is the same Dick Spottswood who a few years later would play Blind Willie Johnson's "Praise God I'm Satisfied" over the telephone for a young John Fahey, who'd called up demanding it, causing Fahey to weep and nearly vomit).

McKune was never an object freak: like Fahey—who went looking for Skip James largely in hopes of learning the older man's notoriously difficult minor-key tunings—he wanted the songs, the sounds, though he searched as relentlessly as any antiquarian. His early "want lists" in *Record Changer* magazine are themselves now collectibles. Hamilton includes the lovely detail that occasionally in his lists, McKune would issue a call for hypothetical records. He might advertise for "Blues on black Vocalion, any with San Antonio master numbers"; that is, records made in the same studio and during the same week as Robert Johnson's most famous sessions (Goethe looking for the Urpflanze!).

What McKune heard when the records arrived transfixed him. Hamilton shows her seriousness and should earn the respect of all prewar wonks by not reflexively dismissing this something as an imagined "primitive" or "rough" quality. Indeed, those were the words that would have been used at the time by jazz collectors who for the most part dismissed this music as throwaway hick stuff, novelty songs created by people too poor to get to New Orleans. We can make conjectures, as Hamilton does intelligently, about the interior mansions of McKune's obscurantism—about, say, whether his estimation of Charley Patton as the greatest of the country-blues singers was influenced by the fact that Patton's records are the muddiest and least intelligible, allowing the most to be read into them—but the rigorous attention underlying all of McKune's listening stands as his defense.

Rarely did McKune attempt published aesthetic statements of any kind, but when he did he repeated one word. Writing to VJM *Palaver* in 1960 about Samuel Charters's then recent book, *The Country Blues*, McKune bemoaned the fact that Charters had concentrated on those singers who'd sold the most records, such as Blind Lemon Jefferson and Brownie McGhee, whose respective oeuvres McKune found mediocre and slick. McKune's letter sputters in the arcane fury of its narcissism of minor difference, but the word he keeps getting stuck on is *great*. As in "Jefferson made only one record I can call *great*" (italics McKune's). Or, "I know twenty men who collect the Negro country blues. All of us have been interested in knowing who the *great* [his again], country blues singers are not in who sold best." And later, "I write for those who want a different basis for evaluating blues singers. This basis is their relative greatness."

When I saw that letter in Hamilton's book, it brought up a memory of being on the phone with Dean Blackwood, John Fahey's partner at Revenant Records, and hearing him talk about his early discussions with Fahey over the phantoms project. "John and I always felt like there wasn't enough of a case being made for these folks' greatness," he'd said.

"You've got to have their stuff together to understand the potency of the work."

Before dismissing as naive the overheated boosterism of these pronouncements, we might ask whether there's not a simple technical explanation for the feeling being expressed or left unexpressed in them. I believe that there is and it's this: the narrative of the blues got hijacked by rock 'n' roll, which rode a wave of youth consumers to global domination. Back behind the split, there was something else: a deeper, riper source. Many people who have written about this body of music have noticed it. Robert Palmer called it Deep Blues. We're talking about strains within strains, sure, but listen to something like Ishman Bracey's "Woman Woman Blues," his tattered yet somehow impeccable falsetto when he sings, "She got coal black curly hair." Songs like that were not made for dancing. Not even for singing along. They were made for listening, for grown-ups. They were chamber compositions. Listen to Blind Willie Johnson's "Dark Was the Night, Cold Was the Ground." It has no words. It's hummed by a blind preacher incapable of playing an impure note on the guitar. We have again to go against our training and suspend anthropological thinking here; it doesn't serve at these strata. The noble ambition not to be the kind of people who unwittingly fetishize and exoticize black or poor white folk poverty has allowed us to remain the type who don't stop to ask if the serious treatment of certain folk forms as essentially high- or higher-art forms might have originated with the folk themselves.

If there's a shared weakness to these two books, it's that

they're insufficiently on the catch for this pitfall. "No one in the blues world was calling this music art," says Wald. Is that true? Carl Sandburg was including blues lyrics in his anthologies as early as 1927. More to the point, Ethel Waters, one of the citified "blues queens" whose lyrics and melodies had a funny way of showing up in those raw and undiluted country-blues recordings, had already been writing self-consciously modernist blues for a few years by then (for instance, "I can't sleep for dreaming . . . ," a line of hers I first heard in Crying Sam Collins and took for one of his beautiful manglings, then was humbled to learn had always been intentionally poetic). Marybeth Hamilton, in her not unsympathetic autopsy of James McKune's mania, comes dangerously close to suggesting that McKune was the first person to hear Skip James as we hear him, as a profound artist. But Skip James was the first person to hear Skip James that way. The anonymous African American people described in Wald's book, sitting on the floor of a house in Tennessee and weeping while Robert Johnson sang "Come On in My Kitchen," they were the first people to hear the country blues that way. White men "rediscovered" the blues, fine. We're talking about the complications of that at last. Let's not go crazy and say they invented it, or accidentally credit their "visions" with too much power. That would be counterproductive, a final insult even.

There's a moment on those discs of Gayle Dean Wardlow's interviews, the ones in Revenant's Patton set. Wardlow is talking with Booker Miller, a minor prewar player who knew Charley Patton. And you can hear Wardlow, who was a deceptively good interviewer—he just kept coming at a person in this *Rain Man* style that would leave anyone feeling the less awkward one in the room—and you can tell he's trying to get Miller to describe the *ritual* of his apprenticeship to the elder Patton. "Did you meet him at a juke joint," asked Wardlow, "or on the street?" How did you find each other? It's precisely the sort of question one would ask.

"I admired his records," answered Booker Miller.

THE LAST WAILER

In early July 2010, I flew to Jamaica in hope of contacting Bunny Wailer, the last of the Wailers, Bob Marley's original band. If you don't know who he is—and of the people who read this, surely a goodly percentage won't know; to the rest it will seem asinine to ID such a major figure; either way, though, this is worth doing—find a computer clip of the Wailers performing "Stir It Up" on *The Old Grey Whistle Test,* a music show that used to run on the BBC. It was 1973, their first real tour. Bunny is off to Bob's left, singing the high part and doing a little repetitive one-two accent thing with brushes on snares. He's wonderfully dressed in a tasseled burgundy Shriner's fez and abstract Rastafarian sweater-vest. All three of them look like they could have been in Fat Albert's gang. Possibly no group of musicians has ever looked flat cooler. Peter Tosh was a tall, purple sphinx with an inexplicably sweet falsetto. If Elvis had walked in, Tosh might have nodded.

It had long been a dream of mine to meet Bunny Wailer—a pipe dream, sometimes a literal one in the sense that I dreamed it while holding a pipe. I don't know what it is about Jamaican music, but creatively it just seems to take place at a higher amperage. It may be an island effect. Isolation does seem to produce these intensities sometimes. You think of Ireland, for instance, a backwater in so many ways, and yet: Yeats, Beckett, Joyce, in one century—how does that happen? Consider that in Kingston, in one decade, you had the emergence of Bob Marley and the Wailers, Toots and the Maytals, Jimmy Cliff, Desmond Dekker, the Pioneers and the Paragons, the Melodians and the Ethiopians, the Heptones and the Slickers, the Gaylads, plus an index of people whose names you maybe don't know but who, once heard, are never forgotten. A vortex of world-class talents. The majority of them came from the same housing projects and were singing in large part to get out of them. Partly it's this yearning, a brilliant hungriness, that you hear.

There's more to it, though. The reason the great Jamaican stuff deepens over time, over years, not with nostalgia but with meaning and nuance, is that it's a spiritual music. That's the anomaly underlying its power. It's spiritual pop—not in a calculated way, like Christian rock, but in a way that comes from within. Rastafarianism, when it seized Kingston's emerging record industry as a means for expressing its existence and point of view, made this possible. In the States, rock 'n' roll is always on some level a move away from God into the devil's music, but in Jamaica the cultural conditions were different. Pop grew toward Jah.

Getting in touch with Bunny turned out not surprisingly to be hard (he's known for his reclusiveness). E-mail addresses gave back replies from other people saying to e-mail different addresses, call different numbers. Finally, at one point, I got a message. Unexpectedly it came directly from him. It said, *You may come.* Actually, the language of the e-mail was "Greetings. You may continue with your travel arrangements. One Love, Jah B." The name that came up on the in-box was Neville Livingston, Bunny's real name (Neville O'Reilly Livingston).

Since then there'd been absolute silence. For all I knew, the invitation had come from some stoned joker in Denmark. Also, I'd seen things saying that Bunny moves back and forth between Kingston and a farm in the mountains. What if I got there and he was somewhere in the interior, inaccessible?

Llewis (*sic*) picked me up at the airport. We'd spoken several times beforehand, via phone. Someone recommended him to me as a person who knew Kingston. For some reason, Llewis hadn't wanted to hold a sign for me in baggage claim. Not that I requested it, but it would have been easiest. Instead, he instructed me to approach the dispatch girls, in yellow vests, and tell them I was looking for him; they'd show me where he was. I went up to them.

"There he is," they said, pointing outside to a tall guy who seemed younger than he'd sounded. White polo shirt, shades. Getting closer, I noticed he had a sign after all. Someone else's name was on it.

"Hi, Llewis?" I said.

"John?" he said.

"Yes."

He put down the sign. "I was just holding that for a friend," he said, "doing him an honor."

Yet he carried the sign to the parking lot. Llewis never explained the no-sign/wrong-sign muddle in a way that made any sense, nor how he'd come to have two *l*'s at the front of his name, a question to which he simply refused to speak. I left Jamaica still curious about those things. They were the only two enigmas of that sort, however. At all other times he made conspicuous efforts at straightforwardness. I recommend his services to anyone visiting Kingston. (P.S. He later sent me a message saying his mother had seen it spelled that way in a book, though other people told him it was an error; "LOL, I love it even if it's an error," he wrote.)

We climbed into a white box-van, for which he apologized, saying his good car had been in the shop but would be out tomorrow. I didn't mind the van, though; it gave a clear vantage point from which to see Kingston, passing through jerking freeze-frames of brightly colored intersections. Llewis had been doing research and knew the locations of certain places that dealt in secondhand vinyl records. He introduced me to some stuff from the early eighties I'd never heard. We listened to Papa Michigan and General Smiley's "Diseases" from 1982. It was lyrically disturbing and musically thrilling. It warned all those who would "worship vanities" that "these things unto Jah Jah not pleases." If you're intent on pursuing them anyway,

> *Mind Jah lick you with diseases!*
> *I said the most dangerous diseases.*
> *I talkin' like the elephantitis.*
> *The other one is the poliomyelitis.*

It was summer. The gas-and-garbage smell of the city, the starkness of Kingston's industrial shoreline, made you alert. The humidity was so high it made the atmosphere sag, like the clouds were on your shoulders. The way General Smiley said "poliomyelitis" was beautiful somehow; he pronounced it like *polya*, polyamyelitis.

Llewis hadn't seemed fazed at all by the idea that a person would come to Jamaica looking for Bunny Wailer with no concept of where he lived and only the vaguest intimation of interest or consent on Bunny's part. For all Llewis reacted, it was as if I'd told him I was there to look into import/export opportunities. He'd seen Bunny perform at a festival in the city two years before and found him still electrifying. Bunny looks more and more like a desert father onstage, with his robes and white beard. Llewis quoted a talk-poem he had delivered to the crowd, something about those who want to take the *fruit* of reggae but don't want to water the *root* of reggae.

If you had been to Kingston, it would have seemed changed. "I've never seen it like this," Llewis said. "It was never like this." People had their heads down; you could see that the city's psychic burden had been increased by the violence of what they already called "Bloody May."

What happened is this: A wave of violent gun battles overtook inner-city Kingston, creating a state of internal siege. The U.S. Department of Justice had filed an extradition request asking Jamaica's prime minister, Bruce Golding, to hand over the island's biggest and most powerful drug boss, Christopher Coke (real name). They call him Dudus, which I'd been hearing on the news as Dude-us, but Llewis informed me it's pronounced Dud-us. "Dude-us would be the fancy version," he said. "Too fancy."

A short, thick, somewhat pan-faced man who keeps a low profile and always seems to be smiling at an inward joke,

Dudus is loved by thousands for his Santa Claus qualities when it comes to helping cover the rent or making sure soccer teams get jerseys. According to the FBI, his gang, the Shower Posse, has fourteen hundred (known) murders attached to it.

The Jamaicans felt no great desire to go after Dudus. Jamaican politics is fantastically corrupt, and plenty of ministers had ties to him. Golding tried wishing it away, even hiring an American law firm to lobby against the request, but eventually Washington applied pressure.

Coke gathered his forces, calling in fighters from all over Jamaica, small-time mercenaries from the country who were good with guns. Finally the police and security forces went in to extract him. He had snipers on the rooftops. He had CCTV cameras everywhere, spies among the police and in the ministry. The battle lasted a month. Scores of people were killed, including many civilians—we don't know how many, since the government in all likelihood significantly downplayed the total, desperately trying to save the shreds of the year's all-important tourist economy.

It ended in farce. Dudus got stopped at a roadblock on a highway outside Kingston. The man driving was his spiritual adviser. They claimed they were on their way to the U.S. embassy so Dudus could turn himself in, but to the Americans, not the Jamaicans. Dudus had a black, curly woman's wig on his head and a soft black Gucci cap on top of that and wore old lady's wire-rim glasses. Some said the police dressed him up this way for the mug shot, to make him look weak and to discourage his still-loyal fighters, but it's likely he was using the disguise to get around. One of the soldiers present said later that Dudus had seemed strangely happy when they were cuffing him. He'd been so certain they'd kill him that when he realized it would go down legit, he experienced a rush of relief. Now he was in New York, having pleaded not guilty.

One of the most cryptic things that happened during the buildup to the Dudus war was that Bunny Wailer put out a pro-Dudus dancehall record titled "Don't Touch the President." (President, or Pressy, is one of Dudus's many nicknames.)

Don't touch the president, inna di residen'.
We confident, we say him innocent.
Don't touch the Robin Hood, up inna neighborhood
Because him take the bad, and turn it into good.

Why would an elder statesman of Jamaican culture take the side of these crowds they were showing on TV, in the streets of Kingston, screaming and putting themselves in the way of justice? (The international news cameras had zeroed in on a nuts-seeming woman with a handwritten cardboard sign comparing Dudus to Jesus Christ, and this was rebroadcast in a hundred countries for weeks as a typical expression of Caribbean chaos.)

Traffic was thick now. Llewis turned up the crappy radio in the van as we moved toward the hotel. The DJ played a song called "Slow Motion" by Vybz Kartel, probably the hottest dancehall singer in Jamaica right now. At that moment, Vybz was in jail, suspected (in the vaguest terms) of having gotten involved in Dudus-related violence. "But we're hoping he'll get out soon," said Llewis as he drove. "Maybe this Friday." This was the music Llewis loved best, not the old stuff (which he knew and respected). If the Wailers were playing now, this is what they'd be into. A young couple in a car next to us grinned and bobbed their heads to it as we rolled by. I'd never been wild about dancehall, but now I realized it was because I'd never really heard dancehall. You can't just "listen" to dancehall. It happens; you have to be there for it. The DJ was mixing together three or four different songs. Kartel's hypnotic voice floated over the top of beats that would suddenly vanish, leaving only spacey bass-throbs, as the words kept running. "So this is now?" I asked. "Right?" "This is right now," Llewis said, stabbing his finger at the radio. "This is Right. Now."

At the hotel, I downloaded "Slow Motion." It was somewhat limp, in this version. It sounded like a karaoke mix of what we'd heard in the car. Vybz did not live on the computer. He was in the air over Kingston.

I called Bunny. "Yes," the voice said. Not "Yes?" Yes. "Mr. Wailer?" (What else was one supposed to say? I wasn't about to call him Jah B.) We talked for a bit. "We can do this," he said. He gave me an address, a few blocks off one of the main boulevards, not a particularly upscale part of Kingston. We set a time. "Bless," he said.

I passed out listening to a song that had been on a loop in my head in the weeks leading up to that trip, "Let Him Go," a song Bunny wrote in 1966, when Bob Marley was off in Delaware working as an assistant in a DuPont laboratory and going by the name Donald. It's a Rude Boy number, one in a series of songs and answer-songs that took over the Jamaican sound systems between 1965 and '67. Rudies, as the growing numbers of reckless youths who terrorized and fascinated middle-class Kingston were called, had become a national menace. Half the major ska stars weighed in with a message. There were pro–Rude Boy songs, anti–Rude Boy songs, and songs that weren't clearly one thing or another. With the whole island paying attention, a focused competitiveness (never lacking in Jamaican music) elevated the songwriting. Many classic songs resulted.

None of them is quite on a level with "Let Him Go," the one Bunny Livingston wrote. The backing band included a few of the Skatalites, moonlighting. They laid down a buoyant, brassy rhythm that had just a little tug at the end, a little slur, a groove that, listening back, was transitional between ska and rocksteady. When I hear it start, I feel like a puck on an air-hockey table that's been switched on. *Ooo-ooo-ooo-ooo*, the voices add to one another in layers, building a chord that becomes final right before they break into

> *Rudie come from jail 'cause Rudie get bail.*
> *Rudie come from jail 'cause Rudie get bail.*

There's a sound on that recording, a vocalized *So!* right between the ninety-ninth and one-hundredth seconds: the Wailers, defending Rudie as always, have just sung, *Remember he is young, and he will live long.* And then someone—you can't tell who—makes this noise. Intones, rather. It doesn't seem to come from inside the studio—doesn't belong, that is, to the texture of the session; it emanates from miles away and has arrived through an open window. Somewhere in the interior of Jamaica a goat herder with a staff has leaned back and loosed this sound into a valley, intending it for no ears but Jah's. *Soooo!*—the vowel fading quickly without an echo, pure life force. Was that Bunny doing that?

Llewis arrived twenty minutes early the next morning, and he did have the nice car, a blue Toyota model you don't often see in the States, somehow German-looking, which turned out to be appropriate, because one thing I'd learned about Llewis and would have occasion to learn better over coming days was that he passionately supported Germany's national soccer team and, no matter what else he was doing, avidly followed their unimpeded progress in the World Cup with half his brain. He was perhaps the only person in Jamaica who felt like that. He talked all about them, about their teamwork, as we drove around.

I asked him if he wanted to sit in on the interview with Bunny. "Sure," he said. "It might loosen him up."

"You think I'll make him uptight?" I said.

"He's pretty reclusive, right?" Llewis replied diplomatically.

Bunny lived in an area with only every fourth or fifth road sign intact. I was keeping my finger on the map while Llewis counted lefts, U-turning around till we found the curving lane that had to be his. It looked like Cuba, but more drab. The roads were viciously rutted. The houses were miniature compounds; everybody who could had high walls with glass shards or wire on top. Inside, however, there might be civility, shade, nice colors. You didn't want to show any of that.

I won't say I was shocked to find that Bunny Wailer lived in a poor area. It wasn't a slum, and he has always preferred to live humbly. (When he ditched the Wailers' first world tour in 1973 over disagreements about the direction of the band, he famously went and lived in a ramshackle cabin by the beach, surviving on fish from the sea and writing songs.) Still, the degree of shabbiness surprised me, and Llewis remarked on it, too. How long has Bunny Wailer's music—songs that he participated in making—been in every dorm room, every coffee shop, and he was driving an aged and dusty Japanese sedan? That was serious baldhead math.

There were two tall corrugated-metal gates with giant

Rastafarian lions on them that parted creakily to let you in. A tin sign hung on one. It read, JAH B WILL BE AWAY UNTIL MARCH 15TH. It was July 6. I was guessing he didn't mind the overall message. He was standing there in the courtyard, small and every bit as wiry as he is in the well-known picture of him playing soccer, dreadlocked and shirtless. He had on an excellent brown collarless suit that looked like something Sammy Davis, Jr., would have worn to a hip party in 1970. His beard was long, wispy, and yellowish white. He wore his dreads swirled atop his head into a crown and kept in place with bands.

He greeted us with great politeness but seemed not to want to waste time. He addressed Llewis as "Soldier"! He'd put out chairs for us under a lime tree. His wife, Jean Watt, a gracefully aged woman, brought out orange juice, saying, "Bless, bless."

"Well," I began. "It's an honor to meet you."

"Well, it's an honor to be here, on the earth," he said. "You know what I mean? So we at one. What's up with you, now?"

One was intimidated, but not in a way that felt inappropriate. That was Bunny Wailer, who taught Bob Marley what harmony was. When we'd come in, I had asked if we could maybe take him to lunch, anywhere he liked. Llewis had warned me to say specifically that it would be an "ital" restaurant, one that served food appropriate for Rastas. "Thanks," Bunny answered, pausing, "but . . . the Blackheart Man is very skeptical. He'd rather eat from his own pot."

The notebook read, *"No. 1, ask him about what's happening now, the stuff with Dudus,"* but we hadn't even gotten through the turning-on-the-recorders part when Bunny embarked on an hour-long, historically footnoted breakdown of exactly how the Dudus crisis had come about, tracing it back to the birth of the garrisons in the sixties.

In order to understand anything about Jamaica and why it's statistically one of the most violent places on earth, you have to know something about garrisonism, the unique system by which the island's government functions. Before you turn away in anticipation of boredom, let me say that you may find yourself intrigued by the sheer fact that something this twisted is occurring on a U.S.-friendly island five hundred miles from our coast. Garrisonism has been described—in a Jamaican report put out by a specially convened panel—as "political tribalism." (Bunny called it "a political tribal massacre" in his classic "Innocent Blood" thirty years ago.) The history of garrisonism can be supercrudely summarized as follows. In the 1960s, the island's two rival parties—the liberal People's National Party (PNP) and the conservative Jamaica Labour Party (JLP), Jamaica's version of Democrats and Republicans—started putting up housing projects in Kingston's poorest neighborhoods. Once the buildings were up, whichever party had built them moved in its own trustworthy supporters and kicked anybody who didn't want to vote their way out of the neighborhood. Families and groups of friends were shattered. Children had to change schools because their old school's party affiliation had shifted. Many of these displaced ended up in squatters' camps.

When it was all a question of local island politics, nobody much cared, just as nobody much cares today outside Jamaica about the situation there, or didn't until Dudus went rogue. Things changed, however, in the seventies, when Michael Manley, the PNP leader, expressed sympathy with Castro. The CIA was terrified about Cuban communism spreading to the other Caribbean islands. It backed the Reaganite JLP leader, Edward Seaga. Now there were more, and more serious, guns flowing into the garrisons. It was Manley against Seaga, socialism against capitalism, PNP against JLP, with the garrisons pitted against one another, fighting on behalf of their parties for control of the island. Kingston emerged as a miniature front in the Cold War.

Only in the eighties did drug running enrich certain dons to the point that they no longer needed the state as much. The garrisons were becoming quasi-states. The dons could afford their own guns; they could supply forces. They started dictating terms to the ministers. That is, if the ministers still wanted all the thousands of votes the dons controlled.

"What I'm saying in 'Don't Touch the President,'" Bunny told me, "is that if you remove Dudus, there's gonna be an-other Dudus, until you get rid of the source," namely min-isterial corruption. He said Dudus had been a good don. Actually, what he said was, "He's taking bad and turning it into good, like Jesus Christ." I asked if he'd ever met Dudus. Maybe at one of the *passa passas*, neighborhood concerts hosted by the don?

"Never seen him in my lifetime," he said.

He had the metal gates chained up and padlocked again. A sweet but mean-looking mutt was patrolling the patio. Bunny sat forward on his chair, bouncing his toes. His two cell phones went off incessantly. Llewis would back me up on that. Incessant. "And the amazing thing was," Llewis said, "he never looked to see who it was, but he never turned them off, either." It was true—he just let them ring and ring. I got used to it.

A little kid came by and knocked. I gathered that people did this fairly often, asking for help. "Who that? Who that? No, wrong time here, check me back likkle more, hear, soldier? Check me back likkle more, right now me in a serious meeting." The kid wasn't listening. We could see his eyes through a chink in the gate. "CHECK ME BACK LIKKLE MORE!" Bunny screamed. Every now and then one of his sons walked through the leafy patio. A poster of his daughter, the burgeoning singer Cen'C Love, stood against a wall. This was a good castle for the Blackheart Man.

It seemed he was in a mood to talk, and not only that, but to talk about the old days. I hadn't wanted to push that too hard, treat him like a fossil. He's still writing songs occasionally, going on mini-tours. With some artists, if you ask too much about their old stuff, they take it as a criticism.

Bunny started talking about the young Bob Marley, what he was like when they attended the Stepney All Age School in St. Ann together. Back then they had called Bob Nesta, his first name at birth.

"A lot of people don't know the nature of the individual," Bunny said. "From a childhood state, Bob was cut out to be this icon, this saint." The pain of being biracial had deepened his sensitivity early on. His father was a white man, a captain in the British military, Norval Sinclair Marley. The influence of this side of Bob's childhood had been underemphasized, Bunny felt. Bob had grown up "in the condition of a nobody." In the Jamaica of that time, "the biracial child was like a reproach, because he brings shame on the family of the white man and shame on the family of the black woman.

"Bob would look at you and say, 'You think God *white*? God BLACK!' Ah-haa!" Bunny raised his finger. "And his father is a white person, Captain Marley, and his genes is also in Bob." Bunny had clearly worked through this. He laughed darkly, shaking his head. "Aha, still the captain," he said.

Bob was *from* the country, but Bunny's family had only

moved to the country; they came from Kingston. Bunny brought knowledge of music—he'd been a champion child dancer. At the revivalist church in St. Ann where Bunny's father preached, he banged the drum during the songs. "I was a great drummer, you know," he said. "Sometimes they had to use my influence to build up the vibes of the church."

Bunny would play his self-made guitar there in the village, and Bob saw how many people came to listen. "It was the only little amusement in those dark woods," Bunny laughed. He showed Bob how to make one.

The fervor with which Bob picked up music startled Bunny. "I did it as a hobby, for entertaining the community," he said. "Bob took it as a weapon, to get him out of that kind of condition of being a nobody to being a somebody, a musician." Bunny spoke about the first, not especially successful Bob Marley singles, issued under various names (one was "Bobby Martell") by the pioneering Chinese-Jamaican ska producer Leslie Kong. One of them, a song called "Terror," is a kind of holy grail in the world of Jamaican record collecting. No copy has ever been found. Bunny implied that it had been too radical for release, the government wouldn't have liked it. "A lot of people don't know about that song," Bunny said. "Terrible song, that." He meant terrible as in fearsome. He blew my mind by quoting a verse of it:

He who rules by terror
Doeth grievous wrong.
In hell I'll count his error.
Let them hear my song.

"Them hide it," Bunny said. "That song nobody know, them hide it. It hidden."

I realized later that these are lines, fiddled with here and there, from an Alfred, Lord Tennyson, poem, "The Captain: A Legend of the Navy." A poem Bob had been made to memorize in school, maybe? It tells the story of a ship—a phantom precursor of the ship in "Slave Driver"—on which the captain is so cruel that the men commit mass suicide, rushing in to attack an enemy vessel at his command, then laying down their arms, letting the ship be blown to smithereens. Captain Marley, seven years dead, surely haunts this song. He'd abandoned Bob as a toddler. Bob's mom then became the mistress of Bunny's father. During different stretches, the two boys lived under one roof together. They knew each other so well that years later, Bunny could remember (and recorded a version of) a song that Bob had written as a boy, a sing-songy thing called "Fancy Curls."

At this point, Bunny excused himself and went off for a lunch/siesta retreat of some kind. Llewis and I sat there on the patio for about an hour, talking quietly. He'd been right; his presence had put Bunny at greater ease. Whenever I expressed surprise—that exaggerated surprise it's somehow impossible not to affect when you're interviewing people: "Really?!"—Bunny would point at Llewis and say, "True, soldier?" And Llewis would say, "One hundred percent true."

When Bunny returned, his mood was suppressed. He sat farther back. His eyelids were lowered, and his phones rang shrilly in his pockets, utterly ignored. His silence during the preceding month was much less baffling. I asked about Joe Higgs, the man who made the Wailers happen. Higgs—there's a neglected genius of Jamaican music. His 1975 *Life of Contradiction*, recently rereleased, is desert-island good. He died fairly young, of cancer. In 1959, during a wave of political uprisings by militant Rastafarians, he was beaten and jailed. (Bunny himself would be imprisoned on ganja charges eight years later.)

When Higgs got out, he started hosting informal music sessions under a fruit tree in the open yard by his place. "Trench Town in those days didn't have any real separation from yard to yard," Bunny said. "There was no fence, nothing, so Joe Higgs's yard was a place that had activities related to gambling, a table, the lady who sells fried dumplings, fried fish . . . It was a popular corner."

Higgs became a mentor to the Wailers, whose potential he sensed right away. Bunny said that the older man actually put his career on hold for a couple of years to train them. "He was paying so much attention to the Wailers," Bunny said, "he started to believe in the Wailers more even than himself." He taught them harmony, breath control, and the rudiments of composition, which young Bob especially was hungry to learn. According to Bunny, Higgs used Mr. Miyagi–like methods. He would come knocking at one-thirty in the morning, waking them up and making them play, saying, "If you can't sing dem hours, then you can't sing." He would lead them deep into May Pen Cemetery (the same cemetery where bodies are said to have been covertly buried during the Dudus riots), then demand that they harmonize among the graves, reasoning, "If you're not afraid fe sing fe duppy [a Caribbean spirit], the audience *caaan't* frighten you."

"That was the kind of teacher he was," Bunny said. "It pumped bravery in us." He mentioned that in all the years he'd been touring, since 1969, "I've never sexed a woman in my work." He laid out his theory that a man's energy is contained in his sperm. "Every time you discharge, you're liable to lose five pounds." He encouraged me to try it next time, weigh myself afterward.

"Maybe *you* lose five pounds," Llewis said. Bunny laughed.

He was getting tired. It was strange to realize, after hearing all these stories about that cradle period, that Bunny was entering his mid-sixties. Because Peter and Bob and Joe Higgs and so many others weren't destined to become old, you didn't expect it to happen to Bunny, somehow. He looks like a little Rastafarian wizard. He'll live much longer; he has that skinny-man longevity. How had he done it? I asked him. How had he alone stayed alive? "I put my trust in the Most High," he said, "Jah Rastafari." He told us we could come back tomorrow at the same time.

In the morning, we pulled up to Bunny's place as before and banged on the gates, but the scene had changed. An older Rasta, hollow chested in his thinness and wearing gnarled gray dreads, greeted us, saying, "Africa love." When I think about it, he was probably greeting only Llewis that way.

Bunny couldn't come out, the man explained. He was in a serious meeting. We should try again later.

We decided to see Trench Town. On the way, Llewis gave me an idea of where the different garrisons lay, which ones were PNP, which ones were JLP. We drove toward Tivoli Gardens but hit a roadblock and got turned around. "He is press," Llewis said. "I am press," I said. The young cop looked at us silently. He just repeated the circling motion with his finger, with his left hand over the machine gun.

Things got palpably more tense as you moved toward these neighborhood streets. Dudus's supporters didn't know what to do. Jamaican politics is a perpetual *1984*-style standoff meant to be endlessly perpetuated while the ministers enrich themselves. It doesn't know how to behave in a vacuum.

I was frankly shocked by the appearance of the Trench Town Culture Yard. It's in a slum. That's an insensitive word, but when they have sledgehammer holes in the walls for windows, and women with babies on their arms are openly begging on the street, wanting to be paid to have their picture taken, and groups of ownerless dogs with skin diseases are going around, that's a slum. There's a lovely little area right there at the entrance, though, shaded with trees, and it has benches. Hummingbirds. A bunch of Rastas were hanging out. The air was sickly sweet with the smell of torched hemp.

Llewis and I talked and decided that a nice gesture would be to procure some good herb and bring it to Bunny. He'd been more generous with his time than any applicable obligations required. We soon met a young moped-riding gentleman capable of filling our need. We explained who it was for—they know Bunny well in Trench Town. They call him "Bunny Wailers" there, with an *s*. They also understood without needing it explained that he's unlikely to be a person who plays around with dry-ass gray you-have-to-smoke-four-joints-to-feel-it rope-weed. The guy promised to bring back the best he had. I happily overpaid, as Llewis seemed to feel that the guy was not overly bullshitting us about the quality.

Back at Bunny's, however, the same Rasta guy met us again at the gate. Jah B was sorry. The meeting looked to run longer than expected. Come back that night. Bunny did want to see us, the man said, but they were discussing serious matters.

It was late afternoon now. We were heat-drunk and fatigued and still hadn't really even begun. We discussed some more and agreed that we should take the opportunity to smoke some of the weed I'd bought, to make absolutely sure that it wasn't shit, that we wouldn't be inadvertently insulting Bunny with it. We would be like the king's tasters, I suppose. Where could this be done safely, though? Contrary to what you might think, Jamaica is not a place where you can just lie around in a park and smoke ganja all day.

Llewis said that he knew of some clubs. We drove for a while, toward the edge of the city. A security guy met us at the gate and let us through. There was a big open-air bar. "Mind if we smoke?" Llewis asked. The guy said he didn't. We rolled a two-sheeter, under a giant sign that said NO GANJA SMOKING. Inside it was a strip club; out here it was just mellow. The girls inside had no customers. Dudus had killed Kingston tourism. They kept wandering out looking bored. Naturally we offered them hits from the joint, which they were evidently allowed to take, and did. We tipped them, just for existing, I suppose. They were all from the country. The cheapness of their lingerie was sad, and so was the horrible clacking eighties-era American pop they kept playing inside, real Casey Kasem nightmare stuff.

They rolled out a TV. A World Cup match was on. I hadn't even thought about the fact that Llewis had been prepared to miss it, his beloved Germany versus Spain, had the original schedule with Bunny happened. He'd put money on this match, too, it turned out. Llewis, what a solid dude. And now, by this magic, we got to watch the soccer after all, while smoking and drinking and waiting to go see Bunny. We had hours to kill.

The weed turned out to be way up there powerwise. I was straight confused for a while. Possibly this had something to do with making Germany's loss extra crushing to Llewis. He couldn't take it. To him it seemed not only perverse but insane that Spain had won. The litany of explanations, both technical and moral, that he delivered to the few assembled bar patrons and dancers became a discourse. He was lecturing. He slipped entirely into patois, and that's how the others spoke to him, so I fathomed little of what they said, while nonetheless seeing my role as to reassure Llewis of Germany's superiority.

We had a sort of hungover dinner at T.G.I. Friday's, Llewis somewhat morose. But on the way to Bunny's for what we hoped would be the last time, we listened to "Diseases" again, and "Diseases" would cheer up a dry drunk at a Cabo sales retreat.

Llewis taught me something. At high school in Jamaica, he said, when your team lost, it was traditional to chant, on your way out of the grounds, "We no feel no way! We no feel no way!" Meaning essentially, we're not sweating it, we didn't really give a shit anyway. I sensed real psychological depth in this chant and didn't need to be urged more than once by Llewis to beat on the dashboard and join him in it, which we did the rest of the way to Bunny's, and in that manner Llewis seemed to exorcise his disappointment.

Now it was dark. We knocked on the gate. The same guy came back, but this time he said Jah B had given instructions for us to be let in. We stepped through, back into the patio, and saw that Bunny was sitting around a table with a number of other Rastafarians. They were having a "reasoning," to use Bunny's word. He gestured to us and said that the meeting was wrapping up. It had been going for seven hours.

The guy carried in two chairs and placed them in the corner of the patio, away from the table, motioning for us to sit. We sat while they continued to discuss business. Llewis and I felt out of place and awkward. A couple of the women present were vocal about not wanting us there. At one point we stood up and tried to signal our willingness to wait outside or something, but the man who'd let us in said to the women, "Jah B wants them here, they are special people to Jah B," and everything calmed.

The meeting went on for maybe another hour. It began to rain, and we were allowed to bring our chairs closer. They prayed. Then there was an hour of goodbyes. The Rastas waved to us cordially as they were leaving. Bunny sat in his office, with the door open, conferring privately with one of the sisters. We heard crying, and then they were praying, and Bunny made curious whooping sounds. It was revivalist-sounding.

When he was done with that, he came out and spoke to us, told us he needed to bathe and freshen up, get restored. During our last visit, he'd said that he didn't sleep much, got most of his best work done at night.

I had a couple of decent-size roaches in my shirt pocket. We huffed those in the shadows of the courtyard. We could hear singing from a church across the street, the sound of many raised voices inside a tightly closed box. Bunny had an old poster leaning against one concrete wall, a portrait of Marcus Garvey. Llewis sang Burning Spear, *Do you remember the days of slavery?* After each hit he took, he'd say, "Irie." He wasn't a Rasta; he was being sort of tongue in cheek, the way we might say something in a Southern accent after taking a shot of whiskey. He said he'd dabbled with Rastafarianism once, after high school, but had come to a place where he didn't believe in religion, period.

Bunny appeared silently as a dark shape in the light from his office, wearing a full formal dress khaki Haile Selassie Ethiopian military uniform. His dreads were freshly coiled. He motioned for us to sit. "What was that a meeting of?" I asked. He explained it had been a gathering of a group calling itself the Millennium Council, which contained a representative from each of the thirteen "mansions" of Rasta (like denominations—Bunny is Nyabinghi, one of the elders of that mansion). They were meeting to discuss Jamaica's participation in an upcoming international Rastafarian conference.

He began to tell us the story of how he had become a Rasta. "I knew of Rasta from I was a little child," he said, "but the Blackheart Man was the name given to the Rastaman, to make every youth stay far from that individual, 'cause he's likely to cut your heart out and eat it and all that kind of stuff. And when you disobeyed or did anything that wasn't appropriate within the family, they would say, 'If you don't do this here, I'm gonna call the Blackheart Man on you.'"

In Kingston, in Trench Town, when kids were late to school, they used to run by the gullies to get there faster. Rastas lived in the gullies. The city gave them waste grounds for making their camps. "The Blackheart Man lived in the manhole," Bunny said. "Check that—that's Rastaman." Sometimes one of these dreadlocked mystics would come out of his shanty "to fill his little butter pan with water," and when the children saw him, they'd run the other way. Bunny remembered a couple of his friends getting cut and bruised, they ran so fast to get away. But for some reason—maybe it was the influence of Joe Higgs—this youth, Neville, started asking himself why he ran. He'd noticed that as he and his friends ran from the Rastas, the Rastas were calmly walking back to their holes. "So when him comes out, I took a brave heart, and he just look at me as if, 'Aren't you running, too?'"

Bunny questioned the man, asking what made him live like he did. "I find out he has an intellect, someone like a lawyer or a doctor when he opened his mouth," he said. "Then he tells me that Haile Selassie the First inspired him to walk this route. 'Seek first the kingdom of Jah, and all other things shall be added.' *Rastaman*. Not me hear them thing out no Bible—*Rasta* taught them things, and me understand immediately."

In spring of 1966 occurred the visit of His Imperial Majesty Haile Selassie, the Ethiopian emperor, the black man on the cover of *Time* who had taken his place at the white man's highest table, in the United Nations, and who many Jamaicans, on fire with a Marcus Garvey–inspired Pan-Africanist Zionism, held to be a coming of Christ. When Ras Tafari (Prince Fearless, in his native Amharic) arrived at the Kingston airport, he was so overwhelmed by the intensity of the crowd's reception that he immediately turned and went back into the plane, worried for his life. A Rastafarian leader, dressed in a simple forest tunic like John the Baptist, gained permission to go on board, where he explained to Selassie that the surging of the crowd owed purely to their love for him. It is said that Selassie wept. Bunny Livingston was there that day. "Who didn't see His Imperial Majesty didn't want to," he said. Like many in the crowd, he felt the emperor's eyes on himself individually and at the same time on everyone. There were many other such "mystics" (showings forth of the divine). A shower passed, and thousands were soaked and flash-dried on the spot. Some Rastas lit chalice for herb, and a plane flying overhead exploded. They'd been given powers. Bunny saw a band of Moravian sisters, all dressed in white with black faces, dancing down the road waving palms and singing hosanna, "because He was Who He was," Bunny said, "because He is Who He is."

I'd brought a little digital speaker setup with me. We listened to "Fighting Against Convictions," the song he wrote during his fourteen-month stint of hard labor, much of it spent at Richmond Farm Prison in 1967. It begins, *Battering down SEN-tence* . . . with a sudden rising note on *SEN*. I told him what an unusual melody I thought that was, immediately gripping. Some of the senior wardens wouldn't let him sing it, he said, even when the other prisoners requested it. "You see, the t'ing about it is," he said, "the melody has to sing the message of how you feel. In the prison, it has to have that kind of a *wailing* type of melody that suggests you are actually experiencing something, you're not just singing about something that you heard about."

Around this point, I underwent what I can only assume was a momentary hallucination of some type. Strange things were happening to Bunny's face as he spoke. Different races were passing through it, through the cast of his features—black, white, Asian, Indian, the whole transnational human slosh that produced the West Indies. The Atlantic world was passing through his face. I was having thoughts so crypto-colonialist, I might as well have had on a white safari hat and been peering at him through a monocle. Out of nowhere, Bunny started talking about fruit, all the different strange fruits that grow in Jamaica. I dug his physical love for his home, the reason he could never leave. "You're talking about soursop, you're talking about sweetsop.

You're talking about naseberry, you're talking about June plum. Breadfruit." (That tree the original Wailers met under in Joe Higgs's yard was a "coolie plum." I ate one in Trench Town. Quite toothsome.)

"We have guinep," Bunny said. "I've never gone anywhere in the world and seen guinep. We got one called stinking toe. So dry that you gotta be careful how you eat it—it might choke you, the dust from the pollen." He jumped up. A spry man. "I got some of it here," he said. "I got some stinking toe right here. I'm gonna put some liquid glucose on it, make jelly out of it. Just taste it," he said. He scooped some from the bottom of the bucket. The West Indian locust, *Hymenaea courbaril*. He warned me that it would be the driest thing I would ever eat. My mouth was already cottony from the weed. I don't know how long it took to eat that single bite. The process of excavating it from my teeth afterward alone took twenty minutes. But the sweetness that is at the center of locust fruit is the strangest, most unexpected sweetness. It's like crawling through the desert for days and coming upon a tiny bush that gives extremely sweet fruit. There's a page of my life that is the eating of that bite of stinking toe, with Bunny watching me and cackling at my expressions as I progressed through the Willy Wonka–esque wonders of this fruit.

"And it's a stimulant," Bunny said, thwacking my knee. "It gives you a hard cock. It's like the shell—it makes your dick hard as a shell."

The singing across the road had stopped long before; so had the rain. It was getting very late. There was one last thing: I wanted to sit with him and listen to "Let Him Go" on the little player. While I cued it up, he ran through the other Rude Boy songs of those years. He remembered them all. "This one, now, just *ended* the [Rude Boy] war," he said. "'Let Him Go' stopped them in them tracks." It was never answered. The song came on, and Bunny sang along. He sounded fantastic. That crackling tone.

You frame him, you say things he didn't do,
You rebuke him, you scorn him, you make him feel blue.
Let him go . . .

He threw back his head. "Lloyd Knibbs," he said, referring to the Skatalites' drummer. The three of us were leaning forward. Bunny had his hands pressed between his thighs. The music, even over my little Target-bought sound system, filled the shed with a golden vibe.

As the *So!* approached, I caught his eye. "This thing coming up," I said over the music, "that *So!* Who's doing that?"

Bunny slapped his chest. "That's me, mon!" As if he were disappointed in me for asking.

He demonstrated, rising from his chair. I leaned back to take him in. "Here's Vision," he said (meaning Constantine "Vision" Walker, who stepped in for Bob in 1966). Bunny moved his hand in a wavy pattern as Vision sang, *Remember he is smart, remember he is strong.* "And here's me," Bunny whispered. He thrust his head forward and ghosted his long-ago line into an imaginary mike: *Remember he is young, and he will live long.* Pulling back quickly, he pointed his finger in the air—like, "Aha!"—and shouted, *Sooo!*

It was him.

Three months after my visit, relations between Bunny and me soured. Not even the mystical sweetness of stinking-toe jelly could have redeemed them. The magazine sent a world-class photographer, Mark Seliger, over to Kingston, with a crew, to photograph him. I got involved in the negotiations surrounding the portrait. Bunny didn't want to do it, but in the end (at least as I understood our conversations) he agreed. We were asking almost nothing, an hour, at his house. But we were also asking a lot: we wanted his face. I sympathized and tried to be delicate. But he grew increasingly hard and suspicious on the telephone. A legal letter arrived. This all happened after our crew was in Kingston. Hotel fees, per diems, plane-ticket changes. My last talk with Bunny degenerated into hostility. He called me a "ras clot" and a "bumba clot," the worst things you can call someone in Jamaica. I'm not 100 percent sure what those words mean, but apparently they have something to do with an ass rag or used tampon. He accused me of having boxed him in, with the whole photo-shoot business, and of then trying to guilt him. Possibly I did this, on some level. He ranted. He reminded me that he was a revolutionary commander. Didn't I know that he needed to hide his face? "Do you know Bunny Wailer?" he asked. "Do you know I and I?"

I admitted that no, I didn't.

He summoned a dark cloud of patois cursing. I couldn't follow for minutes on end. Then he hung up. He never would call me back. I became an unanswered ring in the pockets of his marvelous suits.

I was fine with it. It felt right to be rejected by Bunny Wailer. "What can *GQ* magazine do for I and I?" he had demanded. The answer was nothing. We'd come from Babylon; he sent us back there, to our garrisons. The last transmission I got said, "Greetings, John, Here are photos. One Love. Jah B. Wailer." There was a snapshot of him in a parking lot, wearing a white sailor suit, saluting. You could read it any way you wanted.

The real gift he gave me was the gift of saying no. It was the gift of remaining the Blackheart Man. That had been the hook the whole time—that he is still alive.

VIOLENCE OF THE LAMBS

Human history is mainly the history of human customs,
and we know very little of animal history from this point
of view. Nevertheless animals do change their customs.
—JOHN BURDON SANDERSON HALDANE, British Geneticist,
What Is Life?, 1947

Animals are changing, and I cannot tell you why.
—INUSIQ NASALIK, 88-year-old Inuit Elder, September 6, 2004

Last year I was asked to write a magazine story about the future of the human race, a topic on which my sporadic descents to the crushing mental depths of pop-rock culture crit had quite predictably made me the go-to guy. Nonetheless I undertook in all good faith to fulfill the assignment. The future of the human race is something we ought to take seriously, since despite all the fortunes spent on those giant space-monitoring radio dishes and the exploratory satellites and whatnot, there exists not a shred of conclusive evidence to contradict the rational assumption that away from this blue ball we live on, the universe is an infinity of unfeeling matter. So let's keep this thing going, is my take.

In search of insight I spent a couple of days at the Future of Humanity Institute, at Oxford University in England. I called the woman I'd been told was the most farsighted person at FEMA. I talked to any self-identifying and not instantly, palpably insane futurologist who'd answer a query—Bill Lilly at the New School for Human Advancement proved especially accommodating. I spoke with someone at the Vatican. The Vatican actually has a future expert, essentially a house book of Revelation wonk. In short, I want you to know that I tried and tried, for months, to write about something other than what I've ended up writing on here, a tangent that popped up early in the research but immediately screamed career-killer and was repeatedly shunted aside in favor of things like out-of-control nanotechnology of the near future (which, you'll be glad to hear, is something they're deeply concerned about at the Future of Humanity Institute). But as I tried every way I knew to find some legitimate half-truths about the future for you to read about on your flight to Dallas or wherever your loved ones live—and I do suggest that you visit them soon, as in this year, I really do—the problem became that people who make a profession of thinking seriously about the future won't really tell you anything that isn't cautious, hedged, and quadruple-qualified, because, as I came slowly to comprehend and deal with, no one knows what's going to happen in the future.

My surprise at this pretty obvious-seeming realization showed me the extent to which, thanks to Hollywood or my own paranoia or whatever, I'd unconsciously internalized a belief in the existence of some person, some prematurely middle-aged guy, either Jewish or Asian (or, in the comedy version, Irish), who sits in a room in the bowels of some governmental building and actually knows what's going to happen in the future, whose mutterings need to be heeded, whose moods must be tracked with concern if not alarm, and whose very existence is a cause all over the world of slight, constant anxiety, and properly so. Is this a dying spasm of the religion gene? Probably. All I know is that it came as a great liberation to me, to have this creature expunged from my imagination, with his alert levels and his survival kits and all his total crap that he goes on about while with the left hand building nukes and starting wars. I reminded myself that incessant potential catastrophe is the human condition, is in fact the price of possessing consciousness, and I determined to live with greater ease from now on, and not to let anyone scare me about the future, because the truth is, the worst thing that could ever happen to you is death, and that's going to happen despite all your worry and effort, so it's simply irrational not to say fuck it. I'm not saying start chain-smoking cloves and having unprotected sex with seaport trannie bar girls, though neither am I saying to abjure those things if they're what make you feel most alive. I'm just saying, take courage. That and pretty much that alone is never the incorrect thing to do. And these thoughts were so edifying to me, and I really looked forward to sharing them with you, hoping they might lighten your load along the road.

Then I was introduced to a person called Marcus Livengood.

Good day, sunshine.

A question that lately has been getting knocked around a lot in the better biology departments is this: As we intrude on, clear-cut, burn, pollute, occupy, cause to become too hot or too dry, or otherwise render unsuitable to wildlife a larger and larger percentage of the planet, what will be involved in terms of the inevitable increased human exposure to remnant populations of truly wild fauna? Not just for us but for them. What sort of changes, adaptations, and responses might we look for in the animals themselves as the pressures of this global-biological endgame start to make themselves felt at the level of the individual organism? We have in mind here not micro-evolutionary changes to existing species but stress-related behavior modification, so-called phenotypic plasticity, the sort of thing we know numerous animal groups to be capable of, though it is rarely witnessed. Or was rarely witnessed. Now it seems to be cropping up everywhere, as even a casual viewer of nature shows can attest. Across numerous species and habitat types, we are seeing, in crudest terms, animals do things we haven't seen them do before.

I tiptoe around saying anything direct here because of what I hope is an understandable sheepishness in reporting on this subject at all, so sharply does it smack of quackery and gullibility; on top of that, it should be clear by now that I take no pleasure in freaking anyone out. What I can tell you is that this thing is real, that it has proved harder rather than easier for reasonable and informed people to deny, and that, however modest and obscure continues to be the small community of researchers and analysts and bloggers who have thus far commented on it and made the first steps toward charting its dimensions, you will hear a lot more about it in the next ten to twenty years. Even the Future of Humanity Institute folks are going to want to pay attention to this one, though its origin lies rather far, academically speaking, from the stone paths of Oxford.

Centerbrook, in southern Ohio, embodies a type of small-town college familiar to anyone who grew up or was educated in the Midwest. It started out in the nineteenth century as some sort of vocational academy, a normal school or a technical school, and accrued its university status over time, adding a department here or a professor there as qualified academics moved back from the Northeast to retire or take care of Mom, until one day all that remained undone was to stamp it a liberal-arts institution. No one ever got a good job just by saying they went to Centerbrook, but the students, on the days I visited, seemed sharp and ambitious. Many of them were a good decade past eighteen to twenty-two. And although the campus isn't pretty—it's all naked brick and parking lots—there was an atmosphere of seriousness about what they were up to there.

Professor Marcus Livengood, who goes by Marc to the point of indulging "Mr. Marc" among his students, attended Centerbrook before getting his Ph.D. in comparative zoology at UC Santa Clara. He then came back to a job in the life-sciences department at his undergraduate alma mater. When I showed up forty minutes late for our appointment, he was alone in his surprisingly gigantic office.

I've never seen a person easier to describe physically. He looks like a young George Lucas. Same head shape, same beard, squint, everything, only taller and not pudgy yet and without the gray. Also, Mr. Livengood wears a ponytail. He wore as well the heavy square glasses that rogue scientists are commanded to wear when they're inducted into the Rogue Scientist Lodge.

With what struck me as no mean feel for theater, as if we hadn't already been e-mailing for weeks, Livengood said, "So you're here to talk about the animals?"

Whatever process led to this interview had begun about a year before. I fear I'll be trading away some much, much needed credibility by confessing this up front, but it began for me on the Internet. Not on kook sites, mind you; I wouldn't spend any time on the kook sites until a good bit later, until after I'd got mixed up with Marc, in fact. No, this was at AOL, America Online, which I, like many others, use to connect to the Internet every day and check my messages. One thing that happens when you connect via America Online is that this little list of news headlines pops up on the welcome page, and you can follow them to the relevant articles. You know all this. Well, someone at AOL, in a pulsating cubicle on the company's editorial floor, a person entrusted with sifting through all the different wire reports from all over the planet and deciding what merited attention, started seeing something, a pattern. I wish there were a way to determine this person's identity (I've tried), because these days I consider him or her a curious sort of brother or sister in arms. In any event, it seemed like every day, once a week at a minimum, there'd be a far-out animal-attack story.

Not just that. An animal-attack story is a mountain lion pouncing on a jogger, a bear busting into someone's car, a surfer losing a leg. Mind you, those cases look to be on the rise, too, in many parts of the world. But that's a story we know. Species self-protection + everybody loving the outdoors = occasional kills. We're talking here about stories that have to do with changes in the nature and lethality of animal aggression. Let's go ahead and escort an elephant out of the room here and just say it: we're talking about things like what happened to Steve Irwin.

Yes, the Irwin story has long since turned into a butt for online commenters' macabre jokes. I won't make them myself: the man had a little girl, little Bindi. Indeed, it was while filming scenes for her show that Irwin perished. (My daughter watches her show and owns merchandise related to it. The theme song goes, "The Croc Hunter taught her, / Now his only daughter / Is Bindi the Jungle Girl."

The fact remains that in roughly three hundred years during which human beings have been both (a) swimming, unknowingly or not, above giant stingrays in shallow water and (b) recording unusual things that happened to them in the ocean generally, there has been not a single instance of a stingray spiking someone to death in the heart, which is what happened to Irwin. The barbed end of the stingray's tail— over which, I'm told, rays have unholy power of control and accuracy; they kill tiny, tiny fish with it—passed directly in between two of Irwin's ribs and into his left ventricle. He stood up, pulled it out, and died. There was video of this, but the Irwin family has destroyed it. In the weeks following, Australians began slaughtering rays in the coastal waters. Police and beachcombers were finding mangled carcasses. But Michael Hornby, director of Irwin's Wildlife Warrior fund, issued a statement disavowing these acts and making clear that it would "not accept and not stand for anyone who's taken a form of retribution" on the rays.

Freaky things happen all the time in the world. I suppose everything has to happen for the first time at some point. Which is what you told yourself about the Irwin story. We'd gone three hundred years without an incident like this; if we could go three hundred more, we'd be all right. Clear snorkels.

As it was, we went six weeks. On October 19, 2006, in the waters off Boca Raton, Florida, a man named James Bertakis was boating with a family friend when a giant stingray leapt out of the water and into his lap. It's important to visualize this correctly. The animal landed on his actual lap, with

Bertakis in a sitting position, empty-handed—he had no rod—and the ray landed facing him, so they were eye to eye. This scene was described in some detail by the woman present. Bertakis and the ray were staring at each other, and it was flexing its tail. And then, bang. Up over its body and directly into the heart muscle, the heart flesh, inches deep.

Reporters immediately asked the internationally regarded marine biologists at the University of Miami if there could be any connection, but Dr. Bob Cowen, the researcher put forward as spokesperson by the department, responded that he could "not imagine any connection" and that the attacks were "just two really unusual situations."

"Except not," said Livengood.

We were sitting now, and I'd just read off that skeptical quotation, along with several others, in order to suggest—politely, I hoped—that the position held by those in his profession who could be called mainstream is that what may seem like an evolution in global animal behavior is really just an increase in media attention, or a string of coincidences that get stitched together on the Internet, or most charitably, an increase in the exposure of individual human beings to undomesticated animals, as our habitats expand and the animals become more desperate for food sources, more willing to venture out.

"What do you mean, 'Except not'?" I asked.

"Except they weren't unusual."

I assumed, of course, that he meant there'd been other barb-to-heart ray attacks, and was prepared to ask if he'd share the data.

"Rays? No," he said. "Or at least those are the only two

we've seen. But everything else . . ." He looked up into the corner with his head tilted as if I'd told him to pose for a picture that way. Then he popped to his feet.

"You want to see our file?" he asked. He'd wandered over to another, larger computer in the corner of his office and was messing around on it.

I'd already shown him my file, when we first sat down. Mine was in a manila folder. It contained cutouts and print-outs of all the articles I'd archived in the preceding year plus. Most of them I'd e-mailed first to friends, with little jokey subject headers along the lines of Gird Thyself. It was one of the lucky recipients who replied, after the thirtieth or forti-eth message, "Did you know there's actually a guy who be-lieves this is happening?" When I wrote back saying, "Yes: myself," he sent another message, saying, "Right, but this guy studies animals."

When I showed Livengood my folder, he gave out a sin-gle loud laugh, and said, "That's what we get in a week, since people found out about us."

I won't play dumb with you—I already knew, by this point, that by "us" Livengood meant not him and his colleagues but him and a bunch of isolated obsessives—bloggers and amateur naturalists and sci-fi people dizzy with their first taste of contrarian legitimacy and also, I suppose, people like me who'd become helplessly fixated for no honorable reason on a cabalistic pattern in the news. This "us," if it's even an "us," doesn't have a good acronym yet and hasn't given any papers at conferences or generated much of a media profile at all, really, apart from a few stray "opposing point of view" quotes in wire-service articles like the ones I'd gathered.

"Check this out," Livengood said, sliding his chair to the side to make room for me. On the screen was a large parti-color map of the world, in a circular shape like an old navigational map. The landmasses and coastlines were thickly riddled here and there with tiny black dots, about pencil-tip size. There were maybe twenty-five stray black dots on the open seas. Livengood said—breezily, like someone giving an office tour to the new guy—"Those are all confirmed, and most of those are from the past six years."

"What are they, exactly?"

"Start clicking on them!" he said, like he'd been wondering when I'd get to this.

I sat there for at least half an hour. At one point, Livengood got up and went off down the hall. It was true that the sheaf of articles I'd been so proud of was a Cracker Jack flipbook in comparison with what Livengood and his various TAs had collected. I should say that for an item to make his list, it must stand up to the admittedly soft but at least not nonexistent test of being (a) not a hoax—that is, independently verifiable as an incident through follow-up research—and (b) not the result of some obvious confusion. I invite you to verify these things as well, through Google or LexisNexis or in a few cases an article in *Animal Behavior Abstracts* (a complete-looking set of which sat on the shelves behind Livengood's desk); you won't find them in the *Weekly World News*, either, but on the BBC website, the AP, *Science*, and *Nature*, places that have a vested interest in not getting fooled. Anyway, I assure you I don't know enough about even the normal goings-on in the animal kingdom to fabricate this many anomalies.

I figured out that some of the little dots, when you clicked on them, led to multiple incidents, signifying vectors of

activity, usually but not always confined to a single specie.
There are four small English seaport towns, for instance,
where various seabirds have started targeting people. A swan
came out of the water there and took a dog under. Indeed,
when measured in actual numbers, birds may be the single
most active species in terms of manifesting whatever lies beneath this shift. In Boston, for the past few years, there's
been what can only be called an ongoing siege of wild tur-
keys. Children and old people getting attacked. In Sonoma
County, California, the chicken population not long ago
carried out "a flurry of attacks on neighborhood children."
The mother of one of the victims told a reporter, "It's not
charming when you have to see your baby attacked . . . seeing the blood going down his face and seeing him screaming . . . I can't sleep at night."

A fair share of the new violence is animal-on-animal.
Needless to say, it garners less attention in the media. In the
Polish village of Stubienko, in June 2000 (one of the earlier
blips in Livengood's collection), the storks went crazy and
started slaughtering chickens, hundreds of them. (There
were, I'm seeing only now, additional reports of "sporadic attacks on humans" at the time.) Observers were "at a loss to
explain the aberrant behavior."

You see what I mean, I hope, about there being something *off* in these stories. The storks started slaughtering the
chickens.

Much of the intra-animal violence seems to suggest sheer
madness. Chimps have repeatedly been documented engaging in "rape, wife beating, murder, and infanticide." Elephants
on the African savanna have been raping rhinoceroses,
something that is evidently just as startling to zoologists as
to the layperson.

Indeed, if you've paid attention to one particular facet of this story as it's unfolded, it's probably the work of Gay Bradshaw, a psychologist and environmental scientist who's been tracking the accelerated mental degeneration of elephant populations in severely destabilized areas of Africa and Asia. She's an extremely well-regarded researcher whose work is adding up to maybe the most persuasive proof yet mounted that the overlap between our psyches and those of the more developed animals has been massively underestimated when it comes to affection, suffering, stress, and we don't even know what areas. That's how I understand her work, at any rate. Earlier this year, a major magazine brought her to national attention, and she has a book deal, and to make a long story short, she declined an interview, for which I blame her not even slightly; if I were an internationally respected animal scientist, I'd drive cold muddy hours out of my way to avoid even a Rumsfeld-and-Saddam-style meeting with Marc Livengood, not that I don't personally find him heroic. Nonetheless there is perhaps more of a kinship between their respective working theses than either would care to admit. (Livengood regards Bradshaw with a bit of jealousy and eyerolling, I'm sure you'll be shocked to learn.)

Bradshaw's focus doesn't stray onto the animal-on-human part of the elephant crackup—nonetheless, they are killing us, too, in numbers never imagined. More than a thousand victims in less than a decade. Forty-four Nigerian communities "erased" by rampaging elephants in a single migratory season. Some of the incidents have been quite spectacular, with multiple animals working in concert (as opposed to isolated or "rogue" males, which frequently act up); they're storming through neighborhoods, turning on crowds. If you've ever seen an elephant attack a human being, it's very personal-looking anyway. They keep going after you when you're down. And at first, at least, you're conscious, while they basically knock the bejeezus out of you with their trunks and then stomp you into the earth. In one place, the animals first rampaged, clearing the town, then broke into unprotected casks of locally brewed rice beer, then hurled themselves against electrified fences and died. Bradshaw writes, "Some biologists think that increased elephant aggression might comprise, in part, revenge against humans for accidental or deliberate elephant deaths." Not to be outdone, "angry villagers" are poisoning to death an average of twenty elephants each year, according to *The New York Times*.

As suggested by the tortured-ray carcasses that washed up in the wake of the Irwin killing, swift acts of human retaliation have not infrequently followed the more dramatic of the late attacks. In Salt Springs, Florida, where gators went berserk a year and a half ago and killed three women in a week, the citizens "declared war on alligators." That's how one busy trapper described it. "People are really going crazy," he said. In other cases, cooler heads have prevailed and more peaceful measures have been adopted. One example: in Bombay, earlier this year, a pack of leopards entered the town—just sauntered out of the forest at the heart of that city—and assassinated a total of twenty-two people. J. C. Daniel, an environmentalist who has monitored the wildlife in that forest for forty years, said, "We have to study why the animal is coming out. It never came out before." But the people responded creatively. In hopes of calming the beasts—and with a gesture that had weird overtones of sacrificial offerings to assuage angry cat gods—officials in the area are releasing hundreds and hundreds of little pigs and rabbits into the forest. (2 Kings 17:25: "And when they began to dwell there, they feared not the Lord: and the Lord sent lions among them, which killed them.")

In China it's the pets that are changing. The AP reported, "About 90,000 people in Beijing have been attacked by dogs and cats in the first six months of this year, up almost 34 percent for the same period last year, the government said." In America, where animals have perhaps a freer recourse to weapons, at least four people have been shot by their dogs in the past two years. One incident involved a stun gun. One reportedly took place while the animal was being beaten, its owner hoped to death. That killing, then, could accurately be described as self-defense. (In a third incident, in Memphis, a dog shot its owner in the back while the man was arguing with his girlfriend—this one may have been accidental.)

A pack of two hundred dogs descended out of the mountains—this was in Albania—ran straight into the middle of the town of Mamurras, and just started going after people, old people, young people, "dragging them to the ground and inflicting serious wounds." One witness spoke of a "clearly identifiable leader." (Lest we assume this to be a seasonal occurrence in Albania, the town's mayor, Anton Frroku, stated, "Even in the movies, I have never seen a horde of two hundred stray dogs from the mountains attacking people in the middle of a town.")

"Clearly identifiable leader": Elsewhere, too, there are suggestions of organization, cooperation. In India one of the country's busiest highways has been repeatedly taken over and brought to a standstill by what the BBC has described as "troops" of "monkey raiders," two thousand at a time. "We have already seen that new troops have entered the area in recent weeks," a local official tells the BBC. There was talk of "relocating" them. In Britain, where the rat population has increased by 40 percent in the last decade, and old people are saying they haven't seen anything like it since the Blitz, scientists have pinned the otherwise inexplicable surge on the fact that the rats "have been learning from other rats how to avoid the poisons." Again, look at these numbers. We're consistently seeing increases not of 4 or 5 percent but on the order of 40, 50 percent.

In at least one situation, clearly discernible technological innovation has entered the picture. A community of chimpanzees living on the edges of the savanna in Senegal has learned to fashion and use spears, which they sharpen with their teeth. These are chimps we've been observing for two hundred years; they have never used spears. Now they've begun spiking little bush babies with them. The bush babies hide in hollow trees. The chimps do a sort of frog-gigging number on them and pull them out like fondue. Within a year of the first chimp having been observed using a weapon this way, nine others had caught on and were recorded doing it in a total of twenty-two observed instances, suggesting that at least at the simian level these fairly radical behavioral changes are taking place within the span of a single generation.

The science behind all this is, you might say, disturbingly fundamental. As the planet warms, evolution speeds. We've known this for a long time. You learn it in college biology. Things evolve faster nearer the equator. Heat speeds up molecular activity. You have a population of squid—it divides. One branch hangs out up by Alaska, the other goes down to the coast of Peru. Go and visit them fifty thousand years later. The group up by Alaska is slowly subdividing into two species. The one down by Peru has turned into twenty-six species and is no longer even recognizable. Well, these days the whole planet is experiencing that effect. More heat, more light. The animals are doing things differently; they're showing up places they're not supposed to go, sleeping at different times, eating different things. Talk with any field-worker and it's a truism that the guidebooks are becoming obsolete at ten times the speed. As a researcher told the BBC in 2001, "There is a genetic change in their response to daylight. We can detect this change over as short a time period as five years. Evolution is happening and it is happening very fast." And he was talking only about a particular species of mosquito. Dr. Christina Holzapfel, at the University of Oregon in Eugene, has been watching changes *among* Canadian red squirrels. "Phenotypic plasticity is not the whole story," she told *Science*. "Studies show," a source quoted her as saying, "that over the past several decades, rapid climate change has led to heritable, genetic changes in animal populations." Most recently a piece in *Smithsonian* stated, "Lately there has been evidence that plants and animals are changing much faster."

What this means is that we picked a bad time to have all the animals enraged at us, since just at the moment when their disposition might be expected to turn, they happen to be evolving like crazy.

What stuck out above all else, as I clicked through Livengood's dots, was the same tendency that had presented itself when I was still just idly following news items on the Internet, namely the extraordinary number of "first time" attacks. That is, not simply unprecedented types of attack, such as leopard packs going forth and killing in a crowded city, but rather pure cases of animals that have never shown a desire to kill human beings before, killing them.

It was only a couple of years ago, in an October 2006

posting on the website of the Institute for the Future—an "independent nonprofit research group" headquartered in the States, that puts its considerable budget toward working "with organizations of all kinds to help them make better, more informed decisions about the future"—that the first tentative red flag was raised on this whole issue, insofar as it marked the first time a group of nondismissible, intellectually clubbable types had gone so far, had been explicit:

"File this under the wildest of wildcards, but are the number of attacks by animals formerly thought to be relatively harmless or difficult to provoke on the rise? Are there other interesting statistics suggesting an increase in the number of attacks by animals that previously were not especially aggressive?"

Blogger and fellow seeker Alex Soojung-Kim Pang, there sure as hell are.

Attacks of dolphins on humans are noticeably up, with a particularly violent population repeatedly attacking dozens of swimmers off the coast of Cancún, killing at least two, with several more unexplained drownings that may have been "take under" incidents. Every marine biologist reached for comment after those confirmed attacks said the same thing: "There's no such thing as a fatal dolphin attack."

This news would be startling to Henri Le Lay, president of the Association of Fishermen and Yachtsmen at the port of Brézellec in Brittany, who spoke with reporters about "a psychotic dolphin," nicknamed Jean Floch, that has been going after fishermen in their boats. "He's like a mad dog," Le Lay said. "I don't want to see any widows or orphans. This could end badly."

Sea lions, too, are going after human beings for the first time. Not accidentally bumping into them but pursuing them through open water. In Alaska one jumped into a boat, knocked a fisherman overboard, and took him down. Sea lions are famous for fleeing any sort of conflict. Expert opinion? "Abnormal behavior."

Unlikely as it may sound, given the myth, in the history of the European occupation of North America there is but a single recorded fatal attack by a wild but healthy (that is, nonrabid, nonstarving) wolf on a human being. It happened in 2005, in Alaska. The guy went out to take a pee or maybe just to look at the stars. When they found him, he'd already been worked over by scavengers.

In Uganda and Tanzania, chimps "struggling to survive amid the destruction of their forest habitat are snatching and killing human babies." They've taken sixteen in the past seven years and had killed half of those before anyone found them. The eating of babies is "a recent development," said the article.

Click, click, click—they just kept coming. In Belarus the beavers have been attacking people ("first recorded attack [in that country's long history] of a beaver on a human"). This has happened again, in Lindesberg, Sweden, quite recently; a woman was hospitalized. The decidedly non-Swedish response of the townspeople, as reported by a city official? "Four of the beavers in the river have been shot, and the rest will be exterminated. Then the beaver house will be blown up to prevent other families from taking it over." Not comforting is a related report out of Washington, D.C., that states, "Beavers are expanding rapidly into cities."

For every account that seemed a little far-fetched and made me think a few qualifying facts must have been left out, there'd be another that, while admittedly bizarre, had the instant ring of stuff you wouldn't make up, like the jogger in southeastern North Carolina who witnesses saw get surrounded on the boardwalk by a squadron of oversize male hermit crabs, which approached him, kung fu–style, with that one bulging claw forward, and appeared to attempt to drive him off a pier. And as always with cases like these, the quote from the zoologist comes around like a mantra: first recorded . . . not known to have occurred previously . . . relevant literature was searched but no prior instances retrieved . . . experts shocked . . . abnormal . . . unheard of . . .

When Livengood came back, I was six inches lower in the chair; I probably looked like a person whose mind had just been destroyed by a satanic video game.

"Still 'skeptically curious'?" Livengood said. (When we'd first spoken on the telephone, he'd asked me what my "take" was, and I'd replied, "Skeptically curious," which I'd intended to mean essentially nothing—but oh man, it stuck with him.)

I mumbled something. To which Livengood replied, with a sigh and a fake-bored tone, "Oh yeah. Something's happening." Then he bounced for a minute in his black office chair, tapping his fingertips together.

I said, "It's impossible."

Then he looked at me and said, as if not having heard me, "Hey! You need to go to Africa with me!"

We were en route to a dry, formerly nomadic region in the northeast of Kenya, about 350 miles northeast of Nairobi, just before you hit the Somali border, a place called Mandera, although Marc insisted on saying repeatedly that we were "going to ground zero."

In the year 2000—which Marc, displaying a certain stubborn lack of subtlety that I was beginning to see as not unrelated to his nonexistent status in the academic world, repeatedly referred to as "year zero"—there were two separate incidents within a single month's time, not far from each other, in villages occupying this area. Marc refers to them as "the battle site" and "the kill site."

He'd arranged for us to be met by a tall, extraordinarily upright young woman from Dakar named Sila Fall. Her hair was in braids, and she wore all white with a blue bandanna around her neck. She was the UNICEF liaison for this district. She took us down a road to a village; it looked more like a camp. But the people here were healthy. UNICEF was overseeing the digging of a new well. They asked us to sit and watch a sort of play, performed in Kikamba. I could just make out the plot. One man was sick; he was the patient. Another man came, the healer. They spoke to each other— that ancient bond. They danced.

We walked behind Sila Fall, who walked very fast. She showed us all the improvements UNICEF had made— though not so much with pride as with restlessness, as if to say, We've at least done this. The clinic. The school. "In 2000 it was not like this," she said. "In 2000, if it didn't get thrown from the back of an army truck, we didn't have it. We were dying."

"The woman lives here," she said, pointing but without stopping. "They say she is at her sister's today." Seconds later, in front of another, identical hut, we did stop. I saw now that Marc was manifesting excitement through physical agitation, moving from foot to foot and emitting little *herm* sounds. From the shaded interior of the hut materialized a middle-aged woman in a long skirt and T-shirt. Sila Fall spoke to her in Kikamba, she spoke to Sila Fall in Kikamba, then Sila Fall said to Marc in English, "She says that she welcomes you, she . . . knows who you are, and she will show you the place that you want to know about." This, then, was Kakenya Wamboi, or as Marc called her in e-mails to me, "the veteran."

It's known that in the spring of 2000, when the drought conditions were at their worst in this district, there occurred a two-hour pitched battle between monkeys and human beings over access to three newly arrived water tankers. As the four of us walked beyond the narrow outskirts of the village, about two hundred yards down an ovenishly hot road, Kakenya Wamboi, who participated in that event, was speaking through Sila Fall, answering Marc's extremely precise, prepared-sounding questions, telling Marc and me the story of the fight, how the human beings had rushed to draw water from the tankers, yet within seconds an entire troop of monkeys had appeared. They ranged themselves along the edges of the tankers. Others came from across the road. "They bit us and clawed at us. They threw stones at us from the top of the truck. My husband is dead, but until he died he had a mark on his forehead from where one of the stones cracked his skull. You don't know how strong they are! They struck ten people. Badly enough that we all ran off. The men went back with axes. The monkeys were drinking all of the water. My husband said that they could work the valves. The drivers were still in the trucks. They were scared. The men went at the monkeys with axes and had to kill eight of them before the rest ran off. The drivers would not stay in this village overnight as they usually do, so we had to draw all the water off in a rush; we didn't get it all before they started the trucks again. Some of what we got was in bad containers and spoiled, and the monkeys had already taken about a third of it. Of the people that died in that famine, most of them died that spring, and my husband always said the monkeys killed them, that the monkeys won that battle."

She mimed what I suppose was a monkey swinging an ax in victory.

At some point, Sila Fall interrupted her and said that we needed to go, because to reach the other place Marc wanted to see, we had to drive two hours, and we didn't want to be on that road after dark; it skirted the Somali border—she made a machine-gun sign—so we needed to say goodbye. Did Marc have any more questions?

"What sort of calls were they doing during the attack? What sounds were they making? Or weren't they making sounds?"

Kakenya Wamboi said that they were chattering the entire time. Not screaming. More like talking. Then she said something else. Sila Fall said, "She says that she is glad to meet you and help you and that you see that she is very poor, you see her house, and she knows you are good people, and that she hopes you will help her." To his credit, Marc looked at me.

Knowing Marc Livengood a little now, you may appreciate the profundity of the Livengood silence during this car ride with Sila Fall. The man was contemplating some heavy thoughts. Sila Fall drove and talked, mostly about a period of years she spent in the United States. I was dying to ask her if she knew why Livengood was here or what it was that Livengood believed, but could neither do this in front of Marc nor figure a way to get them apart. Finally, the van swerved and slowed and through the seat we could feel the tires meeting the sudden resistance of sand. We got out and started to walk. I asked Sila Fall, "Have you seen this place?"

She nodded. "I grew up here."

We walked for twenty minutes through a gap in a low sandstone formation. We came to what must have been the remnant of a sinkhole, a cavity in the earth the shape of an upside-down yarn cone. At the bottom was a pool of water. "Healthy water," Sila Fall said. There was one spot along the rim of the hole where you could slide and clamber down. "I wasn't here in 2000," Sila Fall said, "but if it was as dry as they say, there was only a puddle down there. It was probably the only water for miles."

In late February of that year, a herder named Ali Adam Hussein slid down to that puddle, probably not to slake his own thirst but to gather a little water for his cows. He looked up and saw several monkeys looking down at him. Presumably, he went to go for his weapon. The monkeys responded by lifting several stones and hurling them directly at his head. He died hours later of what a nurse back in Mandera, where we'd just come from, described simply as "severe head injuries."

Marc did not ask Sila Fall's permission before he himself skidded down into the deep natural watering hole. Both Sila Fall and I watched him, somewhat stunned. He seemed to have acted on a sudden impulse. At the bottom, however, he immediately displayed purpose. He stood with his hip cocked, his ponytail jutting out through the back of his khaki Centerbrook University cap, grinning up at me through his beard. I said, "Tell me what you're thinking."

"I'm standing where he stood, John." Marc Livengood is a man who likes to say your name at the end of sentences when he talks to you.

"And what does that mean?" I said. (These were not real questions; he just sometimes liked to force me to go through the whole production of baiting him, and I'd adapted to it.)

"What does it mean?" he said. "It means I'm standing where the First Victim stood." He said the two words in such a way that I feel I have to capitalize the first letter of each. "It means we are all three standing on the site of an incident unknown to the annals of natural science, and it is unstudied. You heard the same stories I heard today; you tell me what that means." Then he took pictures for forty minutes.

Able at last to converse with Sila Fall somewhat normally, I asked her, "Do you know why he's here?"

"He's a scientist," she said.

"Specifically, I mean? You don't? Specifically, he believes that the animals are turning on us, that we're about to experience a war of animals on human beings, and that it's going to begin here. That it may already have begun here."

"Do you believe that?" she asked.

"I don't think so," I said. I didn't know how to tell her that she didn't need to be polite with me. She was there in a professional capacity. I suppose I was, too, in some deformed way. Really, it was stupid of me to be accosting her. But I'd been listening to Marc nonstop since we'd left the airport in Nairobi, and she seemed very adjusted.

"Most people would probably think he's insane," I said.

Sila Fall shrugged her shoulders. "It's possible," she said.

"Possible that he's insane or that there's about to be an animal-human war?"

She shrugged her shoulders again.

———

The story runs into obstacles here, because shortly after we arrived back in the States, Marc Livengood was fired from Centerbrook. Neither he nor anybody at the school will talk about it except to confirm that he's suing. From someone in the town who shall remain unidentified, I learned that he's living with his father, a retired engineer, in Dayton, or was as of two months before. The one time I got him to return a phone call and was able to ask him what had happened, he replied, in an almost boastful tone, "John, when the story of this comes out, you . . . Let's just say Marc Livengood is not going to be what's disgraced by this. Okay?" He refused to clarify that and hung up within maybe half a minute, sounding disgusted. A guy in the tech department at the school, whom I'd called in a Hail Mary way, told me he'd heard his boss talking about it on the telephone and that it was all "computer-related."

Needless to say, it's been challenging, with Livengood underground, to push the narrative forward. I couldn't get anybody else in the field to say anything about him, because nobody really knows anything about him; it had always just been an Internet thing. Even his colleagues at the school thought he was involved, as his chair put it to me, in "a kind of curatorial project." He'd once been the subject of a profile in a magazine called *Varmint Masters*, published out of Birmingham, Alabama. Once more, I invite you to research this. It's a real magazine. And these people have radically redefined the definition of the word *varmint*. They hunt feral moose, things like that. Now and then, some country, say Australia, will have a problem with an out-of-control population of some invasive species, camels in one case, and these varmint masters will travel from the four corners with their bunker-busting rifles and such. As of this writing, I haven't been able to find a copy of the Livengood issue, even on eBay, and cannot find contact info for the publisher in Birmingham. Is it possible that Livengood felt some sort of bond with a subpopulation of men who are working to become ever more expert hunters of animals not normally thought of as prey? Now there was no one to answer these and other questions. I got one guy, a marine biologist at a university on the East Coast—he asked me to name neither him nor the school—who remembered Livengood from a conference. He said, "I actually thought some of what he was talking about was pretty interesting, but back then it was just about predatory patterns, dietary disturbances. It sounds like maybe he had some kind of breakdown or something. I mean, I'm hearing about it from you."

I was hearing about it from Livengood. We were all supposed to hear it from him, and may yet. That's in the future, which, as I think we've established, is fairly sketchy terrain to prance out onto without a sure hand to guide you. I present this essay, with its mere sliver of the material Livengood gathered, with its shadow of an approximation of the boldness of thought he would bring to bear on it, as a testament. I think about him every time I see another animal story in the news. The cat at the nursing home in Rhode Island that was able to predict which patients were about to die and would sit on their beds until they'd expired? Marc Livengood has thoughts on that, be assured.

Pet loyalty, in fact, was a recurrent subject of his monologue on our last night together in Nairobi. Which eons of their training would prove genetically more persuasive when, for instance, the dogs were asked by the wolves to choose? Would they turn on us or defend us? Us and them, that's what it would come down to.

That night we sat at an uncomfortably tiny table at an open-air place about a mile from the airport. He talked. I drank with my left hand, my pencil hand flying. He spoke of how it would go, how it would really begin, stopping after every third or fourth sentence to hold up his hands in a "stop" gesture and say, "Speculation! Speculation!"

He conjured up one of the eeriest Armageddons I've ever heard described: existence on a planet that has itself become treacherous. A rapidly approaching period of uncertainty and terror, waves of increased attacks from all over the bio-terrain, creatures coming up from the deep oceans to paralyze shipping, possibly at the sonic command of the dolphins. The forests will no longer be a place to camp. Troops of wildcats, deer, and moose. Ever seen hikers get stomped by a moose? It's like watching cans go through a can cruncher.

For a while, everyone will cling to the hope that it's some kind of phase, and all sorts of comforting theories will be peddled: sunspots, magnetism in the earth's core, a different explanation every week, but always something to suggest that "the power will come back on," as Livengood liked to say.

"You have to understand," he told me, "these are normal biological systems functioning. We are a threat to these animals. They're just doing what nature has designed them to do. In that sense, there's nothing revolutionary at all about what I'm arguing. You could even say there's nothing new about my work. Where it gets interesting is when you remember that we're a different kind of threat, right? We're presenting them with the prospect of more or less total global domination by a single species. The lower orders haven't seen this since the dinosaurs. And keep in mind they were undergoing a period of accelerated evolution then, too. We always make it that the dinosaurs died, then mammals came forward. Why not at least entertain the idea that the mammals played a role?"

"You mean that they took over?"

"Eh . . ." he said. "Intentionality is tricky with natural selection."

We were quiet for a minute, sipping our tea.

"And keep in mind," Marc continued, "that there may be at this moment something like forty dolphins living in the open seas, escapees from marine defense programs. We don't know what they're trained to do. Carry explosives? Kill divers? I'm looking for them to emerge in some sort of overt leadership capacity before 2010. It's the chimps on land, the dolphins in the seas. We can assume they're working out some kind of mutually intelligible signal system now, most likely on the West African coast."

I asked him about the whole interspecies-cooperation thing, which has always and to some degree still does strike me as sheer sci-fi.

"Do you know Kropotkin's *Mutual Aid*?" he asked, and then, when he saw my blank look, added, "Read it. The book's been of print for probably a hundred years, but you should read it. He documented hundreds of instances of this—separate species helping one another. Kropotkin's finding was if two or more species are exposed to a shared threat, we will also see shared defense. The only question concerns the mechanism."

"What's it all going to look like?" This was my question.

"Unrecognizable," he said. "People moving about in packs. Depopulation. We don't know how far down the chain this realignment of animal consciousness is going to travel, for precisely the reason that we don't how far down consciousness penetrates. The insects—will they be involved?

The rodent classes? The reptiles? You're just making arm-chair guesses at that point."

I asked him which animal he was most worried about.

"That's hard," he answered. "I think about the dolphins, not because of their lethality—though it's consistently underestimated—but because I think they understand best, of all the species, what damage we've done to the planet. They get the immensity of it. The other animals are responding to sudden infusions of hormones and little instinct triggers, but I believe that the dolphins are capable of hatred and that their hatred of us is essentially bottomless.

"Then, if you're talking scariest land animal to me, you might want to list the bear. Or rather, a combined chimp-and-bear onslaught, with a sort of Master Blaster power dynamic between chimps and bears. My God, bears can hurt you when they have a mind. Takes ten shots to stop one, routinely. Of course, by then we'll be firing on them with bazookas and whatnot. Hunting codes will be gone. Still, fighting them is going to be the closest thing to fighting a human army. I fear the bears. Definitely, they know how to get into houses and cars. A species-wide rampage will be just . . .

"Fuck, man!" he said, with a sudden dazed smile. "Part of keeping going in a professional capacity for me is keeping my mind off of stuff like that."

He adjusted his glasses and looked around.

"Think about it like this," he said. "In the early eighteenth century, there were massive combined populations of enslaved blacks, embattled Indians, and unhappy poor-white servants living in North America. Added up, a colossal majority. If at any moment those groups had truly woken up to the nature of their plight, which is to say the commonality of their plight, and identified the cause as the agenda of the colonial ruling class, ours would not now be a mainly European continent, genetically speaking.

"The animals are making the same discovery about themselves," he said. "And I don't think they'll squander it."

"So you would say bears are scarier than dolphins in the end?" I asked him.

"You want scariest?" he said. "Scariest is not the animals we know about. It's the animals we don't know about. Have you ever seen the statistics on estimated unknown species globally? We don't know half the crap that's alive on this planet, John. And I mean down at the very bottom of the ocean, in the Marianas Trench . . . that's an undiscovered planet, in terms of what's down there. And who knows what size those animals are, what they're capable of? Well, the animals may know. They may know what's down there, and they may know how to communicate with it.

"Have you ever heard the big Bloop?" he asked. "You should look it up." He was sick of telling me things. He started looking around for the check.

I did look it up when I got home. Six years ago one of the navy's spy microphones, a thing they had hanging way down in the ocean to listen for Soviet submarines, picked up the sound of something alive—its voiceprint made that clear, that it belonged to something biological—only, in order to make a sound this large, the animal would have needed to be vastly larger than any animal we know about. It left a mark on the seismograph something like what a small undersea tectonic event would have done. Microphones three thousand miles apart both captured it. You should look it up.

———

Have fear, that's what Marc Livengood taught me. What he teaches us. And if I've in any way satisfied the expectations of this assignment, it's in coming away with that drop of distilled realism: You want to know what to be afraid of in the next fifty years? Everything that walks and crawls, friends. Everything that moves. Because it hates us. "Why do they hate us?" Remember that? How quaint it already seems, when you think we were so recently asking that question about one another! And yet perhaps the answers are the same; maybe we can apply the lessons of the one to the other. They hate us because they can't be us. Can't have our thumbs, our brains, our music, our beautiful flowing hair. Can't have it can't have it can't have it. And right now, sure, I say that I feel bad about that. But in the moment, in the moment when I'm letting explosive tracer rounds erupt from the mouth of my firemaker, just hosing metal right into the faces of a bunch of screaming giant eagles as they come for my daughter—and my cats, who will never betray me, not ever, or who perhaps have betrayed me and are scratching the hell out of my back while I struggle to aim—will I be thinking, "Ah, too bad, wish we hadn't done you like that"? Don't kid yourselves.

We gave them so much. That's what galls me. What did they have before us? What did they do? We gave them jobs, we put them on television, we cried for their losses. It seems their idea of repayment is the tooth and the claw. I don't think we need them. Everything we need we can make from corn.

Not that I don't hold out hope. If you and I are here in a half century, I hope we'll be celebrating the end of this war. I hope we'll be telling with highest zest, again and again till our great-grandchildren are sick of it, the story of the day of the accord, when we knew it was over. Of little Bindi, a woman now, wind in her face, her feminine beauty still touched by a bit of *Mad Max* dog-boy caninity, as she was escorted out through the waves between white flags to a meeting with Dolphin Leader, where they brokered a détente in the chirpy language Steve had just finished teaching her when he got spiked. We will promise to live in greater harmony with Gaia.

But I'm not sure we'll ever say the world is *ours* again, not sure we'll ever really feel at home here again. That may be for the best. Being brave, after all, means saying in every situation, "I'll comport myself as I think honorable, no matter the risk and no matter what the voice of frowning power has to say about it." That's the kind of thinking that'll get you raped by a rhino.

Takeaway message? Let's be proactive. Starting with a subscription to *Varmint Masters*. We've been working with this settled agriculture for more than ten thousand years. What it's gotten us is a poisoned planet and a bunch of furious, mentally retarded beings with teeth and claws and tusks and tentacles and retractable poisoned darts and venom that they can spit and noses so strong they lift tanks and on and on and on, and what do we have? What were we given in this fight? Opposable thumbs. That's pretty weak, I'm sorry. But guess what? Guess what, *animales*? We did something with those thumbs. We built these weapons. With them we are going to fire on you.

Big parts of this piece I made up. I didn't want to say that, but the editors are making me, because of certain scandals in the past with made-up stories, and because they want to distance themselves from me. Fine.

I made up Marc Livengood. I made up the trip to Nairobi. But I didn't make up the two incidents in Kenya, the battles of monkeys and men and the murder. I did not fabricate a single one of the animal-related facts or stories, the incidents. There's even a real-life guy on the Internet whom I could have used in place of the made-up Marc, but that got messy, because he wanted money, and anyway, he seemed insane.

Editor's note: Gay Bradshaw, Christina Holzapfel, and everyone at the Institute for the Future and the Future of Humanity Institute at Oxford University are serious scholars and researchers who had nothing to do with this story and have never discussed animal violence with the author, much less endorsed any of his assertions, nor would they, presumably.

Author's note: Since this article was first published, they've discovered a hot-pink millipede that can shoot clouds of cyanide from its body. There's a chimp on a preserve in Indiana that's having full-on conversations with its owner. Dolphins have been seen using tools—so far, only for digging. An unprecedented uprising of komodo dragons in Indonesia has led to the death of a fisherman. *The New York Times* just reported that human hospital admissions for dog bites are on the rise. Not slightly but by over 40 percent. Anne Elixhauser, a senior research scientist with the Agency for Healthcare Research and Quality, is quoted as saying, "It's really kind of frightening, and unfortunately, we're at a loss to explain it."

PEYTON'S PLACE

Practically every day, cars stop in front of our house, and people get out to take pictures of it, and of us—me and my wife and daughter—if we happen to be outside. Or they'll take one of Tony, who cuts the whole neighborhood's grass. Tony loves it. He poses for them, with his rake and lawn bags, grinning, one arm thrown wide as if to say, "All this, my friends." I've told him several times to start charging, but he won't even hear it. He does it, he says, because it makes him feel famous. Sometimes it's only one car. Other times it's eight or nine in a day. It depends what time of year it is, and what's happening on the Internet. Once there was an event of some kind in town, and we got more than twenty. I go for long stretches when I forget it's even happening. I really don't see them, since I don't leave the house that much, and they're always quiet, they never make trouble. But a month ago my new neighbor, Nicholas, who just moved in next door, came over to introduce himself. He's a tall thin guy in his fifties, glasses and a white beard. Very nice, very sociable. Before he left, he said, "Can I ask you something? Have you noticed that people are always taking pictures of your house?"

Yeah, I said—pressing PLAY on my spiel—it's silly, I know, but our house used to be on TV, not anymore, those people are fans . . . Isn't that funny?

"I mean, it is constant," he said.

I know! I said. Hope it doesn't bother you. Tell me if it ever gets annoying.

"No, no, I don't mind," he said. "They're always polite. They almost seem embarrassed."

Well, tell me if that changes, I said.

"Okay," he said. "I just can't believe how many there are."

Nicholas and I have had some version of that conversation three times, one for every week he's lived next door. Each time I've wanted to tell him it's going to end, except that I don't know if it will. It may increase.

My brother-in-law sells trailers in the Arizona desert—indeed he professes to "have the trailer game in a chokehold" in that part of the world. Not long ago he told me about the Stamp. He had a boss whose office was across from his in the trailer they worked out of. They sold trailers from a trailer. The boss had a huge, specially made rubber stamp on his desk that read APPROVED. Whenever things were getting tense in my brother-in-law's office, when the boss could hear that negotiations were becoming sticky, usually on the matter of the prospective buyer's gaining loan approval, he would saunter in with the Stamp. Saunter doesn't describe his walk, which my brother-in-law demonstrated. The boss was a little guy, and his legs sort of wheeled out from his body as he walked, like something you'd associate with a degenerative hip condition. He'd come wheeling up to the desk like that and *bam* bring down the Stamp on the application, AP-PROVED, and wheel away, leaving the buyers stunned and, as it dawned on them, delighted. "You understand," my brother-in-law said, "a lot of the people I was selling to were gypsies. As in, literal gypsies. They didn't have mailing addresses."

The story goes some way toward explaining how my wife and I got permission from a bank to buy a giant brick neo-colonial house—also how the world economy went into free fall, but that's for another time and a writer with nothing to do but an enormous amount of research. My wife was eight months pregnant, and we lived in a one-bedroom apart-ment, the converted ground floor of an antebellum house, on a noisy street downtown, with an eccentric upstairs neigh-bor, Keef, from Leland, who told me that I was a rich man—that's how he put it, "Y'er a rich man, ain't ye?"—who told us that he was going to shoot his daughter's boyfriend with an ultra-accurate sniper rifle he owned, for filling his daughter full of drugs, "shoot him below the knee," he said, "that way they caint git ye with intent to kill." Keef had been a low-level white supremacist and still bore a few unfortunate tat-toos but told us he'd lost his racism when, on a cruise in the Bahamas, he'd saved a drowning black boy's life, in the on-ship pool, and by this conversion experience "came to love some blacks." He later fell off a two-story painting ladder and broke all his bones. A fascinating man, but not the sort I wanted my daughter having unlimited exposure to in her formative years. Not my angel. We entered nesting panic. We wanted big and solid. We wanted Greatest Generation, but their parents, even greater. We found it. It had a sleeping porch, and a shiplike attic where I in my dotage would pull objects from a trunk and tell their histories to little ones. We asked for the money, and in some office, somebody's boss came forward with the Stamp.

Around the time it became clear that we'd gotten ahead of ourselves financially—and thinking back, that was a seismic twinge in advance of the market meltdown, a message from the bowels that people like the guy with four cell phones and a Jersey accent working out of a storage unit in Charlotte, who'd loaned us the money, probably shouldn't have been loaning hundreds of thousands of dollars to people like me, not that "magazine writer" isn't right there behind civil servant on the job-security pyramid—that was when we remembered something our buyer's agent, Andy, had said, something about a TV show that might want to use the house, and somebody might be calling us. We had written it down. A guy named Greg.

Often I think of Greg. What an amazing guy. Truly amazing, as in he brought us into a maze. We only ever saw him once. I've never seen him since. And this is a small town— you see people. It was like they flew him in for this meeting. He was a heavy guy in a tentlike Hawaiian shirt. Goatee, sunglasses. Did he tell me he played rugby or did he look exactly like someone I knew who played rugby? He sat across from us at our kitchen table, a thirteen-foot dark wood table that purportedly came in pieces from a Norwegian farmhouse, relic of nesting panic (long table, order). Greg sat across from us. He explained that they'd mostly be using only the front two rooms of the house. This was the place they mainly shot. The rest of our character's house had been re-created on a set, and the transitions would be made seamless in editing.

He laid out the deal they'd struck with the previous owners. We move you into a Hilton. Meals and per diem. We put everything back the way it was. We take Polaroids of your bookshelves to make sure we've put the books in order. That's how thorough we are. We even pay people to come in afterward and clean up. The house looks better than you left it. We'll pay you $—— for an exterior shoot, $—— for interiors.

The combined amount equaled our mortgage.

Yes, I think we can work something out.

"The front two rooms"—that phrase, in particular, we heard repeated: it has a poetic density to it, like "cellar door," so I remember. The front two rooms.

Maroon minivan, Greg gone.

A lot of movies and TV shows are shot here, in our adopted coastal hometown of Wilmington, North Carolina—Wilmywood. It started when the late Frank Capra, Jr., came here to make *Firestarter* in the early eighties. He liked the place and stayed, and an industry evolved around him. Dennis Hopper bought property. Now half the kids who wait on you downtown are extras, or want to be actors. You'll be in Target and realize you're in line behind Val Kilmer. We have studios and a film school, and we're known in the business for our exceptionally wide variety of locations. You can be doing beachy beachy, and suddenly go leafy established suburb, go country hayride, then nighttime happening street, pretty much whatever.

For the last several years, the big ticket in town has been the teen melodrama *One Tree Hill*, which was on the WB and is now on the CW Network. Don't let the off brands fool

.., though, a surprising number of people watch it, maybe even you, for all I know. It's one of the worst TV shows ever made, and I seriously do not mean that as an insult. It's bad in the way that Mexican TV is bad, superstylized bad. Good bad. Indeed, there are times when the particular campiness of its badness, although I can sense its presence, is in fact beyond me, beyond my frequency, like with that beep you play on the Internet that only kids can hear. Too many of my camp-receptor cells have died. Possibly *One Tree Hill* is a work of genius. Certainly it is about to go nine seasons, strongly suggesting that the mother of its creator, Mark Schwahn, did not give birth to any idiots, or if she did those people are Schwahn's siblings.

The *One Tree* character who supposedly lived in our house was Peyton, played by one of the stars, Hilarie Burton, a striking bone-thin blonde. Think coppery curls. I'd seen her on MTV right at the moment when I was first feeling too old to watch MTV. Superfriendly when we met her—superfriendly always. Hilarie has a golden reputation in Wilmington. She's one of the cast members who've made the place home, and she gets involved in local things. When we met, she gave us hugs, complimented the house, thanked us for letting them use it. She disarmed us—good manners had not been what we'd expected.

I don't know how our house became known as a place to shoot. It's not all that special. I think it's sort of immediately sturdy-looking—guys who come here to fix things invariably remark on "how much wood they used on this place"—in a way that's visually useful to a director who wants to say Big Brick House in as little time and with as few subtleties as possible. The studio has scouts who drive around looking for these things. And this is an interesting neighborhood. I learned from a local historian that it was created as a sort of colony by Christian Scientists in the 1920s. Lolita's house from *Lolita*—the Jeremy Irons version—is down the street (it's really pretty). One of the crew guys who came to paint our living room—a short, supermuscular dude with a biker's mustache and cap, who knew a lot of Wilmington film trivia—told me that our house was in *Blue Velvet*, which David Lynch made here. I looked it up. Sure enough. Just for a few seconds. During the car-chase scene, when Jeffrey thinks he's being trailed by psychotic Frank (in Dennis Hopper's immortal performance), but then is relieved to find it's only chucklehead Mike, the moment when the hub cap comes off and goes rolling down the street like a toy hoop (an unintended effect that Lynch reportedly loved in editing, causing him to linger on that moment—if you watch it you can see that the beat is held unusually long, compared with what you'd normally do on a curb-scraping turn, namely cut it off to emphasize speed), that happens in front of our house. There were other shows. The dresser in the guest bedroom had been, we were told, Katie Holmes's on *Dawson's Creek*. They used us as a haunted house in one episode of that series.

Now Peyton lived here, and they needed to bring over her stuff. Greg had given us a choice: Either we can switch our furniture out with yours every time—load up your stuff and haul it away; haul in our stuff, use it, haul it away; reload your stuff—we're actually willing to do that before and after each shoot. Or we can just leave our stuff here. Treat it as your own. We'll take it away when the show is over. Let us decorate your new house for you. They may let you keep a few pieces.

Theoretically that made sense. In reality (a word I can hardly use without laughing), it meant that we lived on a TV set. Of course, they consulted us on everything, showing us furniture catalogues, guiding us toward choices that both suited our taste and looked like something Peyton would have in her home. It meant more tasteful floral patterns than I'd expected, but that was okay. Maybe there was a little Peyton in me.

She was complicated, deeper than the other teens on *One Tree*, which in teen-show terms meant that she often wore flannel shirts. The other teens would come to her for advice. She lived alone. Her biological parents were dead, her adoptive parents missing, or some combination. This created an explanation for how she'd come to possess her own large home while still in high school, and how it was that she often lay in bed with teenage boys in that home, talking and snuggling, unmolested by those awful ogrelike parents who beat on the door and scream, "I don't hear any studying in there!" Peyton Sawyer: Forced to grow up too fast. Harboring an inner innocence.

One thing we did not help choose: these dark charcoal drawings. In my memory they seem to appear overnight. There were a bunch of them, and they were the first thing you saw when you walked through the front door, and they looked as if they'd been executed during art therapy time at a prison. I said something to one of the crewmen at one point, something like, "Gosh, the whole front of the house is filled with some very intense and angry artwork."

"Yes," he said. "Those are not happy paintings."

Petyon was in a tortured-artist period that season.

"You can just put them in a closet when we're not shooting."

When it was quiet again, we sat on the new couch with the baby, taking it in. Wow—the rooms looked great. A little sterile, a little showroom. But we hadn't been able to afford to furnish this place ourselves anyway. What had our plan been, to pick up used stuff off the street that other people had put out for collection? I couldn't even remember. There hadn't been a plan.

I had a high school Latin teacher named Patty Papadopolous, an enormous person—she often needed a wheelchair to get about, for her girth and what it had done to her knees— also a brilliant teacher. She married young, but her husband was killed in Vietnam. Bottle-blond beehive hairdo. She schlepped between public schools, teaching the few Latin courses they could still fill, using a medical forklift thing that moved her in and out of her van. She was captivating on the ancient world. She told us how the Roman army at its most mercilessly efficient used to stop every afternoon, build a city, live in it that night, eat and fuck and play dice and argue strategy and sharpen weapons and go to the toilet in it, pack it up the next morning, and march.

That description sprang to mind when the show arrived for the season's first shoot. With the baby barely two weeks old, we'd felt that she was too small to be moving back and forth from house to Hilton. They did a series of scenes with us in the house, sequestered upstairs.

Boxy light trucks appeared in a row down the street, a line of white buffalo. It was very *E.T.*, the scene where they take him away. Cops were parked on the corners, directing traffic and shooing gawkers. In a nearby field they pitched the food tent, which soon buzzed with crew. The stars ate in a van. I looked out the window—miles of cable, banks of lights, Porta-Pottys. Walkie-talkies.

It was a day shoot, but a night scene. They had blacked most of the windows. Upstairs, where we were, it was afternoon. Downstairs it was about ten o'clock at night. From the sound I guessed there were twenty strangers in the house.

Silence. We listened.

Peyton's voice.

I can't remember the line. It was something like "That's not what I wanted." And then another character said something, footsteps. The director was having Hilarie do the line different ways.

"That not what I wanted."

"That's NOT WHAT I WANTED."

"That's not what I WANTED."

You got a sense, even through the floorboards, of former-kid-star work ethic from Hilarie, giving 100 percent. And *rolling*. And *rolling*. No brattiness, every take usable.

We heard general chatter, and could tell they were breaking off the scene. As the baby nursed, we listened for the next one.

No next one. They were done, moving out. Gone by midnight, traffic barriers picked up. The city vanished. It had existed for about twenty seconds of footage.

When the following shoot came, an exterior this time, we had family in town. That was fun. It gratified us to see them get a little thrill from it all, the occasional celebrity sighting. It also meant that some memorable, life-changing moments from my first days of being a father—of holding my own child in the kitchen and seeing the generations together—happened while Peyton was on the back patio having equally intense times. One of her fathers, who'd been a merchant marine, had come to port, and was trying to get back into her world. I may be slightly off on that, I had to put it together from dialogue fragments.

You could see Hilarie's sweetness in the way she humored our families. The scene called for her to run through the backyard, up the steps to the back screen door, say, "No, Dad!" and slam the door behind her. Each time she executed a take, my mother and ninety-year-old Cuban grandmother-in-law, their faces squeezed together in the window of the porch door, would smile and furiously wave at her through the glass, as we begged them to sit. Hilarie waved back, just absorbing it into her process. "No, Dad." (Slam, smile, wave, turn.) "Dad, no!" (Slam, smile, wave, turn.)

Did she want some black beans? Abuela asked. She was so skinny!

"No, no, I'm fine. Thank you, though." (To my wife, behind the hand, "They're so sweet.")

She had a barbeque going out back. A grill, burgers. Picnic tables. All gone by dark. And at some point the next morning, a check flew in at the door, without a sound. As the ending voice-over of a *One Tree* episode might have put it, things were a little crazy, but we were going to be all right.

One thing did happen during the set-decoration phase. It was small, but the symbolism of it was so obvious, so articulate, I really should have paid more attention. They wallpapered the stairwell, and put up light sconces.

It was the first little toe-wander across the Greg Perimeter, that line around the front two rooms. It was the first shy tentacle tap, the first tendril nuzzle.

"But Greg distinctly said only the front two rooms."

Well, we only shoot in here. But everything you can see from this room has to match her house, too. It's for continuity.

Needless to say we hadn't been around when Peyton had chosen the wallpaper—or when one of her lost parents had chosen it. Not that it was ugly or anything. Just somber. It didn't say newlywed or newborn or anything newly. And it was our staircase. We had to walk up and down it every day. We couldn't avoid it like we mostly came to avoid the front two rooms, treating them as a parlor. Peyton's spirit lived there.

The problem wasn't the wallpaper, though, it was this curious thing the crew guys did with it once they got upstairs. They stopped in the middle of a wall. The paper wrapped around at the top of the stairs, so you'd see it if you were shooting up, and it did start down the hall, but about a foot and a half before it reached the first doorway, the first natural obstacle, it just terminated. That wall was part wallpaper, part paint, divided horizontally. It looked bad, and I'm a person who could live happily in a cardboard box if I wouldn't miss my loved ones.

The next morning, when we pointed out the anomaly, they corrected it instantly. Inconvenience was hardly an issue. The crew were hyperprofessional (film crews almost always are—the constant time intensity of the work creates an autoflushing mechanism, instantly getting rid of the lazy and sloppy). It was rather the oddity of their having done something so glaring, when with everything else, they'd been so meticulous (because it turned out they really did take pictures of your bookshelves). The wallpaper ended precisely where the camera's peripheral vision did. What the camera couldn't see wasn't totally real.

————

If our daughter later in her life finds that she possesses any of those contextless, purely visual, prememory memories, like some people have from their first two years, hers will be of a suite at the Riverside Hilton, in downtown Wilmington, North Carolina. It rises beigely beside the Cape Fear River. My Lord, did we spend some time there. They knew us by sight at the check-in counter. We developed a game with pillows. Not a game, but a child stunt that could be endlessly repeated. We stacked up every pillow in the suite, maybe a dozen, in the center of the king bed, and laid my daughter on top of the highest one like the princess and the pea, and let it crash down onto the bed like a falling tower. She laughed until she gave herself hiccups. She was a toddler by then, of course. You wouldn't toss an infant about like that, although with an infant, they're so easy to balance, you could have done even more pillows, you could have done fifteen or twenty. My Cuban grandmother-in-law was given her own room, and she would watch the baby at night, while we hit the restaurants by the river with our meal vouchers. Mornings I woke around sunrise, before the baby even, and read by the window during that quiet hour. Best was when they gave us a room on the city side. You could watch the dawn invade the streets one by one, and see the old eighteenth-century layout of the town illuminated.

Those junkets gave me a ghostly feeling. It's strange to stay in a hotel in your own city. We had moved here, we'd found property here, and now they were paying us not to stay there, like people who lived elsewhere. People in the lobby would say, "Where are you visiting from?"

It became unsettling, though, when we started to watch the show. The hours of Hilton boredom brought on epic jags of cable flipping (oh, sad and too-hard colorful rubber buttons of hotel cable remotes). In the dark we'd look for the house to come on. We competed like in charades to say "There it is!" first. (Not as a formal competition but spontaneously.)

We formed memories of our house that weren't memories; we'd experienced them solely through television. We hadn't been there for them, yet they'd occurred while we lived there. It felt something like what I imagine amnesiacs feel when they are shown pictures from their unremembered lives. You thought, How could I not remember this, how can I not have known that this happened? Coming back home after a big shoot, and finding everything just as you'd left it, despite your certain knowledge that dramatic and often violent things had occurred there while you were gone, it kept bringing to mind a Steven Wright joke, from one of his comedy specials in the eighties. "Thieves broke into my house," he said. "They took all my things and replaced them with exact replicas."

Once we'd boarded the Hilton gravy train, the Greg Perimeter vanished like a knocked-out laser security grid at a museum. Breached by the wallpaper, it had suffered other small incursions during the early shoots—lights in the upstairs windows, for instance, to boost the artificial sunlight during a night shoot/day scene, a truly disorienting scene, the last we stayed home for, when they made it afternoon in the front yard. Now they were actually setting scenes in other rooms. Peyton and Lucas (Chad Michael Murray's character, the Chachi to Peyton's Joanie) baked cookies in the kitchen. They got into a food fight and started slinging dough at each other. All over our kitchen, dough balls hitting the wall. Splat, in the cracks, on the cupboards, sailing out into the hallway. Surely this was grounds for a lucrative contract readjustment. I checked the terms— Arrgh! I'd signed over the whole property! "Equal to the amount of the mortgage," said the guy on my shoulder.

And besides, when we got home, everything was spotless. Couldn't find a fleck of dough anywhere. Couldn't find a chocolate chip (wish I had—it might be worth something on eBay). The only way the scene had affected us, in a strict material sense, was that we got our kitchen professionally cleaned for free. We'd faced harder challenges.

That's when Psycho Derek appeared.

Much later, when we were no longer on friendly terms with *One Tree*, I caught myself wondering if Psycho Derek had not perhaps been created purely as an instrument for abusing our house, to make sure we never forgot the name Peyton Sawyer. Who was he? Who was Psycho Derek?

In another country, in another world, "Ian Banks" is a young blond Scottish writer. He has a pretty wife, and one night they're out driving. He's drunk and messing with the wheel. Crash, she dies. In his guilt and grief, he goes on the Internet and starts looking for girls who look like his wife. Guess what, his wife looked just like Peyton. He does some research. He learns that Peyton has a biological brother, separated at birth, name: Derek. Lightbulb—he'll impersonate the brother. From behind that mask he worms his way into her world. But Peyton figures out he's a violent obsessive. She cuts him off. That's when he starts to attack. Our house.

He tied up Peyton and her best friend, Brooke, in the basement, as a prelude to raping them (*One Tree* was getting dark, that's where its campiness lost me, with the darkness—I don't see how you get to be teeny-dumb and do psychotic teen rape fantasies, but as I say, the irony of the genre has evolved, found new crevices). In one episode Psycho Derek was pushed down our staircase, violently grabbing at the antique banister to save himself as he fell. In another he got thrown through our bedroom window onto a safety bag on the front lawn. Our house had become the stunt house (they don't care, they're at the Hilton, they need the money!).

The crew couldn't clean up after this stuff as easily. Everything was not the same when we got home. The yard was full of shattered safety glass. The handrail on the stairs was a few centimeters more rickety, thanks to Psycho Derek's heavy grasping (when we watched it on TV we realized that the stunt guy had actually fallen backward onto the rail, with all his weight). Not to mention that in our minds the basement was now permanently a onetime BDSM sex dungeon, and not a mutual-consent swinger dungeon, either. Psycho Derek had created some seriously bad visual associations in the house, ones our daughter might not enjoy discovering come her own teen years—the basement bondage pre-rape had taken place on Peyton's prom night. (Prom was hard on our house: Peyton's friend, Brooke, mad at Peyton for something, had egged it on the day of the prom; deranged Brooke fans later re-created this incident in "reality," hitting our house with eggs in the very same spots; at least we assumed that's who did it. Could have been vandals.)

I can't blame Derek for everything. And I should take this opportunity to thank the real Derek, Peyton's true half brother, who turned out to be black, and showed up just in time, wearing a varsity jacket, to save her from Psycho Derek, and our home from any more trauma. No, Psycho Derek had been neutralized by the time we ended the contract.

What did happen? I don't know how to explain it, except

to say that it was a sort of caveman thing. Instincts that had lain dormant in my genome for generations awoke. Who were these strangers in my rock shelter? Why were they walking in and out without knocking or saying goodbye, why did they keep referring to it as "Peyton's House"? This is my house. The more the story line expanded through the rooms, the worse the feeling became. And of course the crew guys, who'd now been coming to the house for several years—who knew it in some ways better than we did—couldn't help making themselves more comfortable in it over time, sneaking in for more bathroom breaks. On one shoot, I remember, I'd been confused about where they needed to set up, and as a result neglected to clean the bedroom. Later a crew guy— the same one who'd told me about *Blue Velvet*—said, "I'm not used to picking up other people's underwear." I felt like saying, Then don't go into their bedrooms at nine o'clock in the morning! Except he was paying to be in my bedroom.

Isn't there another profession where people pay to be in your bedroom?

One day, we were at the Hilton, and I realized I'd forgotten something. I drove back to the house in the middle of a shoot. On my way out, having found what I needed, I ran into one of the crew. He had dinner plates in his hands. I knew those plates—they were plates we'd been given when we got married.

He got nervous, obviously aware that he'd crossed some line. He told me that the stars, in their dining van, had asked for real plates. These were the first he'd seen. In that awkward moment on the brick path there, something came into my head that my across-the-street neighbor, Arnie, kept saying to me, rather passive-aggressively I thought, when I would pass him on the sidewalk. Inevitably remarking on the

One Tree Hill stuff, he'd say, "The way my wife and I feel is, we don't have much, but it's ours."

By then I was fairly certain that all the neighbors hated us. I'm sure that when we moved in, they were praying we wouldn't resume the previous owners' contract with the show, that the nightmare would end. These shoots couldn't help disrupting the whole psychogeography of the block. To have to be waved through by cops into your own neighborhood, how obnoxious! The lights, the noise (the crew were always scrupulously hushed outside, but when you have that many people, there's a hive hum). I felt how much I'd hate it, if I were one of them. And why our house, anyway? There was just some bad anthropological juju going on in our little barrio. And that's not good. You don't want that. When Armageddon comes and the village is reset to a primitive state, your clan will be shunned and denied resources.

When a disagreement about money came up—we thought we were owed for an extra day—my subconscious seized on it as an excuse (though I didn't really need one, they were unpleasant about the money, which seemed weird, given we'd never been complainers). Finally one day we told them they couldn't film there anymore. It was all too big a pain in the ass. I had a suspicion they were thinking about the attic. I've never had that confirmed, but the attic is neat-looking, and it would have been the next logical step. Psycho Derek isn't dead, he's in the attic, boring peepholes. Our daughter was getting older, old enough to start wondering why we regularly moved out of the house and then right back in again, and who was living there in the meantime? If my brain couldn't handle the metaphysical implications of it all, what chance did she have? A producer called and offered us a lot more money at one point—so Peyton could say goodbye—but it had become a principle thing by then, and it felt good to say no, to reclaim the cave. And so, for primarily petty and neurotic reasons, I made a decision that negatively impacted our financial future. It's called being a good father.

I remember when they came to get Peyton's furniture. Because she'd moved in at the same time as us, her things and ours had mingled at the edges. My wife was at work, and with some pieces, I didn't know whose they were. The guy who was in charge that day held up a vase that had been on the table. "I honestly don't know if that's ours or hers," I said. I suspected it was hers, but had always liked it. "You know what," the guy said, "let's just say it's yours."

They sent painters in, which I thought was classy. Many of the walls had been scuffed by equipment and gaffer's tape and whatnot. My wife gave them a bunch of bold colors, colors we'd never tended to before. The place looks totally different. It's ours again, or rather for the first time. We burned a sage stick. Both literally and metaphorically.

Our only worry was that maybe we'd caused trouble for Hilarie somehow, affected the plotline in some way that made Peyton less essential to the cast, but when we ran into her some weeks later and voiced this concern, she was characteristically ultramature about it, and said, "You know, I think you really helped her grow up." Her being Peyton. The producers had decided to zip forward the story line four years—just skip college, go straight from right after high-school graduation to right after college graduation, with the characters all back home, in order to avoid the dorm-room doldrums that have brought down other teen shows, like *Felicity*. Now Peyton lived downtown. She managed bands.

"She doesn't live in her parents' house anymore," Hilarie said. "She has her own apartment. I think it's about time."

A year passed. We were at the airport in London—my wife had a conference there. Standing in the ticket line, we started talking about the show—probably we'd seen an old episode in one of the hotels we'd stayed at in Scotland—and we were having a what-an-experience type of conversation. At one point, the woman in front of us turned around. Business suit, dark bun. She leaned forward, and in an unplaceable European accent, said, "You have a lovely home." Not in a creepy way. She said it about as nicely as you could say something like that. "Are you a fan of the show?" my wife asked. "Oh, yes," the woman said. "I always watch it." She knew exactly what Peyton's house looked like. She described it for us. The white railing, the hallway.

By then we'd grown inured to fans coming by, frequently knocking on the door. They acted more passionate in the early days, or at least more brazen. They wanted pictures of themselves, of them with you, of you and the house, them and the house, one at a time. They were 90 percent female, teens and early twenties, but lots of their moms came with them. One of the few males, a tall skinny stonery guy, gave me half of a dollar bill, and asked me to hide it inside something on the set. I put it inside a little African-looking wooden bowl that we and Peyton kept by the front door. The bowl had a lid. He thanked us profusely and said that now he could sit at home with his girlfriend, who loved Peyton, and they'd know the other half of the dollar bill was in her house. When they came for Peyton's stuff, it was still in there; I checked.

Nobody was ever scary or rude. One time we did get these Belgian girls. They were perhaps unwholesomely fixated on the show. Six of them showed up, with a Lebanese taxi-van driver who'd brought them straight from the airport, four minutes away. He'd evidently picked them up outside baggage claim and, hearing their talk of *One Tree Hill*, offered to give them a tour of locations. Now here they were. The driver stood behind them the whole time, as if presenting them to us for consideration. We gave them a couple of souvenirs from the show, a script from an old episode that had been lying around, something else I don't remember. At these modest acts of kindness they broke down into tears, which caused my wife to go and get more things to give them, which made them cry harder. I can see them standing in the hallway, these beautiful girls, crying and laughing. They gave us a jar of excellent honey from their country, and an Eiffel Tower key chain that my daughter loved and we still use. Bless you, girls, wherever you are. Watching *One Tree*, probably.

The farthest away that anyone ever came from—another mother-daughter team—was Thailand. "Peyton House?" Mostly Ohio, Florida, places like that.

Just this week, we had two from South Carolina knock at the door. My daughter and I met them on the porch. If I had to guess, I'd say they were about to embark on their senior year of high school. You could tell they were good friends, because they never said a word to each other. They stared at us, and past us into the house.

"Can I help you?" I said.

The smaller girl, a brunet with a haircut somewhat matronly for one so young, said, "Okay . . . Did you know that your house used to be on a show?"

Yes," I said. "In fact, we were living here when they did that filming."

Their eyes widened. "May we come in?" I glanced down at my daughter. She looked excited—big girls!

"Why not?"

The brunet's question had given me a small, surprising tilt of nostalgia. Did we know that we used to be on a show? Did we know that? The time-lapse sands of pop-cultural oblivion, which will not be stayed, had overtaken us in just a few short years. We were trivia. These girls had come, before college separated them, to see something they remembered from when they were even younger, watching it together. Peyton isn't on the show anymore. Hilarie and Chad Michael Murray both failed to return for the most recent season. Contract disputes, they said. Chad, in a wild merging of life and art, ended up marrying a girl from the local high school here, right down the street, New Hanover High. The girl was still a high school student when they met. Chad had to wait for her to become legal, before they could marry. We heard him once in the front yard on his cell phone, on a night we were slow to get out of the house before a shoot, giving her advice about the SATs.

Hilarie's still in Wilmington, doing her own production company, Southern Gothic. Last year we saw her in a serious movie, *Provinces of Night*, based on a William Gay book. Val Kilmer was in it. Hilarie played an "oft-unconscious junkie," and she was good. She can act. She'll be fine.

The girls wanted to see the basement—they remembered the prom episode well—but I said no. I took pictures to make it up to them.

After they left, I was walking back down the hallway with my daughter, who's almost five. She's turned into a lovely child. Little brown helmet of smooth hair. She reminds me of the tiny Martian from Looney Tunes—"Illudium Pu-36 Explosive Space Modulator." Purely in terms of silhouette. She marches around in a very deliberate way.

"Daddy," she said, "why did those girls want to see our house?"

"Remember how I told you this house used to be on a TV show?"

"Yes," she said.

"Those girls love the show, so they wanted to see where it was made."

She stopped.

"Is our house still on TV?" she asked.

"Well," I said, "there are reruns, so, I guess it's still on sometimes."

She got a concerned look on her face. Standing with her feet apart, she threw her arms out, looking from room to room.

"Are we on a show right now?!" she demanded.

I said I didn't think so.

ACKNOWLEDGMENTS

The author would like to thank anyone and everyone who, in either a personal or professional capacity, showed him kindness at deadline time (the period of from four to five weeks on either side of a due date). Please know that he would change everything about his working habits, if he could locate the control panel.

Thank you fact-checkers, copy editors, proofreaders, and art/design people for making these pieces more readable in their primary magazine incarnations.

EVERYBODY AT:

FSG

GQ

The Sewanee School of Letters

The UNCW Department of Creative Writing

The Mrs. Giles Whiting Foundation

The Wylie Agency

The NYPL's Dorothy and Lewis B. Cullman Center
for Scholars and Writers

Dimension Films

Harper's Magazine

Oxford American

The Paris Review

As the author types the following names, he will pause
after each to reflect warmly on his particular debt of gratitude
in that case: Daniel Anderson, Emily Bell, Clyde Edgerton,
Carol Ann Fitzgerald, Devin Friedman, Ben George, Peter
Ginna, John Grammer, John Gray, Pam Henry, Benicia Fraga
Hernandez, Jack Hitt, Roger Hodge, Amos and Maria John-
son, Betsy Johnson, Chris and Becky Johnson, Jackie Ko,
Lewis Lapham, Ben McGowan, Ben Metcalf, Jane Baynham
Milward, the Milward clan more largely, John K. Moore, Jr.,
Raha Naddaf, Woody Register, Ellen Rosenbush, Anna Stein,
Jean Strouse, Beth Sullivan, Jen Szalai, Tom and Bibby Terry,
Worth Wagers, Andy Ward, Matt Weiland, Kevin West,
Sean Wilsey.

LAST BUT MOST:

Jin Auh

Mariana Chloe Johnson

Joel Lovell

Wyatt Mason

Sean McDonald

G. Sanford McGhee

Jim Nelson

Jan Simek

Marc Smirnoff

Lorin Stein